Management for Professionals

More information about this series at http://www.springer.com/series/10101

Steven De Haes · Wim Van Grembergen ·
Anant Joshi · Tim Huygh

Enterprise Governance of Information Technology

Achieving Alignment and Value in Digital Organizations

Third Edition

 Springer

Steven De Haes
Antwerp Management School
University of Antwerp
Antwerp, Belgium

Wim Van Grembergen
Antwerp Management School
University of Antwerp
Antwerp, Belgium

Anant Joshi
Antwerp Management School
Antwerp, Belgium

Maastricht University
Maastricht, The Netherlands

Tim Huygh
Antwerp Management School
University of Antwerp
Antwerp, Belgium

ISSN 2192-8096   ISSN 2192-810X   (electronic)
Management for Professionals
ISBN 978-3-030-25920-4   ISBN 978-3-030-25918-1   (eBook)
https://doi.org/10.1007/978-3-030-25918-1

This Springer imprint is published by the registered company Springer Nature Switzerland AG
The registered company address is: Gewerbestrasse 11, 6330 Cham, Switzerland

Preface to the Third Edition

"Enterprise Governance of IT (EGIT)" is a relatively new concept that is increasingly gaining interest in academia and practice. EGIT is about defining and implementing processes, structures, and relational mechanisms that enable both business and IT stakeholders to execute their responsibilities in support of business/IT alignment and the creation and protection of IT business value. As an example of its growing importance, the International Standardisation Organization (ISO) issued a new global standard in this domain in 2008, which was updated in 2015.

Within the University of Antwerp—Department of Management Information Systems—and the Antwerp Management School—IT Alignment and Governance (ITAG) Research Institute—we have been executing applied research in this domain for many years. With this book in its third edition, we want to provide a complete and comprehensive overview of what EGIT entails and how it can be applied in practice. Our conclusions in this book are based on our knowledge obtained in applied research projects, our many years of involvement in the development of COBIT, and our own hands-on coaching and consulting experience in many industries in governance and alignment projects, and international state-of-the-art literature. This way, this book encompasses both academic models and concepts, but also includes practice-oriented frameworks such as COBIT and discusses and analyzes many practical cases and examples from different industries.

The target audience for this book is threefold:

- Master students, for whom this textbook can be used in courses on IT strategy, Enterprise Governance of IT, IT management, IT processes, IT and business architecture, IT assurance/audit, information systems management, etc.;
- Executive students in business schools, for MBA type of courses where IT strategy or IT management modules are addressed;

- Practitioners in the field, both business and IT managers, who are seeking research-based fundamentals and practical guidance related to Enterprise Governance of IT.

This book is organized around six main chapters. Chapter 1 introduces Enterprise Governance of IT as a means to enable business/IT alignment and ultimately IT business value. This introductory chapter defines each of these three core concepts and introduces the relationship between them. As such, this chapter sets the scene of the book. Chapter 2 builds on the first chapter and stipulates a conceptual model to address the challenge of implementing EGIT in practice. This chapter also provides a demonstration of how EGIT mechanisms can be leveraged in practice. Finally, this chapter addresses contemporary EGIT-related topics (e.g., the role of the board of directors and the context of inter-organizational environments). In Chapter 3, the impact of Enterprise Governance of IT on business/IT alignment is discussed. The first question is how an organization can measure and evaluate its business/IT alignment. This discussion is supplemented with a benchmarking case, where business/IT alignment was measured for the Belgian financial services sector. Next, the impact of Enterprise Governance of IT practices on business/IT alignment is analyzed and illustrated. Finally, this chapter discusses the contextualization of business/IT alignment (i.e., a multidimensional perspective on business/IT alignment and social (business/IT) alignment). Chapter 4 discusses the concept of IT business value. It starts with a brief discussion about the IT productivity paradox and the IT productivity cycle. Then, two approaches to measure and manage the value of IT are introduced and discussed (i.e., at the level of investment through the business case process and at the level of the IT function through the IT balanced scorecard). This chapter also includes a detailed case study that demonstrates how the IT balanced scorecard can be leveraged in practice. Chapter 5 introduces and discusses COBIT as a framework for Enterprise Governance of IT. This chapter discusses in detail all the core elements of the COBIT 2019 framework and explains how organizations can leverage the guidance provided by the COBIT framework. The final chapter, Chapter 6, provides some in-depth insights on (specific aspects of) Enterprise Governance of IT derived from performing case study research in real organizations.

To support the reader in understanding and absorbing the material provided, "assignment boxes" are included in the chapters where readers are invited to apply the materials discussed in the book in comprehensive exercises. Also, at the end of each chapter, a summary and study questions are available enabling the reader to cross-check if the insights are absorbed. For people who want more information, each chapter provides hooks to more detailed background material by ways of literature references.

We hope that with this book, we can contribute to further developing the emerging knowledge domain of Enterprise Governance of IT. This book is one of the outcomes of our activities within the University of Antwerp and the Antwerp Management

School–IT Alignment and Governance (ITAG) Research Institute. The communicating author of this book can be contacted at steven.dehaes@uantwerpen.be, welcoming reactions on this book or sharing experiences in the domain of Enterprise Governance of IT.

Antwerp, Belgium   Steven De Haes
Antwerp, Belgium   Wim Van Grembergen
Antwerp, Belgium/Maastricht, The Netherlands   Anant Joshi
Antwerp, Belgium   Tim Huygh

Acknowledgements

We would like to thank all those involved in participating in our research and teaching activities and in writing this book. Without the support of these people, the development of this book could not have been satisfactorily completed.

We gratefully acknowledge the business and IT managers who shared their insights and practices on Enterprise Governance of IT and participated in one or more of our research projects. We appreciated the support provided for this project by the Faculty of Business and Economics of the University of Antwerp and the Antwerp Management School, by our colleagues in these institutions and other international colleagues we had the opportunity and honor to work with. We also would like to thank our master and executive students who provided us with many ideas on the subject of Enterprise Governance of IT and its mechanisms.

We would also like to express our gratitude toward the board of directors, the management committee and all the staff and volunteers of ISACA. Our involvement in the COBIT development activities has been of great value in further progressing our ideas.

We also thank our publisher Springer who showed great interest in our research and book project and from whom we received magnificent support in managing this project.

Last but not least, we would like to thank our families. Wim would like to extend his gratitude to Hilde, Astrid, and Helen who always supported and helped him with every project including this book. Steven wishes to thank Brenda for her loving support and patience and wants to dedicate this book to Ruben, Charlotte, and Michiel. Anant would like to thank his father, Suresh Joshi, for his unconditional love, support, and encouragement. He wants to dedicate this book to his late mother, Sulbha Joshi. Tim wants to explicitly thank his parents for their unconditional love and support, and Sien for her love, encouragement, and patience.

Antwerp, Belgium
May 2019

Steven De Haes
Wim Van Grembergen
Anant Joshi
Tim Huygh

Contents

About the Authors

Steven De Haes is Professor of Information Systems Management at the University of Antwerp and Dean at the Antwerp Management School. He is actively engaged in teaching and applied research in the domains of Digital Strategies, IT Governance and Management, IT Strategy and Alignment, IT Value and Performance Management, IT Assurance and Audit and Information Risk and Security.

He teaches at bachelor, master, and executive level at the University of Antwerp and the Antwerp Management School. His research has been published in international peer-reviewed journals and conference proceeding, and he co-authored and/or edited several books. He is Co-Editor-in-Chief of the *International Journal of Digital Strategy, Governance, and Business Transformation* (IJDSGBT) (https:// www.igi-global.com/journal/international-journal-digital-strategy-governance), formerly the *International Journal of IT/Business Alignment and Governance* (IJITBAG).

He also acts as speaker and facilitator in academic and professional conferences and coaches organizations in their digital strategies, IT governance, alignment, and assurance efforts. He is involved in the development of the international IT governance framework COBIT as researcher and co-author.

He can be contacted at steven.dehaes@uantwerpen.be.

Wim Van Grembergen is Professor Emeritus at the University of Antwerp (UA) and the Antwerp Management School (AMS). He was previously a guest Professor at the University of Leuven (KUL) and had teaching assignments at the University of Stellenbosch in South Africa, the Institute of Business Studies in Moscow, the Queensland University of Technology in Australia, Simon Fraser University in Canada, and the University of Cape Town in South Africa. Over the past 20 years, he conducted research in IT governance, IT audit, IT strategy, IT performance management, and the IT balanced scorecard.

He presented at leading conferences such as the European Conference on Information Systems (ECIS), the Information Resources Management Association (IRMA) Conference, and the Hawaii International Conference on Systems Sciences

(HICSS). Since 2002, he is mini-track chair "IT governance and its mechanisms" at the HICSS conference. He has many publications in leading academic journals and published books on IT governance and the IT balanced scorecard. He is Co-Editor-in-Chief of the *International Journal of Digital Strategy, Governance, and Business Transformation* (IJDSGBT). He is involved in research for ISACA/ITGI on IT governance and was involved in the development of multiple versions of the COBIT framework. Dr. Van Grembergen is a frequent speaker at academic and professional meetings and conferences and has served in a consulting capacity to a number of firms. His e-mail address is wim.vangrembergen@uantwerpen.be.

Anant Joshi is Assistant Professor of Information Management at the Department of Accounting and Information Management at Maastricht University's School of Business and Economics. He is also a visiting scholar at the University of Antwerp and Antwerp Management School (Belgium). He holds a Ph.D. degree in Management Information Systems from Maastricht University, Netherlands. His research interests include Enterprise Governance of IT, Business Value of IT, Digital Transformation, and Corporate Governance.

His research work has been published in Information and Management, Information Systems Management, and various conference proceedings including the International Conference on Information Systems (ICIS), Hawaii International Conference on System Sciences (HICSS), and in the annual meeting of the European Accounting Association (EAA).

He can be contacted at a.joshi@maastrichtuniversity.nl.

Tim Huygh is Ph.D. candidate at the Department of Management Information Systems at the Faculty of Business and Economics of the University of Antwerp, in Belgium. He is also a visiting Lecturer at the University of Antwerp, teaching a course on digital organizations and digital strategy at the undergraduate level, as well as a course on research methods in management information systems at the graduate level. He holds an M.Sc. degree in Management Information Systems from the University of Antwerp, and an M.Sc. degree in Advanced Business Studies from the KU Leuven. His research interests include the governance and management of information and technology, business/IT alignment, and IT business value.

His research has been published in ISI-indexed journals like *Information Systems Management* (ISM) and the *Journal of Global Information Management* (JGIM), and various conference proceedings including the International Conference on Information Systems (ICIS) and the Hawaii International Conference on System Sciences (HICSS).

He can be contacted at tim.huygh@uantwerpen.be.

Chapter 1
Enterprise Governance of IT, Alignment, and Value

Abstract The main title of this book refers to the concept of "Enterprise Governance of IT," a concept that addresses the definition and implementation of processes, structures, and relational mechanisms that enable both business and IT stakeholders to execute their responsibilities in support of business/IT alignment and the creation and protection of IT business value. The subtitle of this book refers to these two other important concepts, namely "business/IT alignment" and "IT business value." In this introductory chapter, these three core concepts are defined and the relationship between them is introduced. Each of these concepts will then be discussed more in-depth in the subsequent chapters.

1.1 Enterprise Governance of IT

Digital disruption is all around us, and many organizations are actively digitally transforming (Valentine & Stewart, 2015). Global IT capital investment has increased by 30% from 2005 to 2015, currently accounting for an estimated 20% of total capital investment (Laudon & Laudon, 2018). IT is considered to be steadily growing into the largest capital expense of organizations (Tiwana & Kim, 2015). Worldwide IT spending was estimated to be 3.65 billion USD for 2018 (an increase of 3.9% compared to 2017) and is forecasted to reach approximately 3.77 billion USD in 2019 (which would be an increase of 3.2% compared to 2018) (Gartner, 2019). Firms are increasingly using digital technologies for strategic purposes, accompanied by fundamentally reshaped (digital) business strategies (Bharadwaj, El Sawy, Pavlou, & Venkatraman, 2013). As a result of this growing pervasiveness of IT, organizational decision-makers are increasingly facing important IT-related decisions at all managerial levels (i.e., operational, tactical, and strategic). Disciplines like IT management (more operationally oriented) and IT governance (more strategically oriented) developed to assist organizations with these issues and ensure appropriate control over their current and future IT use (ISACA, 2018; ISO/IEC, 2015; Peterson, 2004).

© Springer Nature Switzerland AG 2020
S. De Haes et al., *Enterprise Governance of Information Technology*,
Management for Professionals, https://doi.org/10.1007/978-3-030-25918-1_1

It has been stressed many times that the achievement of IT business value relies heavily on good IT governance (Kearns & Sabherwal, 2006; Weill & Ross, 2004; Wu, Straub, & Liang, 2015). As Weill and Ross (2004, pp. 3–4) put it: *"[...] effective IT governance is the single most important predictor of the value an organization generates from IT."* Aside from the potential benefits of good IT governance, there are also potential risks to nonexistent or inappropriate IT governance (Ali & Green, 2012). For instance, IT governance failure has been mentioned in relation to information security breaches (Raghupathi, 2007) and wasted IT expenditure (Davenport, 1998). In summary, organizations have clear incentives to strive for effective IT governance, as this enables the creation and protection of IT business value (Benaroch & Chernobai, 2017; IT Governance Institute (ITGI), 2003).

The issues related to ensuring appropriate control over IT to enable the creation and protection of IT business value fall under the umbrella of the "Enterprise Governance of IT (EGIT)" concept. In the context of this book, Enterprise Governance of IT is defined as stated in Fig. 1.1.

The definition not only refers to Enterprise Governance of IT as an organizational capacity (i.e., instantiated through structures, processes, and relational mechanisms) but also to the outcomes it enables. Indeed, the outcome of Enterprise Governance of IT is the creation and protection of IT business value, which is enabled through the mediating mechanism of business/IT alignment. This relationship between these three core concepts is visualized as a conceptual model in Fig. 1.2. This relationship has also been validated by other researchers, including Wu et al. (2015) who concluded: *"we uncover a positive, significant, and impactful linkage between IT governance mechanisms and strategic alignment and, further, between strategic alignment and organizational performance."*

Assignment Box 1.1: "IT doesn't matter"

Not everybody seems to agree with the increasing strategic importance of information technology. In his article "IT doesn't matter", Carr (2003) makes the comparison between commodities such as water and gas, and information technology. He states, *"As information technology's power and ubiquity have grown, its strategic importance has diminished. [...] By now, the core functions of IT – data storage, data processing, and data transport – have become available to all. Their very power and presence have begun to transform them from potentially strategic resources into commodity factors of production. They are becoming costs of doing business that must be paid by all but provide distinction to none."*

Look up the article of Nicolas Carr and the polemic that resulted after the publication of this article. Summarize your thoughts and present a critical view to your peers.

> Enterprise Governance of IT (EGIT) is an integral part of corporate governance for which, as such, the board is accountable. It involves the definition and implementation of processes, structures, and relational mechanisms that enable both business and IT stakeholders to execute their responsibilities in support of business/IT alignment, and the creation and protection of IT business value.

Fig. 1.1 Definition of Enterprise Governance of IT (EGIT)

Fig. 1.2 EGIT-Alignment-Value conceptual model

It is not easy to pinpoint exactly when the concept of "Enterprise Governance of IT," as we understand it now, originated. Gartner introduced the idea of "improving IT governance" for the first time in their Top-ten CIO Management Priorities for 2003 (ranked third). In 1998, the IT Governance Institute (www.itgi.org) was founded as a think tank for IT governance. In academic and professional literature, articles directly mentioning IT governance began to surface in the early 1990s. In the context of the leading academic conference "Hawaii International Conference on System Sciences (HICSS)," IT governance was defined as an organizational capacity exercised by the board, executive management, and IT management to control the formulation and implementation of IT strategy and in this way ensure the fusion of business and IT (Van Grembergen, 2002).

After the emergence of the IT governance concept, the notion received a lot of attention. However, due to the focus on "IT" in the naming of the concept, the IT governance discussion mainly remained within the IT area. We have experienced this in the context of our research many times, for instance, when we tried to contact the CEO for an interview on IT governance and immediately got referred to the CIO. In practice, many IT governance implementations are driven by IT, while one would expect that the business would and should take a leading role in this context. It is clear that IT business value cannot be realized by IT, but will always be created at the business side. For example, there will be no business value created when IT delivers a new CRM (Customer Relationship Management) application on time, on budget and within functionalities, but the business is not integrating this new information system into its business operations. Business value will only be created when new and adequate business processes are designed and executed, enabling the salespeople of the organization to increase turnover and profit (De Haes & Van Grembergen, 2009; Thorp, 2003).

As such, the involvement of business stakeholders is crucial, which initiated a shift in the definition of IT governance toward "Enterprise Governance of IT (EGIT)" (i.e., focusing on the involvement of the business). As previously defined in Fig. 1.1, Enterprise Governance of IT is an integral part of corporate governance for which, as such, *the board is accountable*. It involves the definition and implementation of processes, structures, and relational mechanisms that enable *both business and IT stakeholders* to execute their responsibilities in support of business/IT alignment, and the creation and protection of IT business value.

Enterprise Governance of IT clearly goes beyond the IT-related responsibilities and expands toward (IT-related) business processes needed for the creation and protection of IT business value. The International Standardization Organization, ISO, also moved into this direction, with the release of a new global standard on the "Corporate Governance of IT" in 2008 (ISO/IEC, 2008), which was updated in 2015 (ISO/IEC, 2015). In this ISO 38500 standard, ISO puts forward six principles for governing the current and future use of IT, addressing both business' and IT's roles and responsibilities. For similar reasons, ISACA complemented its IT governance best practice framework COBIT, focusing on IT processes and responsibilities, with the Val IT framework and Risk IT framework, addressing the business processes and responsibilities in value creation and risk management, respectively. This fusion has been established since the release of COBIT 5 (ISACA, 2012). We have been, and still are, involved in the development of the COBIT framework and have experienced this broadening view toward Enterprise Governance of IT as a very fruitful evolution. The broadened view of end-to-end responsibilities in the Enterprise Governance of IT is now fully embedded in the latest version of the COBIT framework which was issued at the end of 2018 (ISACA, 2018). The COBIT 2019 framework is discussed more in-depth in Chap. 5.

This change in naming and focus from "IT Governance" to "Enterprise Governance of IT" might appear subtle and not groundbreaking, but nevertheless implies a crucial shift in the mindset of business stakeholders. The leading role of IT stakeholders in IT governance has always been paradoxical. The same thing happened in the era of business process re-engineering, where also in many cases IT stakeholders took a leading role in reinventing business processes. It is, however, clear that business processes and business value creation can and should only be in the ownership of business stakeholders. On the other hand, we have to acknowledge that in practice, this mind shift will not happen by itself or by changing the name of the concept. We believe that the CIO, and by extension the CIO office, is often in a unique position to act as a change agent in the organization and to realize the business buy-in over time. This latter point will also be illustrated in the KLM case study as discussed in the next chapter of this book.

1.2 Business/IT Alignment

The definition of Enterprise Governance of IT (refer back to Fig. 1.1) explicitly underscores that the outcome of Enterprise Governance of IT is the alignment of information technology with the business. This section provides some initial insights into the so-called business/IT alignment concept. Note that business/IT alignment is discussed more in-depth in Chap. 3 of this book, including the relationship between Enterprise Governance of IT and business/IT alignment.

What does "alignment between the business and IT" exactly mean? Business/IT alignment is the fit and integration among business strategy, IT strategy, business structures, and IT structures (Henderson & Venkatraman, 1993). It comprises two major questions: "how is IT aligned with the business?" and "how is the business aligned with IT?". Henderson and Venkatraman (1993) were the first to clearly describe the interrelationship between business and IT in their well-known strategic alignment model (SAM) (see Fig. 1.3). The strategic alignment model is based on two building blocks: "strategic fit" and "functional integration." Strategic fit recognizes that the IT strategy should be articulated in terms of an external domain (i.e., how the firm is positioned in the IT marketplace) and an internal domain (i.e., how the IT infrastructure should be configured and managed). Strategic fit is of course equally relevant in the business domain. Two types of functional integration exist: strategic and operational integration. Strategic integration is the link between business strategy and IT strategy, reflecting the external components which are important for many companies as IT emerged as a source of strategic advantage. Operational integration covers the internal domain and deals with the link between organizational infrastructure and processes and IT infrastructure and processes.

Henderson and Venkatraman (1993) argue that the external and the internal domains are equally important, but that managers traditionally think of IT strategy in terms of the internal domain since historically IT was viewed as a support function that was less essential to the business. As such, Henderson and Venkatraman (1993) warn for the problems that may surface when a bivariate approach is used with respect to balancing across the four domains—i.e., IT

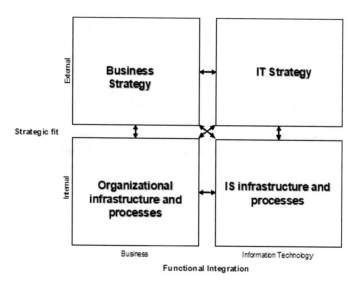

Fig. 1.3 Strategic alignment model (SAM) (Henderson & Venkatraman, 1993)

strategy, business strategy, IT infrastructure, and organizational infrastructure. For instance, when only external issues—i.e., IT strategy and business strategy—are considered, a serious underestimation of the importance of internal issues such as the required redesigning of key business processes might occur. Therefore, the strategic alignment model calls for the recognition of multivariate relationships (i.e., cross-domain alignment), which will always take into consideration at least three out of the four defined domains.

The strategic alignment model demonstrates that alignment is a multifaced and complex construct, often referred to as "the alignment challenge". Weill and Broadbent (1998) contributed to this discussion by depicting a number of difficulties (referred to as "barriers") that organizations have experienced while aligning business with IT. The "expression barriers" arise from the organization's strategic context and from senior management behavior, including a lack of direction in terms of business strategy. This results in an insufficient understanding of, and commitment to, the organization's strategic focus by operational management. "Specification barriers" arise from the circumstances of the organization's IT strategy such as lack of IT involvement in strategy development and business and IT management conducting two independent monologues. This ends up in a situation where business and IT strategies are developed in isolation and are not adequately related. The nature of the organization's existing IT portfolio creates "implementation barriers" which arise when there are technical, political, or financial constraints on the existing infrastructure. A good example of this last barrier is the difficult integration of legacy systems.

Many authors have used the strategic alignment model in further research and have provided comments and additional insights. Maes (1999) for example developed an interesting extension to the strategic alignment model (see Fig. 1.4). The basic idea behind this alignment framework is that the 2×2 dimensions of the SAM is an oversimplification of reality and needs to be extended to a 3×3 model.

In the first place, the internal domain of the alignment framework of Maes is subdivided into two separate areas: a structural and an operational level. This results from the observation that the former area plays an essential role in tuning the long-term strategic vision (which is set in the external domain), and the latter area serves the short-term operational transformation. The IT domain, in turn, is being reshaped into an information/communication level and a technology level. The split of the IT domain results from the observation that most information and communication processes are technology independent and therefore need to be considered separately. This is also in line with the concept of "information governance," which emphasizes first and foremost "the information" as opposed to "the technology."

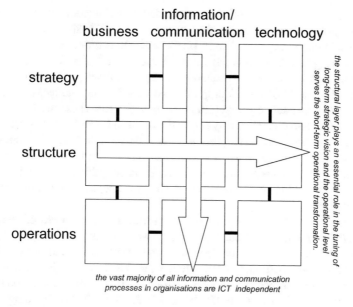

business **information/ communication** **technology**

strategy

structure

operations

the structural layer plays an essential role in the tuning of long-term strategic vision and the operational level serves the short-term operational transformation.

the vast majority of all information and communication processes in organisations are ICT independent

Fig. 1.4 Alignment framework of Maes—an extension of SAM (Maes, 1999)

1.3 IT Business Value

IT business value research is aimed at understanding how and to what extent the use of IT contributes to organizational performance (Melville, Kraemer, & Gurbaxani, 2004). Accordingly, the concept of "IT business value" can be defined as: "*[...] the organizational performance impacts of information technology at both the intermediate process level and the organization-wide level, and comprising both efficiency impacts and competitive impacts.*" (Melville et al., 2004, p. 287). The business value of IT has been a controversial topic in academia and practice. Earlier academic and non-academic publications explicitly doubted the potential of IT (investments) to achieve business value (Carr, 2003; Loveman, 1994), resulting in the widespread use of terms like "IT black hole," or "[IT] productivity paradox" (Bharadwaj, 2000). However, more recent IT business value research consistently finds that IT has a positive impact on (aspects of) organizational performance (Schryen, 2013). Scholars in the field of IT governance are in widespread agreement that IT governance should be about controlling the use of IT in a way that ensures the achievement of IT business value (Buchwald, Urbach, & Ahlemann, 2014; Jewer & McKay, 2012; Schlosser, Beimborn, Weitzel, & Wagner, 2015; Tallon, Ramirez, & Short, 2013; Turel & Bart, 2014; Wu et al., 2015).

The discourse in the practitioner area related to the outcomes of IT governance resonates well with that of academic research, in that IT business value appears to be the focal point in practice as well. ISO/IEC 38500 outlines that IT governance is about ensuring that the current and future IT use creates value for the organization, or in other words contributes positively to organizational performance (ISO/IEC, 2008, 2015). The ITGI (2003) proposed two general outcome areas of IT governance: (1) IT value delivery, and (2) IT risk management. These two outcome areas directly map to two crucial activity sets that have been identified in the context of IT governance, respectively: (1) IT business value creation, and (2) IT business value protection (i.e., counteracting IT business value destruction) (Benaroch & Chernobai, 2017; Goldstein, Chernobai, & Benaroch, 2011). These insights are useful to provide a high-level overview of what is (to be) achieved through effective IT governance.

The concept of "IT business value" also surfaces in the context of research on business/IT alignment. Indeed, a crucial question in the business/IT alignment debate is why the notion is so fundamentally important to an organization's success. In that regard, scholars have demonstrated that business/IT alignment improves (perceived) business performance (Bergeron, Raymond, & Rivard, 2004; Chan, Huff, Barclay, & Copeland, 1997; Sabherwal & Chan, 2001). Building on such evidence, Chan and Reich (2007) categorize alignment as one of the important antecedents of organizational performance.

As such, business/IT alignment appears to be, as an intermediate variable, an important catalyst of IT business value. However, it remains a challenge to demonstrate the achievement of IT business value. Indeed, measuring dependent variables in IS research is a complex endeavor (DeLone & McLean, 1992), often involving both tangible and intangible aspects (King, 1988). There are different instruments available aimed at identifying and quantifying IT costs and IT benefits. When both costs and benefits can be easily quantified and assigned a monetary value, traditional performance measures such as ROI, net present value, internal rate of return, and payback method work well (see Fig. 1.5).

Fig. 1.5 Performance measurement approaches

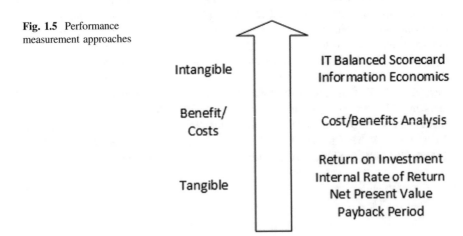

Intangible	IT Balanced Scorecard Information Economics
Benefit/ Costs	Cost/Benefits Analysis
Tangible	Return on Investment Internal Rate of Return Net Present Value Payback Period

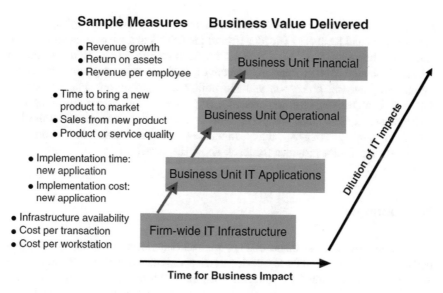

Sample Measures

- Revenue growth
- Return on assets
- Revenue per employee

- Time to bring a new product to market
- Sales from new product
- Product or service quality

- Implementation time: new application
- Implementation cost: new application

- Infrastructure availability
- Cost per transaction
- Cost per workstation

Business Value Delivered

Business Unit Financial

Business Unit Operational

Business Unit IT Applications

Firm-wide IT Infrastructure

Dilution of IT impacts

Time for Business Impact

Fig. 1.6 Business value hierarchy (Weill & Broadbent, 1998)

As these traditional methods need monetary values, problems emerge when they are applied to the use of IT, which often generates intangible benefits such as "better customer service" or "improved decision-making". Moreover, different levels of management and users perceive the value of IT differently. Weill and Broadbent (1998) refer in this context to the "business value hierarchy" (see Fig. 1.6). Very successful IT investments have a positive impact on all levels of the business value hierarchy. Less successful investments are not strong enough to impact the higher levels and consequently influence only the lower levels. The higher we move in the measurement hierarchy, the more dilution that occurs from factors such as pricing decisions and competitors' moves. This dilution means that measuring the impact of an IT investment is much easier at the bottom of the hierarchy than at the top.

Multicriteria measurement methods may solve this problem because they account for both tangible and intangible impacts (refer back to Fig. 1.5), where the latter are more typical for the higher business value hierarchies. One of the best known multicriteria methods is information economics (Parker & Benson, 1989), which in essence is a scoring technique whereby a mix of tangible (typically ROI) and intangible benefits and risks are scored. Another widely used multicriteria performance measurement technique is the balanced scorecard (BSC), which can be applied to IT projects, investments, and even entire IT departments.[1] The BSC, which was initially developed for the enterprise level by Kaplan and Norton (1996),

---

[1]The application of the BSC on IT-related issues will be addressed in Chap. 4 on IT business value.

is a performance management system that enables firms to drive strategies based on measurement and feedback. The idea behind the BSC is that the evaluation of a firm should not be restricted to the traditional financial measures (e.g., ROI) but should be supplemented with a mission, objectives, and measures regarding customer satisfaction, internal processes, and the ability to innovate and prepare for the future. The objectives and measures of a BSC can be used as a cornerstone of a management system that uncovers and communicates strategies, establishes long-term strategic targets, aligns initiatives, allocates long- and short-term resources, and finally provides feedback about the strategies.

1.4 Summary

Given a growing pervasiveness of IT, organizational decision-makers are increasingly facing important IT-related decisions at all managerial levels. Enterprise Governance of IT gradually developed since the 1990s to assist organizations with these issues and ensure appropriate control over their current and future IT use. EGIT addresses the definition and implementation of processes, structures and relational mechanisms that enable both business and IT stakeholders to execute their responsibilities in support of business/IT alignment and the creation and protection of IT business value. As such, EGIT is an important enabler of business/IT alignment. In general, business/IT alignment is about ensuring that IT is aligned to the business needs. This complex construct was formally defined by Henderson and Venkatraman (1993) as the fit and integration among business strategy, IT strategy, business structures, and IT structures. Their strategic alignment model (SAM) describes the interrelationships between these four business and IT components. Business/IT alignment, in turn, is an important enabler of IT business value. IT in itself will not generate business value, as value from IT will only be realized if both IT and the business are involved (and aligned). Measuring and demonstrating IT business value is, however, not an easy task. To effectuate this, multicriteria measurement approaches such as information economics and the balanced scorecard can be leveraged.

Study Questions

1. Define "EGIT" and explain the mind shift associated with moving from "IT governance" toward "EGIT."
2. Explain and discuss the components of the concept of "business/IT alignment" as described in the strategic alignment model (SAM).
3. Discuss why business/IT alignment can be difficult to achieve in organizations.
4. Explain the concept of "IT business value'" and discuss why it is difficult to measure.

5. Discuss a few approaches to measure the achievement of IT business value and discuss their pros and cons.
6. Describe and discuss the relationship between EGIT, business/IT alignment, and IT business value.

References

Ali, S., & Green, P. (2012). Effective information technology (IT) governance mechanisms: An IT outsourcing perspective. *Information Systems Frontiers, 14*(2), 179–193.

Benaroch, M., & Chernobai, A. (2017). Operational IT failures, IT value destruction, and board-level IT governance changes. *MIS Quarterly, 41*(3), 729–762.

Bergeron, F., Raymond, L., & Rivard, S. (2004). Ideal patterns of strategic alignment and business performance. *Information & Management, 41*(8), 1003–1020.

Bharadwaj, A. (2000). A resource-based perspective on information technology capability and firm performance: An empirical investigation. *MIS Quarterly, 24*(1), 169–196.

Bharadwaj, A., El Sawy, O., Pavlou, P., & Venkatraman, N. (2013). Digital business strategy: Toward a next generation of insights. *MIS Quarterly, 37*(2), 471–482.

Buchwald, A., Urbach, N., & Ahlemann, F. (2014). Business value through controlled IT: Toward an integrated model of IT governance success and its impact. *Journal of Information Technology, 29*(2), 128–147.

Carr, N. G. (2003). IT doesn't matter. *Harvard Business Review, 81*(5), 41–49.

Chan, Y. E., Huff, S. L., Barclay, D. W., & Copeland, D. G. (1997). Business strategic orientation, information systems strategic orientation, and strategic alignment. *Information Systems Research, 8*(2), 125–150.

Chan, Y. E., & Reich, B. H. (2007). IT alignment: What have we learned? *Journal of Information Technology, 22*(4), 297–315.

Davenport, T. H. (1998). Putting the enterprise into the enterprise system. *Harvard Business Review, 76*(4), 121–131.

De Haes, S., & Van Grembergen, W. (2009). An exploratory study into IT governance implementations and its impact on business/IT alignment. *Information Systems Management, 26*(2), 123–137.

DeLone, W., & McLean, E. (1992). Information systems success: The quest for the dependent variable. *Information Systems Research, 3*(1), 60–95.

Gartner. (2019). *Gartner says global IT spending to reach $3.8 Trillion in 2019*. Retrieved from https://www.gartner.com/en/newsroom/press-releases/2019-01-28-gartner-says-global-it-spending-to-reach–3-8-trillio.

Goldstein, J., Chernobai, A., & Benaroch, M. (2011). An event study analysis of the economic impact of IT operational risk and its subcategories. *Journal of the Association for Information Systems, 12*(9), 606–631.

Henderson, J. C., & Venkatraman, N. (1993). Strategic alignment: Leveraging information technology for transforming organizations. *IBM Systems Journal, 32*(1), 4–16.

ISACA. (2012). *COBIT 5: A business framework for the governance and management of enterprise IT*. Retrieved from http://www.isaca.org/COBIT/Pages/COBIT-5-Framework-product-page.aspx.

ISACA. (2018). *COBIT 2019 framework: Introduction & methodology*.

ISO/IEC. (2008). *ISO/IEC standard 38500: Corporate governance of information technology*.

ISO/IEC. (2015). *ISO/IEC standard 38500: Information technology—Governance of IT for the organization.*

IT Governance Institute (ITGI). (2003). *Board briefing on IT governance* (2nd ed.). Retrieved from http://www.isaca.org/knowledge-center/research/researchdeliverables/pages/board-briefing-on-it-governance-2nd-edition.aspx.

Jewer, J., & McKay, K. (2012). Antecedents and consequences of board IT governance: Institutional and strategic choice perspectives. *Journal of the Association for Information Systems, 13*(7), 581–617.

Kaplan, R. S., & Norton, D. P. (1996). *The balanced scorecard: Translating strategy into action.*

Kearns, G. S., & Sabherwal, R. (2006). Strategic alignment between business and information technology: A knowledge-based view of behaviors, outcome, and consequences. *Journal of Management Information Systems, 23*(3), 129–162.

King, W. R. (1988). How effective is your information systems planning? *Long Range Planning, 21*(5), 103–112.

Laudon, K. C., & Laudon, J. P. (2018). *Management information systems* (15 ed., global edition). New York: Pearson Education.

Loveman, G. W. (1994). An assessment of the productivity impact of information technologies. *Information technology and the corporation of the 1990s: Research studies* (pp. 84–110). Oxford, UK: Oxford University Press.

Maes, R. E. (1999). Reconsidering information management through a generic framework. *PrimaVera Working Paper, 99*(15).

Melville, Kraemer, & Gurbaxani. (2004). Review: Information technology and organizational performance: An integrative model of IT business value. *MIS Quarterly, 28*(2), 283.

Parker, M. M., & Benson, R. J. (1989). Enterprisewide information economics: Latest concepts. *Journal of Information Systems Management, 6*(4), 7–13.

Peterson, R. R. (2004). Integration strategies and tactics for information technology governance. In *Strategies for information technology governance* (pp. 37–80).

Raghupathi, W. (2007). Corporate governance of IT: A framework for development. *Communications of the ACM, 50*(8), 94–99.

Sabherwal, R., & Chan, Y. E. (2001). Alignment between business and IS strategies: A study of prospectors, analyzers, and defenders. *Information Systems Research.* Retrieved from http://pubsonline.informs.org/doi/abs/10.1287/isre.12.1.11.9714.

Schlosser, F., Beimborn, D., Weitzel, T., & Wagner, H.-T. (2015). Achieving social alignment between business and IT—An empirical evaluation of the efficacy of IT governance mechanisms. *Journal of Information Technology, 30*(2), 119–135.

Schryen, G. (2013). Revisiting IS business value research: What we already know, what we still need to know, and how we can get there. *European Journal of Information Systems, 22*(2), 139–169.

Tallon, P. P., Ramirez, R. V., & Short, J. E. (2013). The information artifact in IT governance: Toward a theory of information governance. *Journal of Management Information Systems, 30* (3), 141–178.

Thorp, J. (2003). *The information paradox: Realizing the business benefits of information technology* (2nd ed.). Toronto: Mcgraw-Hill.

Tiwana, A., & Kim, S. K. (2015). Discriminating IT governance. *Information Systems Research, 26*(4), 656–674.

Turel, O., & Bart, C. (2014). Board-level IT governance and organizational performance. *European Journal of Information Systems, 23*(2), 223–239.

Valentine, E., & Stewart, G. (2015). Enterprise business technology governance: Three competencies to build board digital leadership capability. In *HICSS 2015 Proceedings.*

Van Grembergen, W. (2002). Introduction to the Minitrack "IT Governance and its Mechanisms." In *Proceedings of the 35th Hawaii International Conference on System Sciences.*

Weill, P., & Broadbent, M. (1998). *Leveraging the new infrastructure—How market leaders capitalize on Information Technology.* Boston: Harvard Business School Press.

Weill, P., & Ross, J. (2004). *IT Governance: How top performers manage IT decision rights for superior results*. Harvard Business Press.

Wu, S. P.-J., Straub, D. W., & Liang, T.-P. (2015). How information technology governance mechanisms and strategic alignment influence organizational performance: Insights from a matched survey of business and IT managers. *MIS Quarterly, 39*(2), 497–518.

Chapter 2
Enterprise Governance of IT

Abstract The previous chapter provided a high-level description of the "Enterprise Governance of IT (EGIT)" concept. This second chapter starts with discussing the genesis and evolution of EGIT, both in academic research and practice. Then, this chapter introduces mechanisms that can be used to implement EGIT in practice. Indeed, developing a high-level model for EGIT is the first step, deploying it throughout all levels of the organization is the next challenging step. To effectuate this, EGIT can be deployed using a mixture of various structures, processes, and relational mechanisms. These EGIT mechanisms will be discussed in this chapter, including a demonstration of how such mechanisms were leveraged in the context of KLM, a large international airline company. Finally, specific EGIT-related topics will be discussed such as the role of the board in EGIT, IT governance transparency, the inter-organizational governance of IT, ambidextrous EGIT, and a more theoretical view on EGIT by drawing on the lens of the Viable System Model (VSM).

2.1 Genesis and Evolution of Enterprise Governance of IT

2.1.1 The Initial Stages of Academic Research into the Governance of IT

The term "IT governance" started to appear in academic outlets in the early 1990s. Loh and Venkatraman (1992) positioned IT outsourcing as an innovative IT governance model and researched the drivers of its diffusion. One year later, Henderson and Venkatraman (1993) proposed IT governance as a relevant choice related to how a firm positions itself in the IT marketplace. Nevertheless, issues that would now be placed under the general heading of IT governance were already being studied long before the 1990s. For instance, Garrity (1963) presented survey results that included a focus on IT decision-making authority and control (asking questions like "How many levels below the chief executive is the computer executive?") (Brown & Grant, 2005; Wilkin & Chenhall, 2010). After conducting an extensive

© Springer Nature Switzerland AG 2020

S. De Haes et al., *Enterprise Governance of Information Technology*,

Management for Professionals, https://doi.org/10.1007/978-3-030-25918-1_2

literature review, Brown and Grant (2005) identified two initial parallel research streams related to the governance of IT, arguing that these streams provide the foundation upon which later IT governance research is being built. The first stream of research deals with IT governance forms and the second with IT governance contingency analysis.

The research on IT governance forms is similar to earlier debates on the organizational structure or design of the IT function (e.g., King, 1983; Olson & Chervany, 1980; Tavakolian, 1989; Zmud, 1984) and is concerned with the locus of IT decision-making authority and the types of IT decisions. Early debates in this stream framed the issue as the binary choice between the centralization and decentralization of IT decision-making authority (Brown & Grant, 2005). In a centralized form of IT governance, all IT decision-making authority lies with a central IS unit. Due to centralized integration, this design provides greater opportunities to realize operational efficiencies and synergies. Conversely, IT decision-making authority is distributed to the individual business units in a decentralized form of IT governance, providing flexibility in responding to individual business unit needs (Brown, 1997; Brown & Grant, 2005; Sambamurthy & Zmud, 2000). Scholars quickly realized that this dichotomous classification of "strictly centralized" versus "strictly decentralized" IT decision-making authority was too simplistic and did not reflect the way in which organizations operated. As a result, more complex IT governance forms were proposed. Zmud, Boynton, and Jacobs (1986) proposed a "federal" form, which is about centralizing some IT decision-making authority (i.e., related to IT infrastructure) with a central IS unit while decentralizing other IT decision-making authority (i.e., related to plan, build, and run application systems) to the individual business units. This federal form allows for balancing the hierarchical tradeoffs of control (centralized) versus autonomy (decentralized), supporting organizations in the quest to achieving the best of both worlds (Brown, 1999; Brown & Grant, 2005; Williams & Karahanna, 2013). Other scholars moved away from uniform IT governance forms and proposed non-uniform IT governance forms, which essentially meant a shift in the unit of analysis from the firm level to the business unit level. Brown (1997), recognizing the fact that a changing IS role results in the emergence of new IT governance forms, proposed a "hybrid" IT governance form in which IT decision-making authority related to systems development is decentralized to some but not all individual business units.

The research on IT governance contingency analysis deals with understanding the factors that influence the choice for a structural form of IT governance. The rationale for this research stream lies in the unanimous recognition that "*a universal best IT governance structure does not exist*" (Brown & Grant, 2005, p. 703), but is instead contingent upon a variety of factors. This research stream therefore draws on contingency theory (e.g., Brown, 1997; Lawrence & Lorsch, 1967). Early debates in this stream focused on the individual factors (e.g., industry, firm size, corporate strategy, and corporate structure) influencing the adoption of a uniform IT governance form, without considering possible interactions among the contingency factors (Brown, 1997; Sambamurthy & Zmud, 1999). Quickly, researchers started to realize that the assumption of non-interacting contingency factors might be unrealistic and started to shift their focus toward multiple contingency analyses (e.g., Sambamurthy & Zmud, 1999). Research in this stream also mirrored the increasing complexity of the research on IT governance forms, resulting in studies dealing with interacting contingencies related to non-uniform IT governance forms (e.g., Brown & Magill, 1998).

2.1.2 The Quest for Balancing Academic Rigor and Relevance for Practice

Later researches appeared that converged and aggregated these two initial research streams. Weill and Ross (2004) proposed an IT governance framework that maps six mutually exclusive IT governance forms (which they refer to as "archetypes"[1]) against five key types of IT decisions,[2] while also addressing numerous contingency factors. Nevertheless, Brown and Grant (2005) identified, post-Weill and Ross (2004), multiple paths for the further development of the IT governance research domain. Scholars might (1) continue with the converged and aggregated stream as initiated by Weill and Ross (2004), (2) remain focused on the individual initial research streams, or (3) develop an entirely new research stream. The last option was supported by an earlier call made by Sambamurthy and Zmud (2000, p. 105), who stated that the accumulated knowledge related to IT governance "*[…] might be inadequate in shaping appropriate insights for contemporary practice.*" Schwarz and Hirschheim (2003, p. 151) further specified: "*[…] researchers need to change their views of IT 'structure' to embrace a more social and dynamic existence.*" Brown and Grant (2005) echoed: "*[…] researchers may have to reframe the assumptions underlying IT governance research in order to develop alternative conceptualizations suited to the realities facing contemporary organizations*" (Brown & Grant, 2005, p. 709). In other words, the research community started to realize that an alternative conceptualization of IT governance might be beneficial for the progress of the field, but especially for ensuring its relevance for practice.

---

[1]Each archetype identifies the decision-makers involved in an IT decision. The following archetypes are proposed: (1) business monarchy (i.e., top managers), (2) IT monarchy (i.e., IT specialists), (3) feudal (i.e., each business unit making independent decisions), (4) federal (i.e., combination of the corporate center and the business units, with or without IT people involved), (5) IT duopoly (i.e., IT group and one other group, e.g., top management or business unit leaders), and (6) anarchy (i.e., isolated individual or small group decision-making) (Weill & Ross, 2004).

[2]The following types of IT decisions are proposed: (1) IT principles (i.e., clarifying the business role of IT), (2) IT architecture (i.e., defining integration and standardization requirements), (3) IT infrastructure (i.e., determining shared and enabling services), (4) business application needs (i.e., specifying the business need for purchased or internally developed IT applications), and (5) IT investment and prioritization (i.e., choosing which initiatives to fund and how much to spend) (Weill & Ross, 2004).

Brown (1999) started to look past the initial issues that dominated the two initial IT governance research streams. Further drawing on the work of organizational theorists (e.g., Mintzberg, 1979), the study argued for structural and non-structural horizontal linking mechanisms to facilitate cross-unit collaboration to promote the coordination of IT activities (specifically across corporate/division boundaries). Brown (1999, p. 421) explicitly mentioned that these coordination mechanisms were an appropriate response to an "*[...] increased environmental complexity and uncertainty [...].*" Furthermore, bringing these formal (e.g., steering committees) and informal (e.g., physical collocation) coordination mechanisms in the mix, Brown (1999, p. 446) claims to take "*[a] more holistic approach [...]*" than previous studies. As part of their call for reframing the IT governance research agenda, Sambamurthy and Zmud (2000) proposed a "platform organizing logic" (consisting of IT capabilities, relational architectures, and integration architectures) as a novel underlying assumption for IT governance research. They thereby also directly hinted at the importance of relationships and integration mechanisms (both traditional integration structures and process-related integration mechanisms). A few years later, the "extended platform logic model" by Schwarz and Hirschheim (2003) extended the work of Sambamurthy and Zmud (2000) by including the dimension of identifying IT success metrics, while also underscoring the importance of relationships (between IT and the business) in the context of IT governance.

In line with these prior steps, Peterson (2004, p. 7) presented "*[...] a holistic view of IT governance [...],*" emphasizing that IT governance needs to be about the allocation of formal IT decision-making authority as well as the ability to coordinate and integrate IT decision-making across business and IT. Such coordination can be achieved through horizontal integration capabilities (i.e., structural capabilities, process capabilities, and relational capabilities). The structural IT governance capability concerns "*[...] structural (formal) devices and mechanisms for connecting and enabling horizontal, or liaison, contacts between business and IT management (decision-making) functions*" (Peterson, 2004, p. 14). The process IT governance capability is about "*[...] the formalization and institutionalization of strategic IT decision-making or IT monitoring procedures*" (Peterson, 2004, p. 15). Finally, the relational IT governance capability refers to "*[...] the active participation of, and collaborative relationships among, corporate executives, IT management, and business management*" (Peterson, 2004, p. 15). Putting forward these three types of IT governance capabilities (of which specific examples are presented in Table 2.1), Peterson (2004) criticized prior IT governance research for being solely concerned with the allocation of formal IT decision-making authority (i.e., the structural forms), and called for a new IT governance paradigm in which sufficient attention is given to such horizontal integration capabilities.

Weill and Ross (2004) also contributed to the discussion about the specific components of an IT governance arrangement, proposing that IT governance can be implemented through a set of decision-making structures (i.e., units and roles responsible for IT decision-making), alignment processes (i.e., formalization of how the IT decisions are being made), and communication approaches (related to IT

Table 2.1 Three types of IT governance capabilities (Peterson, 2004)

Structural mechanisms	Process mechanisms	Relational mechanisms
CIO and DIO	Balanced scorecard analysis	Active participation by key stakeholders
IT program managers	Critical success factors analysis	Partnership rewards and incentives
IT relationship managers	Scenario analysis	Shared understanding of business/IT objectives
IT account managers	Cost/benefit/risk analysis	Active conflict resolution (non-avoidance)
IT project office	SWOT analysis	Cross-functional business/IT training and job rotation
IT executive councils	Service-level agreements	Business/IT collocation
IT steering committee	IT chargeback system	Business/IT "virtual connection" and "communities of practice"
IT project committees	IT delivery management	
E-commerce advisory board	IT benefits' management	
E-CRM task force	IT performance tracking	
Centers of competence and excellence	Shared IT performance database	

governance principles, IT policies, and the outcomes of IT decision-making) (Table 2.2).

As part of the research that led to the first edition of this very book, De Haes and Van Grembergen (2009) further advanced research into how IT governance can be implemented. Building on Peterson (2004), but therefore also in line with Weill and Ross (2004), it was proposed that an IT governance arrangement should consist of structures, processes, and relational mechanisms. The main deliverable was a list of 33 IT governance mechanisms and empirical evidence of a positive relationship between IT governance and business/IT alignment. These mechanisms for implementing Enterprise Governance of IT are introduced and discussed in the next section, and a demonstration of how such EGIT mechanisms were leveraged in practice is included in the section that deals with the KLM case study.

Huang, Zmud, and Price (2010) provided insights on how two specific IT governance mechanisms (i.e., IT steering committees involving senior management and IT governance communication policies) contribute to an organization's success in using IT. Their study revealed the value of establishing formal IT governance mechanisms combined with developing and maintaining personal relationships between business and IT senior management. Joachim, Beimborn, and Weitzel (2013) searched extant literature for SOA governance mechanisms and classified

Table 2.2 Common IT governance mechanisms (Weill & Ross, 2004)

Decision-making structures	Alignment processes	Communication approaches
Executive or senior management committee	Tracking of IT projects and resources consumed	Work with managers who do not follow the rules
IT leadership committee comprising IT executives	Service-level agreements	Senior management announcements
Process teams with IT members	Formally tracking business value of IT	Office of CIO or office of IT governance
Business/IT relationship managers	Chargeback arrangements	Web-based portals and intranets for IT
IT council comprising business and IT executives		
Architecture committee		
Capital approval committee		

them according to the taxonomy of IT governance mechanisms by De Haes and Van Grembergen (2009). They then empirically investigated which SOA governance mechanisms contributed to achieving two anticipated SOA benefits (i.e., IT flexibility and service reuse). An interesting finding of this study is that implementing new, dedicated structural governance mechanisms for SOA-related decision-making hampers the ability to achieve anticipated SOA benefits. Instead, integrating SOA-related decision-making into existing structural IT governance mechanisms is recommended. Tallon, Ramirez, and Short (2013) proposed a more inclusive view of IT governance by uncovering mechanisms that can be used to govern information. Building on the taxonomy of IT governance mechanisms proposed by Peterson (2004), they discovered structural, procedural, and relational mechanisms for information governance. Furthermore, a conceptual model is provided that includes the antecedents (enablers and inhibitors) and consequences of these mechanisms. One of the key recommendations of this study is that it is preferable for organizations to not treat the governance of physical IT artifacts and the governance of information as separate issues. Instead, it is advised to jointly govern both types of artifacts under a common umbrella of mechanisms, by using the same governance structures, or to link the structures through shared membership or the exchange of ideas. Therefore, while Joachim et al. (2013) and Tallon et al. (2013) each defined a specific scope for the object of control of IT governance (i.e., what is governed—respectively, SOA and information), they both reached similar conclusions. Indeed, while SOA and information are put forward as important attention points in the context of IT governance, their effective governance does not seem to require dedicated decision-making structures.

Starting from the mid-2000s, scholars were increasingly focusing on the actual mechanisms for IT governance implementation. While some scholars were using exploratory research approaches to discover IT governance mechanisms, others were using these discovered mechanisms to operationalize the IT governance construct and validate proposed nomological networks. For instance, Schlosser, Beimborn, Weitzel, and Wagner (2015) studied the role of IT governance mechanisms in achieving social alignment between business and IT, and Wu, Straub, and Liang (2015) studied the effect of IT governance mechanisms on organizational performance through the mediating effect of strategic alignment between business and IT. With this shift in focus of scholars towards the actual mechanisms for IT governance implementation, academic research seemed to become better aligned to practice in the mid-2000s. In other words, it seemed that Sambamurthy and Zmud's (2000) call to deliver appropriate insights for practice did not go unnoticed. However, academic literature still remained largely silent about several issues that were prevalent in the practitioner literature (e.g., the role of the board of directors in IT governance). The existence of these gaps can possibly be attributed to the fact that academic research into IT governance was stemming from different roots than how practitioners approached the concept.

2.1.3 Practitioners' View on the Governance of IT

In the late 1990s, IT governance also sparked the interest of the practitioner community. The Information Systems Audit and Control Association (ISACA) founded the IT Governance Institute (ITGI) in 1998 as a think tank for IT governance, recognizing an increasing importance of IT for organizations and with that the growing need for effective control over this IT. The practitioners' view on IT governance seemed to be primarily influenced by corporate governance, as is evident from ITGI's (2003) influential publication that positions IT governance as an integral part of a broad framework of corporate governance. Accordingly, IT governance is explicitly put forward as the responsibility of senior management and the board of directors (IT Governance Institute (ITGI), 2003). This last point was also echoed by the more practitioner-oriented academic research. For instance, Ross and Weill (2002) emphasized the need for the involvement of senior business executives in IT decision-making, and Nolan and McFarlan (2005) emphasized the need for involvement of the board of directors in IT governance. As discussed in the previous chapter of this book, these insights thereby initiated a shift in the definition of "IT governance" toward "Enterprise Governance of IT (EGIT)" (i.e., focusing on the involvement of the business). The practitioner literature was also providing specific guidance under the form of structural mechanisms through which the involvement of the appropriate stakeholders could be achieved. For instance, a board-level IT strategy committee was proposed, as well as an IT steering committee at the executive management level (IT Governance Institute (ITGI), 2003).

Corporate governance received worldwide attention following a series of scandals involving major accounting fraud. The heavily publicized Enron and WorldCom scandals in 2001 were for instance the major drivers for passing the

Sarbanes–Oxley (SOX) Act in 2002 as an attempt by the US government to legislate a set of good practices for corporate governance (Ailon, 2011). In the 2000s, many countries released or updated their corporate governance codes. Due to its explicit link with corporate governance, combined with the fact that accounting information usually resides in information systems, attention was then also devoted to developing standards for IT governance (Wilkin & Chenhall, 2010). With the King III corporate governance code, South Africa even released a corporate governance code that contained specific guidance related to the governance of IT (Institute of Directors in Southern Africa, 2009), thereby integrating guidelines for corporate and IT governance in a single document.

The Australian Standard for Corporate Governance of Information and Communication Technology (AS 8015-2005) developed by Standards Australia was one of the first standards for IT governance. The standard provided *"[…] a framework of principles for Directors to use when evaluating, directing and monitoring the information and communication technology (ICT) portfolio in their organizations."* (Standards Australia, 2005, p. 2). The AS 8015-2005 standard presented a model of IT governance based on a cycle of "Evaluate–Direct–Monitor." This model later served as foundation for the ISO/IEC 38500 international standard for IT governance, which was initially released in 2008, and updated in 2015. The objective of this international standard is *"[…] to provide principles, definitions, and a model for governing bodies to use when evaluating, directing, and monitoring the use of information technology (IT) in their organizations."* (ISO/IEC, 2015), which clearly shows that it grew out of AS 8015-2005. ISO/IEC 38500 defines IT governance as *"The system by which the current and future use of IT is directed and controlled."* (ISO/IEC, 2008, 2015). This definition shows the strong link with corporate governance, as the definition for corporate governance provided in the so-called Cadbury Report is: *"The system by which companies are directed and controlled."* (The Committee on the Financial Aspects of Corporate Governance, 1992). The "Evaluate–Direct–Monitor" cycle which is central to ISO/IEC 38500 is composed of three main tasks: (1) evaluating the current and future use of IT, (2) direct preparation and implementation of plans and policies, and (3) monitor, through appropriate measurement systems, the performance of IT (ISO/IEC, 2008).

Within the practitioner community, ISACA (i.e., the founding organization behind the ITGI) is well known for the "Control Objectives for Information and Related Technology (COBIT)" framework. The first version of this framework was released in 1996 (version 1), with updates in 1998 (version 2), 2000 (version 3), 2005 (version 4), 2007 (version 4.1), 2012 (version 5), and 2018 (version 2019). Insights gathered through the ITGI helped to evolve COBIT toward a mature framework for IT management and IT governance (De Haes, Van Grembergen, & Debreceny, 2013). The COBIT framework (and more specifically its latest version COBIT 2019) is discussed more in-depth in the fifth chapter of this book.

2.1.4 Practitioners and Academics: A Converging View

Post-2010, academic scholars became increasingly interested in more specific issues that were deemed relevant in practice. For instance, Jewer and McKay (2012) studied board-level IT governance by leveraging (1) strategic choice theory to study relationships between a board's composition and its involvement in IT governance and (2) institutional theory to study relationships between organizational factors and board involvement in IT governance. Furthermore, they provided evidence for a positive relationship between board involvement in IT governance and the contribution of IT to organizational performance. Turel and Bart (2014) empirically examined the antecedents (i.e., the organization's mode of IT use) and organizational performance consequences of board-level IT governance. Important findings were that involvement of the board of directors in IT governance was dependent on the organization's mode of IT use and that this involvement improved organizational performance (regardless of the organization's mode of IT use). Other scholars studied issues like inter-organizational IT governance (e.g., King, 2013; Xiao, Xie, & Hu, 2013; Wilkin, Campbell, & Moore, 2013), the governance of cloud computing (e.g., Choudhary & Vithayathil, 2013; Winkler & Brown, 2013; Vithayathil, 2018), the governance of service-oriented architectures (Joachim et al., 2013), and the governance of information (Tallon et al., 2013). The COBIT framework has also been leveraged in academic research to understand the impact of IT governance in practice (e.g., Kerr & Murthy, 2013). In summary, scholars are increasingly studying IT governance-related topics that are deemed relevant in practice, thereby providing a more inclusive view of IT governance. This book provides further insights on some emerging IT governance-related topics (e.g., board-level IT governance, ambidextrous IT governance, inter-organizational IT governance) in the final section of this chapter.

While academia becomes increasingly interested in specific IT governance(-related) issues that are deemed relevant in practice, the practitioner area is increasingly looking at academic research for substantiation. In November 2018, the successor of COBIT 5, i.e., COBIT 2019, was officially released. This most recent COBIT update is aimed at facilitating a more flexible, tailored implementation of effective "Enterprise Governance of Information and Technology (EGIT)" and is now explicitly anchored in leading academic research that puts forward EGIT as an enabler of downstream IT business value, mediated through business/IT alignment (ISACA, 2018). The COBIT 2019 framework is the subject of the fifth chapter of this book.

2.2 Mechanisms for Implementing Enterprise Governance of IT

Starting from the mid-2000s, scholars were increasingly focusing on the mechanisms that can be leveraged for the implementation of EGIT. This research interest followed from the understanding that the development of a high-level EGIT model does not imply that EGIT is effectively functioning in the organization. Indeed, developing a high-level model for the Enterprise Governance of IT is the first step, deploying it throughout all levels of the organization is the next challenging step. Building on Peterson (2004), but therefore also in line with Weill and Ross (2004), our research (i.e., De Haes & Van Grembergen, 2009) showed that organizations can and are deploying Enterprise Governance of IT by using a holistic mixture of various structures, processes, and relational mechanisms.

EGIT structures include organizational units and roles responsible for making IT decisions and for enabling contacts between business and IT management decision-making functions (e.g., IT steering committee). This can be seen as a kind of blueprint of how the EGIT framework will be structurally organized. EGIT processes refer to the formalization and institutionalization of strategic IT decision-making and IT monitoring procedures, to ensure that daily behaviors are consistent with policies and provide feedback to decisions (e.g., portfolio management). Finally, EGIT relational mechanisms are about the active participation of, and collaborative relationship among, corporate executives, IT management, and business management and include job rotation, announcements, advocates, channels, and education efforts. This typology of EGIT mechanisms, including some examples, is visually presented in Fig. 2.1.

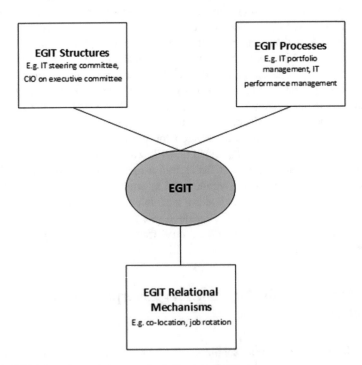

Fig. 2.1 EGIT structures, processes, and relational mechanisms

Our research clearly indicated that organizations are indeed leveraging a mix of structures, processes, and relational mechanisms to implement EGIT in practice (De Haes, Gemke, Thorp, & Van Grembergen, 2011; De Haes & Van Grembergen, 2009). Of course, it should be noted that a "silver bullet" is not possible or desirable. Indeed, "*a universal best IT governance structure does not exist*" (Brown & Grant, 2005, p. 703), but is instead contingent upon a variety of factors. As a result, each organization has to select its own set of EGIT mechanisms, suitable for its specific context (i.e., sector, size, culture)

Based on extensive case study research, we observed that organizations tend to find it much easier to implement EGIT structures in their organizations as opposed to EGIT processes. However, we also observed that many of these EGIT structures cannot be effective without supporting EGIT processes. For example, an IT steering committee cannot make appropriate investment decisions without an appropriate and mature portfolio management process, including the development of solid business cases. It also appeared that EGIT relational mechanisms, such as training, awareness building, receive a lot of attention in the early stages of an EGIT implementation project and become less important when the EGIT framework gets embedded into day-to-day operations. This is not surprising as the introduction of an EGIT arrangement should be regarded in the first place as a large change program within the organization.

Another interesting finding to pinpoint is that, despite our EGIT definition implying a crucial role of the board of directors (as part of their role in overall corporate governance), specific mechanisms to achieve this involvement of the board in EGIT such as "IT expertise at level of board of directors" are less common in organizations. This can possibly be explained by the fact that making the board of directors more IT literate is not easy to achieve, or that the board is still not fully aware of the strategic importance of IT. The role of the board of directors, and the challenges related to it, in the context of EGIT is discussed more in-depth as part of the "capita selecta" section at the end of this chapter.

More recently, the idea of "IT leadership" emerged in many discussion fora. IT leadership can be defined as the ability of the CIO, or a similar role, to articulate a vision for IT's role in the company and ensure that this vision is clearly understood by managers throughout the organization. If the CIO is not able to communicate in business-oriented terms at the executive level, the CIO's impact at that level will be minor. This mechanism is highly dependent on the individual competencies of the CIO and not many methods are available to manage it. However, we have seen that good leadership can be a very powerful catalyst to bring EGIT in an organization to a next level. A good balance between IT-related leadership and the appropriate EGIT structures and processes needs to be ensured (De Haes & Van Grembergen, 2009).

To better understand how organizations can implement EGIT, we have supplemented our case study research with Delphi research, leveraging an expert panel of academics, business, and IT managers and consultants, to list and evaluate structures, processes, and relational mechanisms that contemporary organizations are using in implementing EGIT (De Haes & Van Grembergen, 2009). This exercise resulted in a list of 33 EGIT mechanisms (see Table 2.3) and their

Table 2.3 EGIT mechanisms (i.e., structures, processes, and relational mechanisms)

	#	IT governance mechanism	Definition
IT governance structures	S1	IT strategy committee at level of board of directors	Committee at level of board of directors to ensure IT is regular agenda item and reporting issue for the board of directors
	S2	IT expertise at level of board of directors	Members of the board of directors have expertise and experience regarding the value and risk of IT
	S3	(IT) audit committee at level of board of directors	Independent committee at level of board of directors overviewing (IT) assurance activities
	S4	CIO on executive committee	CIO is a full member of the executive committee
	S5	CIO reporting to CEO and/or COO	CIO has a direct reporting line to the CEO and/or COO
	S6	IT steering committee at executive/senior management level	Steering committee at executive or senior management level responsible for determining business priorities in IT investments
	S7	IT governance function/officer	Function in the organization responsible for promoting, driving and managing IT governance processes
	S8	Security/compliance/risk officer	Function responsible for security, compliance and/or risk, which possibly impacts IT
	S9	IT project steering committee	Steering committee composed of business and IT people focusing on prioritizing and managing IT projects
	S10	IT security steering committee	Steering committee composed of business and IT people focusing on IT-related risks and security issues
	S11	Architecture steering committee	Committee composed of business and IT people providing architecture guidelines and advise on their applications
	S12	Integration of governance/alignment tasks in roles & responsibilities	Documented roles & responsibilities include governance/alignment tasks for business and IT people
IT governance processes	P1	Strategic information systems planning	Formal process to define and update the IT strategy
	P2	IT performance measurement (e.g. IT balanced scorecard)	ITperformance measurement in domains of corporate contribution, user orientation, operational excellence and future orientation
	P3	Portfolio management (incl. business cases, information economics, ROI, payback)	Prioritization process for IT investments and projects in which business and IT is involved (incl. business cases)
	P4	Chargeback arrangements – total cost of ownership (e.g. activity-based costing)	Methodology to charge back IT costs to business units, to enable an understanding of the total cost of ownership
	P5	Service level agreements	Formal agreements between business and IT about IT development projects or IT operations
	P6	IT governance framework COBIT	Process-based IT governance and control framework
	P7	IT governance assurance and self-assessment	Regular self-assessments or independent assurance activities on the governance and control over IT
	P8	Project governance/management methodologies	Processes and methodologies to govern and manage IT projects
	P9	IT budget control and reporting	Processes to control and report upon budgets of IT

	P10	Benefits management and reporting	Processes to monitor the planned business benefits during and after implementation of the IT investments/projects
	P11	COSO/ERM	Framework for internal control
IT governance relational mechanisms	R1	Job rotation	IT staff working in the business units and business staff working in IT
	R2	Co-location	Physically locating business and IT people together
	R3	Cross-training	Training business people about IT and/or training IT people about business
	R4	Knowledge management (on IT governance)	Systems (e.g. on the intranet) to share and distribute knowledge about IT governance framework, responsibilities, tasks, etc.
	R5	Business/IT account manager	Bridging the gap between business and IT by means of account managers who act as in -between
	R6	Executive/senior management giving the good example	Senior business and IT management acting as "partners"
	R7	Informal meetings between business and IT executive/senior management	Informal meetings, with no agenda, where business and IT senior management talk about general activities. Directions, etc.
	R8	IT leadership	Ability of CIO or similar role to articulate a vision for the role of IT in the organization and ensure that this vision is clearly understood by managers throughout the organization
	R9	Corporate internal communication addressing IT on a regular basis	Internal corporate communication regularly addresses general IT issues
	R10	IT governance awareness campaigns	Campaigns to explain to business and IT people the need for IT governance

respective evaluations in terms of perceived effectiveness and perceived ease of implementation.

Based on the expert panel's answers regarding perceived effectiveness, a "minimum baseline" was constructed, taking the form of a list of EGIT mechanisms that an organization should have as a minimum. After several review rounds, the expert panel categorized these 10 minimum baseline mechanisms (shaded light gray in Table 2.3) as key EGIT instruments. This minimum baseline contains a mixture of more strategic-oriented (e.g., IT strategy committee at level of board of directors) and management-oriented (e.g., IT project steering committee) mechanisms. It is also clear that mechanisms such as IT steering committee, portfolio management, project governance/management etc. constitute the core framework to describe how investments in organizations emerge, how they are prioritized and how they are realized. In that sense, most of these mechanisms clearly contain both business and IT-oriented roles and responsibilities.

Assignment Box 2.1: IT Steering Committee Charter

You are working for an international bank and the CEO has asked you to create a charter for a new IT steering committee. Using the template below, provide a description of how you see the role, responsibility, participants and frequency of meetings. Be prepared to defend your solution.

IT Steering Committee - Charter
• Role
• Responsibility (decision power)

• Frequency	• Participants

Assignment Box 2.2: Assessment of EGIT Mechanisms in Practice

If you have access to an organization, assess the presence and maturity of the EGIT mechanisms as discussed in this section. You can use the list of mechanisms provided in Table 2.3, each time indicating whether the mechanism is not present (0) versus very mature (5) in the organization. Also provide a corresponding rationale for each rating you make. You can also add other mechanisms in the list that were not discussed in this chapter.

A generic indication of the maturity scale is provided below. To make the analysis in-depth, the scale should be made specific for each of the mechanisms (e.g. what do you expect if portfolio management is at level 5).

0   Non-existent: There is a complete lack of any recognizable EGIT mechanism.
1   Initial/ad hoc: The organization has recognized that EGIT issues exist and need to be addressed.
2   Repeatable but intuitive: There is awareness of EGIT objectives, and mechanisms are developed and applied by individual managers.
3   Defined: The need to act with respect to EGIT is understood and accepted. Procedures have been standardized, documented and implemented.

4 Managed and measurable: EGIT evolves into an enterprise-wide practice and EGIT activities are becoming integrated with overall enterprise governance.
5 Optimized: EGIT and overall enterprise governance are strategically linked, leveraging technology and human and financial resources to increase the competitive advantage of the enterprise.

2.3 Principles for Enterprise Governance of IT

In practice, organizations often try to express a number of "principles," which clearly state how business and IT will collaborate in the organization. These principles are to be defined jointly by business and IT stakeholders and constitute a kind of contract between business and IT. They are often a good starting point to use as reference for designing and implementing EGIT structures, processes, and relational mechanisms.

Examples of principles used in real-life organizations are provided in Table 2.4. Each of these principles of course requires more detailed definitions and descriptions

Table 2.4 Example EGIT principles

• IT is a professional organization that effectively and efficiently manages its resources in alignment with the needs of the organization.
• IT is the exclusive provider of IT services. Outsourcing is always organised in joint partnership between business and IT.
• IT is proactively engaged in further developing and innovating the organization.
• IT primarily develops and maintains competencies that are aligned to and required for supporting the expertise available in the organization.
• The priorities within IT are aligned to the strategic goals of the organizations through integrated planning cycles.
• All IT applications comply with rules and policies as mutually agreed upon by business and IT
• IT is proactively engaged in reviewing and designing efficient business processes.
• IT and the business collaborate based on fixed agreements. Based on a scope definition, impact analysis and capacity reviews, both business and IT commit for timely delivery within quality requirements.
• There is transparency on the required service quality that IT must deliver to the business, and this service quality is continuously monitored.
• Starting from the initial development of a new business project, the potential impact on IT needs to be analysed.

of what exactly the implications are toward the required EGIT structures, processes, and relational mechanisms. In that sense, such principles become the starting point to "design" a tailored and appropriate EGIT model for the organization. In the next section, by means of the KLM case, a demonstration is provided of how such principles can be translated to required EGIT structures, processes, and relational mechanisms.

Assignment Box 2.3: Understanding EGIT Principles
Discuss in group the meaning of the EGIT principles as presented in Table 2.4. Describe which structures, processes and relational mechanisms you would proposed to design an EGIT model that allows these principles to be realized in the organization. Present and discuss the results in class.

2.4 Case Study: Enterprise Governance of IT at KLM[3]

KLM Royal Dutch Airlines is a global airline company based in the Netherlands. It is the world's oldest airline still operating under its original name (founded in 1919). KLM has its home base and hub in Amsterdam Airport Schiphol (The Netherlands). In 2004, KLM merged with Air France, after which both companies continued to operate as separate airlines, each with their own identity and brand, and each benefiting from each other's strengths. In 2013, KLM employed 32,850 people worldwide and managed a fleet of 199 aircraft. That year, KLM had operating revenues of 25.6 billion euros and operated flights to 131 destinations in 65 countries servicing a total of 25.8 million customers.

This case focuses on the KLM activities within the Air France–KLM group. The organizational structure of KLM is visualized in Fig. 2.2. The KLM Executive Committee is composed of the CEO, CFO, managing director, and all executive vice presidents (EVPs) of the major business units and services (commercial, in-flight services, operations, ground services, cargo, engineering and maintenance, IT, and HR). The EVP of the IT service domain is the CIO, who therefore also has a seat at KLM's executive committee. In 2013, KLM IT employed close to 1000 (internal and external) FTEs, with an IT budget of around 738 million euros. As shown in Fig. 2.2, KLM's IT service domain is organized around IT development activities, IT operations activities and the CIO office addressing aspects of the enterprise/IT architecture, IT strategy, value and portfolio management, sourcing strategy, and risk and security. The mission of the IT department is "*to create*

---

[3]Acknowledgment: We would like to express our special gratitude toward John Thorp and Dirk Gemke for their very inspiring thoughts and contributions in the development of the KLM case study on enterprise governance of IT.

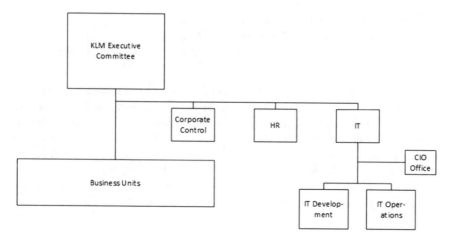

Fig. 2.2 KLM's organizational structure

business value by delivering reliable IT services to the business processes, and innovative IT solutions to enable and support business changes." The following strategic goals for IT support this mission:

- IT is a world-class information services provider and will be able to deliver the best value to the company.
- The IT cost levels will be at a competitive industry level.
- The IT architecture and infrastructure will enable the growth ambitions of KLM (and the Air France–KLM group).

2.4.1 KLM's Trigger Points to Start the EGIT Journey

IT is a business-critical enabler for KLM, yet, at the same time, can be a source of both success and discontent. In 2001, the balance had tilted toward dissatisfaction due to a lack of trust in what was perceived as a very costly and unresponsive IT department. This was happening in a business climate that was increasingly challenging and which became dramatically more so after the 9/11 terrorist attacks. After that event, KLM's CEO seized the opportunity to make a structural break with the past and the decision was made to re-examine and transform KLM's enterprise and IT governance. The executive vice president (EVP) of the operations control center was appointed as the new CIO. It was felt that having the CIO coming out of the "real business" would help in getting the IT governance discussion out of the IT area and have it put on the business executives' agenda. The newly appointed CIO received three clear IT governance-related priorities:

1. Provide the reasons why, or why not, to outsource IT.
2. Create a business/IT board to organize joint success.
3. Design simple governance principles to restore control and steering by the executive vice presidents (EVPs) and the CIO.

In that context, the CIO office was established as a support function to the CIO, consolidating a number of already existing, loosely coupled, and different functions such as an IT Strategy Office, Programme Management, and business/IT liaison roles. In the words of the Vice President (VP) of the CIO office: *"In the scenario that we would outsource IT, both IT operations and development would mainly be sourced outside KLM, but the activities of the of CIO office would be kept internally, as it governs IT strategy, architecture, security, business/IT alignment, etc. The goal of the CIO office is to enable effective IT, in support of business needs."*

2.4.2 Embarking on the EGIT Journey

It was decided that, out of the three IT governance-related priorities stated above, the primary focus should be to design and implement better governance principles and mechanisms (i.e., priority 3). A project called "IT: A Collaborative Effort" was launched, focused at enabling all stakeholders to better understand the cost and value of IT, which in turn would enable them to make more informed decisions on what and how to potentially outsource (in support of priority 1). In support of priority 2, a business/IT board was established, composed of the CEO, CIO and all business unit EVPs, meeting every quarter to discuss and decide on IT-related strategic issues.

With regard to priority 3, the CIO office, in collaboration with the business, designed a set of principles that would significantly simplify IT-related governance. The starting premise was that these principles should put the business in full control of all IT demand and IT spend. In support of these principles, a number of EGIT mechanisms were introduced in the business and IT organizations, including the establishment of the business/IT board and demand management functions for each business domain. These governance principles and mechanisms were introduced as "the only way of working" between business and IT for all business units and activities. The principles also supported the creation of portfolio management processes driven by the business units. The portfolio management processes evolved from being IT resource- and supply-driven toward business demand-driven with an innovative and rigorous approach to evaluation and selection.

2.4.2.1 Governance Principles and Mechanisms

The definition of the first draft set of governance principles and mechanisms was mainly driven by the CIO office. The principles and mechanisms were later refined with the involved business parties and are now shared in the organization through the intranet. According to the Director Value Management and Alliances (member of the CIO office): *"These principles and mechanisms are still challenged from time to time. Our position is that we are always open for discussion for each of these principles and mechanisms, but up till now, we have each time in the end reconfirmed them."* The stated principles apply for all business units and are presented in internal KLM presentations as shown in Table 2.5. The involved parties acknowledge that this list does not really distinguish between principles and mechanisms and presents these in a mixed way, but it was felt to be a pragmatic and practical list that was workable for KLM. The CIO office developed more detailed background information and internal documentation to explain the impact and consequences of each of these principles and mechanisms.

The first EGIT principle (1) states that, for the business, there should be no difference in dealing with an internal or external IT provider. This recognizes that the business should be in full control of all IT demand and IT spend (supply). Related to the latter, criteria were developed regarding choosing between allocating work in-house for customized development or through external IT providers for standardized solutions. These "selective sourcing" agreements are internally referenced as the "Stay on the Surfboard Principle" (Fig. 2.3). Generic business processes that bring no competitive advantage (such as office support, collaboration, and payroll) will be supported by generic (low development cost, off-the-shelf) applications. Business processes, which have the potential to create competitive advantage (such as CRM, revenue management), can and will be supported by in-house (higher development cost) custom-built applications. The VP CIO office

Table 2.5 KLM's EGIT principles

1. For the business, there should be no difference between working with an internal or external IT provider.
2. Differentiate between WHAT and HOW (and WHY).
3. Improve the demand function by creating a Business Demand Office per business domain.
4. Improve the supply function by creating an Innovation Organizer and a Service Manager per business domain.
5. Create monthly decision meetings of WHAT and HOW (management and IT).
6. Focus on the costs that can be influenced in full and those that can be influenced in part: Split between innovation and continuity.
7. Each innovation (investment) has one business owner to which all costs are charged.
8. Each service (continuity) has one business owner to which all costs are charged.
9. Top-down budget framework and simplified budget process.
10. Activity-based costing applied to process primary cost to product cost.

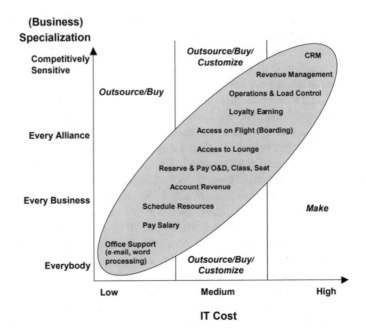

Fig. 2.3 "Stay on the surfboard"—principle for outsourcing at KLM

explains: "*In the past, we evolved to a situation where many commodity services were built and maintained in-house, when businesses were only interested in a good service at low cost for these mainstream applications. The surfboard helped in the discussions on what and what not to outsource, and to bring the debate on 'we want more IT for less money' to another level, oriented towards 'we need different IT for different businesses'.*"

The next set of EGIT principles (more specifically 2–5) define a clear split between IT-related activities in terms of the WHAT activities and HOW activities, or in other terms between demand and supply. Before 2001, IT demand came in via 14 information management committees and numerous informal channels. According to the VP CIO office: "*In the old situation, demand came in through too many different channels, and there was no coordination between those channels. For example, it could be that five similar investment requests were put forward, initiated from different business lines.*" Moreover, as reinforced by the Director Value Management and Alliances, "*some of the Information Management groups also managed a separate IT development team, leading to a very scattered approach.*" To improve the demand function, all business demand for investments and innovation is now channeled via Business Demand Offices (BDOs) for the five business domains of KLM (i.e., engineering and maintenance, cargo, passenger commercial, passenger operations, corporate).

These BDOs are formally positioned in the business department in close contact with their EVPs and with a reporting line to the CIO. Commenting on this, the VP

Finance and Control Ground Services says: "*Putting the BDOs directly in the business was a very important governance design decision, as it enabled them to really act as business representatives.*" Each BDO has a dedicated counterpart or mirror-role on the IT supply side, called the "innovation organizer," responsible for all HOW activity (see Fig. 2.4). Realizing this split was a challenge, as the VP CIO office explains: "*This clear distinction between demand and supply seems obvious, but it implied a huge effort in terms of company meetings, consultations and moving people.*"

As stated in the 6th EGIT principle, a clear differentiation is established between the innovation cost that can be fully influenced by the business and the continuity cost (i.e., cost to "keep the lights on") that can only be partly influenced. The innovation budget includes all manpower, purchases, work by third parties, and other out-of-pocket project costs required to build new IT services and functional changes to existing IT services (i.e., "enhancements"). The BDOs register agreed "innovation" work on the basis of which the innovation organizer coordinates IT development, time accounting, and charge-out. The continuity budget includes cost for IT services, desktops, data communication, and telecommunication and is managed, in terms of volume and quality, by the "exploitation manager" on business side, together with the "business service manager" on IT supply side (refer back to Fig. 2.4). The objective of these business service managers is to deliver continuity of the KLM operations in an efficient way and at lowest IT cost.

This split between the innovation (i.e., program) portfolio and the continuity (i.e., service) portfolio is internally explained with the image of "the bicycle" (see Fig. 2.5). This "bicycle" is mainly used as a visual aid to internally communicate at a high level the split and relationship between the continuity and innovation budget. As visualized, the business/IT strategy drives the definition and application of the governance principles and priority rules and the definition of business cases. The approved business cases are managed in the program (innovation cycle), which,

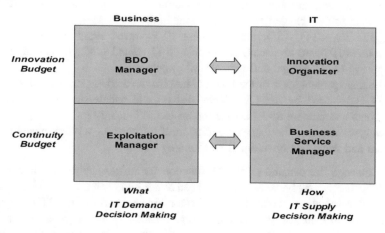

Fig. 2.4 Mirror roles between business and IT at KLM

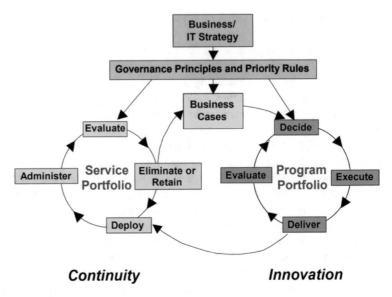

Fig. 2.5 "Innovation-continuity bicycle" at KLM

after delivery, become operational services being deployed and administered in the service (continuity) portfolio. As a result of ongoing evaluation, services may continue with no change, re-enter the innovation cycle through a new business case, or be eliminated (retired).

All these roles created different decision platforms for IT-related governance, as shown in Fig. 2.6. There are a number of scheduled activities, involving different stakeholders and occurring at different frequencies, which occur throughout the year:

- Twice a year, the Group Executive Committee is updated on how IT will respond to new challenges and directions in the businesses.
- The CEO, CFO, CIO, and Business EVPs meet every 2 months in the business/IT board to discuss and decide on IT-related strategic planning and to approve the IT budget and portfolio of programs.
- The management team of the IT provider plus the 5 BDOs meet monthly in the MT-IT, chaired by the CIO. They discuss and decide on tactical planning matters and prepare decisions for the business/IT board.
- Every two weeks, the management team of information services meets to discuss and decide on operational and running issues.

To manage the demand of the IT function for infrastructure investments, for which business cases have traditionally been difficult to justify, a separate BDO for the IT department was created. The Director Finance and Control IT Operations argues: "*If, for example, you have a storage technology which cannot be virtualized, you may be able to build a business case to migrate to a new storage*

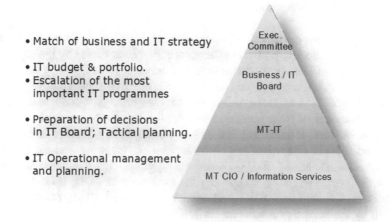

Fig. 2.6 EGIT decision platforms at KLM

technology where virtualization is possible, resulting in lower business service costs. But for other infrastructure type investments, such as the migration of operating systems, the business case will be built on a risk avoidance and cost of future operational support." The IT-BDO, part of the CIO office, analyses future needs and capacity based on the incoming business cases of the businesses. Potential investments are then translated into an IT business case and are discussed with the other BDOs in the "Information Security and Architecture Meeting" (ISAM). Once approved, the CIO office takes ownership to implement these infrastructure services. If possible, such investments are linked to other business investments that are being planned.

Finally, EGIT principles 7–10 address the budgeting and cost accounting processes. The previous process of charging out IT costs to the business, with more than 3300 technical cost components being charged to more than 3400 cost account centers, was unwieldy and provided little useful management information. The VP Finance and Control Ground Services concluded: "*As a result, business perceived IT as a black box which they could not control, and therefore as something that was very likely to be too expensive.*" Drastic simplification of the budgeting process was needed, essentially from charging hundreds of technical items to hundreds of departments of users, to charging only seven products with associated cost: two for innovation and five for continuity, to twelve respective single/unique business owners (units). All budgets and costs (both continuity and innovation) are managed, forecasted, and made transparent through a cost portal, driven by activity-based costing principles, enabling clear and active ownership of the business of all IT-related costs.

2.4.2.2   Portfolio Management

The EGIT principles discussed above were needed as key building blocks in support of having effective portfolio management processes driven by the business units. The design of these portfolio management processes (see Fig. 2.7) was done by the portfolio management office (part of the CIO office). Three approval stages are defined, going from "idea selection" to "program go" and "investment approval." For each of these phases, clear decision thresholds were defined. For investments between 150,000 and 500,000 euros, the EVP, Director Finance and Control and BDO of a business unit could approve the go/no-go decision in each phase, investments above 500,000 euros are approved by the Business Unit Investment Committee (BIC), comprising the business unit COO, EVP, Director Finance and Control, and BDO and investments above 5,000,000 euros are approved by the executive committee (EC).

The initial phase (1) addresses the initiation of the investment proposals or idea generation. In this phase, all business ideas are gathered and captured by the BDOs (demand process) and turned into potential initiatives for which a high-level business case (HLBC) will be developed. These high-level business cases include descriptive information, classifications, and high-level cost/benefits estimates and risks. The VP BDO Passenger Operations clarifies: "*It is often hard to quantify*

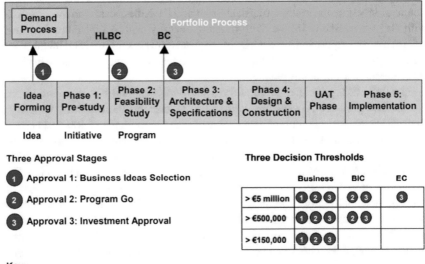

Fig. 2.7 Portfolio management process at KLM

some benefits at this stage. For example, the cost avoided of an aircraft not needing to land on another location because of better support systems. But still, we try to make as good as possible educated estimations." If an initiative is approved (2), it is turned into a program for which a full business case (BC) is developed based on a detailed feasibility study. To enable common and comparable business cases, a business case template was developed as a mandatory instrument for all investments above 150,000 euros.

To be able to prioritize all these business cases, it is crucial to know what the organization's business drivers are. The Director Value Management and Alliances states: *"Our experience was that it was often difficult to obtain a clear list of business priorities from a business unit. However, we needed these priorities to enable the selection of 'the right things' and for that reason we used a methodology to help us and the business in making these business priorities transparent."* The business drivers of a business unit are captured by the CIO office through interviews with the business unit executives. In the example of the Passenger Operations business unit, seven different business priorities were identified (see Fig. 2.8). Next, each of these business drivers is ranked through a pair-wise comparison technique. Instead of just ranking the drivers from 1 to *n*, this technique relates each driver to the other drivers in terms of relative importance, ranging from "extremely less" toward "extremely more" in five sequential steps (e.g., "competitive unit cost" is relatively more important than "quality in physical comfort"). After completion of this pair-wise comparison by each of the executive directors, a prioritized list of the defined business drivers is created and converted into percentages that sum up to 100%, as illustrated for Passenger Operations below.

In the following step, the same pair-wise comparison technique is used to determine the contribution of the investment proposals to each business driver. For each investment proposal, the contribution to each of the business drivers is

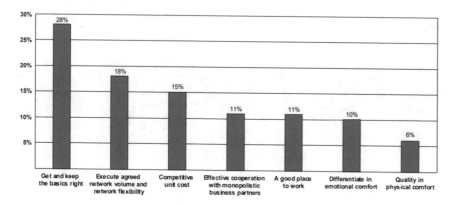

Fig. 2.8 Business drivers for the "Passenger Operations" business unit at KLM

determined, ranging from "low" to "extreme." The result of these steps is an initial portfolio containing a ranked, but still unconstrained, list of all investment proposals at business unit level. The VP BDO Passenger Operations explains the importance of this process: *"These priorities are the basis to build a 'business plan' for the BDO of a specific business unit, describing all the things that the BDO-office of a business unit can be held accountable for. I have even turned this business plan into a video clip on YouTube, to demonstrate to all our business and IT stakeholders our commitment for the next year."*

After this prioritization, total demand of all business units typically exceeds the budget made available by the executive committee. The Director Value Management and Alliances describes how this is handled: *"Instead of using a 'cheese slicer' and, for example, forcing all business units to cut 30% out of the project portfolio, a process of informal discussions is initiated between the BDOs to determine how the portfolio can best be optimized. As long as this process works, this approach is preferred instead of escalating to the next management level."* This process generally works well, and as a result, the business/IT board receives an overview of the major programs and just has to endorse the outcome of the portfolio management process. The Director Value Management and Alliances concludes: *"Through a good portfolio management process, we strive for seamless decision-making."*

Once the portfolio of programs is determined, the business investment committee (for project above 500,000) or executive committee (for project above 5,000,000) still has to release the funds before design, construction, user acceptance testing (UAT) and implementation can start. This might appear as a duplicated decision structure, but it acts as a final check and it also gives the final authority and decision power back to the business executives. The VP BDO Passenger Operations explains: *"In the end, the business executives decide. This approach helped in getting them engaged in the portfolio management process because they get their control back, although until now they have never 'used' it. Another important aspect in this context is that we try to make the time between the business idea and approval on the investment committee as short as possible, as this period is perceived as 'IT being slow'."*

Assignment Box 2.4: Identifying EGIT Mechanisms Leveraged by KLM
Revisit the KLM case study and identify the EGIT structures, processes and relational mechanisms leveraged by KLM. Make sure you can clearly explain each of these mechanisms and its role in the context of KLM's enterprise governance of IT.

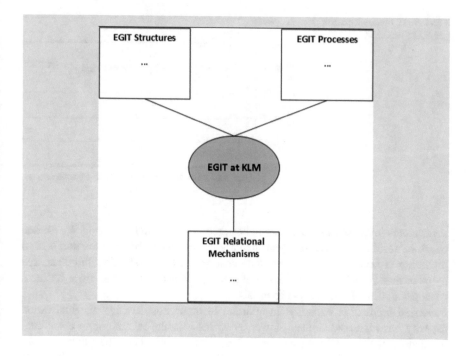

2.4.3   Reported EGIT Benefits

During our interviews with the stakeholders in this case study, the following benefits of the improved Enterprise Governance of IT, which are discussed further in the following paragraphs, were consistently mentioned:

- Lower IT continuity cost per business production unit;
- Increased capacity for innovation;
- Increased alignment of investments to strategic goals;
- More trust between all involved stakeholders; and
- Moving beyond cost thinking toward a value culture.

Lower IT continuity cost: A primary goal of the CIO office is to continuously promote, improve, and demonstrate the value of the EGIT principles and mechanisms in ensuring that IT-enabled investments contribute to real business value. In this effort, one of the metrics reported by the CIO office is the relation between all IT continuity costs and "equivalent available seat kilometers" (EASK), the key metric used to monitor airline production, which represents the total number of seats and cargo capacity multiplied by the total number of kilometers flown by the airline fleet. The graph (Fig. 2.9) shows that (even though many business

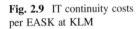

Fig. 2.9 IT continuity costs
per EASK at KLM

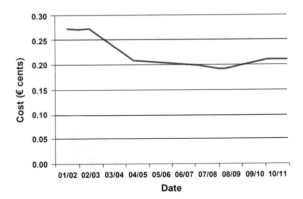

investments involving IT, such as e-tickets, more Web-based sales, and Web-based check-in, resulted in a year-on-year increase in the total IT budget) the unit cost of providing IT services (i.e., IT continuity cost) per airline production unit decreased by more than 20%.[4] This substitution of labor by IT also resulted in lower business costs per unit, as IT is cheaper than labor.

Increased innovation capacity: In addition to direct cost savings, the innovation capacity has increased. Indeed, lower, or at least stable, IT continuity costs contributed to freeing up financials for IT-based innovation. The CIO office also developed metrics to demonstrate this outcome, of which an example is shown in Fig. 2.10. This bar chart shows a relative stable IT continuity budget, enabling the increase of the total IT budget to go almost entirely to new innovation, which has increased from 25% in 2004/2005 to 39% in 2010/2011.

Increased alignment of investments to strategic goals: The use of an innovative and inclusive process to capture and prioritize the business drivers of business units has enabled investment decisions to move beyond what was previously a fairly arbitrary process (in the case of cost reductions), or a largely subjective and emotional discussion (in the case of new innovations), to a more objective one. The new process, which involves discussions with and between business units and the CIO office, is based on the contribution of existing or proposed IT spend to business drivers. It has resulted in increased alignment of investment and IT spend with business unit drivers and strategic goals and increased confidence in the decision-making process. This increased confidence has also resulted in the business/IT board spending less time debating the merits of major programs and generally endorsing the outcome of the portfolio management process.

More trust: A fourth reported EGIT benefit is the increased trust between business and IT. The whole governance and portfolio management process has resulted in improved and more transparent decision-making. The results of the business driver prioritization and investment contribution to the business strategy are visible for

---

[4]The slight upward curve for the next 3 years is due to a temporary decrease of production in response to the global economic crisis.

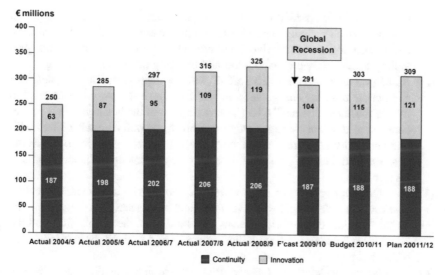

Fig. 2.10 Portion of total IT budget used for "IT continuity" and "IT innovation" at KLM

every stakeholder involved. It makes it difficult for executives to overvalue their own favorite proposals. As a result, there is more trust, and this helps in continuing the "IT: a collaborative effort" journey.

A value culture: Finally, the process of managing the change toward improved EGIT has its own benefits. The communication and discussions on portfolio management have improved management awareness and understanding and supported the transformation from a cost toward a value culture. It also continues to identify additional opportunities to improve the existing EGIT approach.

2.4.4   *Lessons Learned from KLM's EGIT Journey*

Although all organizations, including KLM, face some unique challenges, concerns regarding effective EGIT and the realization of real IT business value are universal concerns. Other organizations can certainly benefit from the experiences and lessons learned by KLM in these areas (De Haes et al., 2011).

The factors that have been key to KLM's successful EGIT journey are summarized below. We recommend that all organizations with an interest in improving their EGIT consider these factors, both in terms of assessing where they are today and in planning the steps they need to take for further improvement. The factors include:

(1) *Senior management commitment*: KLM's success started with their senior management. They had a strong executive leadership team, who moved beyond awareness of a problem, through understanding the causes of the

problem and what needed to be done, to commitment to a sustained program of action which included both clearly communicating direction and priorities, and embedding a "value-driven" culture. They set the tone at the top, promoting teamwork and collaboration and breaking down "silo thinking."

(2) *Business engagement*: Effective EGIT will not happen without adequate and appropriate business engagement. In KLM's case, it was very instrumental to have a "business-oriented" CIO (i.e., coming out of the business). This further demonstrated senior management commitment, as well as establishing credibility and starting to break down the "we versus them"—thinking between the business and IT. This resulted in greater engagement, collaboration, and partnership.

(3) *Distinguishing between the "what" and the "how"*: Making a clear distinction between, and defining respective roles and responsibilities, regarding the "what," i.e., the demand side, versus the "how," i.e., the supply side, and the "investment" versus the "continuity" budget was a difficult, but essential step of the journey.

(4) *Defining key principles and mechanisms*: Developing a small, clearly defined, simple and well-communicated set of EGIT principles and mechanisms focused on putting the business in full control of all IT demand and IT spend. In developing this, KLM did not get stuck in academic discussions about the difference between principles and mechanisms, but presented them in a pragmatic and practical way that "worked for KLM." They also supported these principles and mechanisms with more detailed background information and internal documentation to explain their impact and consequences.

(5) *Positioning demand functions in the business*: Embedding the demand functions (i.e., BDOs) in the business organization was key to having them really act as business representatives, and reinforced the business responsibility for, and ownership of the "what" decisions, and the results of those decisions.

(6) *Clear and transparent business drivers*: A clear and shared understanding of business drivers is crucial in order to be able to prioritize investments and enable the selection of "the right things." KLM used an innovative method to help clarify their business drivers and make them transparent.

(7) *Standard business cases*: While, in some ways, the process of developing a business case is as important as the result, a standard template ensures that the content of the business case is consistent, comprehensive, and comparable. In KLM's case, they developed a standard business case template as a mandatory instrument for all investments above 150,000 euros.

(8) *A strong front-end demand process*: KLM established a rigorous process (through the BDOs) with intense scrutiny applied to the front-end review of each idea, initiative, and business case. This allowed them to allocate funds appropriately by prioritizing the investments in terms of their potential contribution to business drivers.

(9) *A clear and transparent portfolio management process*: The transparency of this process at KLM, with clarity of business drivers and investments' contributions to those drivers, leveled the "playing field," established trust between

all stakeholders, and avoided the traditional decibel, or relationship-based decision-making approach.

(10) *A pragmatic approach*: KLM balanced theory and organizational and cultural reality by taking a pragmatic and practical approach, consisting of well-defined but sometimes small steps, each with their own benefits.

(11) *A strong support group*: There is a need for a function to support the implementation, adoption, and ongoing application and sustainment of EGIT principles and mechanisms. In KLM's case, this was the CIO office, who helped sponsor and embed EGIT in the organization.

2.5 EGIT Capita Selecta

Contemporary academic research is increasingly interested in more specific issues that are deemed relevant in practice. This section discusses a few of those emerging EGIT-related topics, which are also covered in our research activities. More specifically, (1) the role of the board in EGIT, (2) IT governance transparency, (3) the inter-organizational governance of IT, (4) ambidextrous EGIT, and (5) a more theoretical view on EGIT by drawing on the lens of the Viable System Model (VSM) are discussed as part of this section.

2.5.1 Board-Level EGIT[5]

The definition of Enterprise Governance of IT (EGIT) that is put forward by this book, i.e., *"an integral part of corporate governance for which, as such, the board is accountable. It involves the definition and implementation of processes, structures, and relational mechanisms that enable both business and IT stakeholders to execute their responsibilities in support of business/IT alignment, and the creation and protection of IT business value,"* indicates a crucial role of the board of directors. While the need for board involvement in the context of IT governance is widely recognized (ISACA, 2018; ISO/IEC, 2015; IT Governance Institute (ITGI), 2003; Nolan & McFarlan, 2005; Raghupathi, 2007; Trites, 2004), and numerous positive consequences of such involvement have been identified (Turel & Bart, 2014; Valentine & Stewart, 2015), the involvement of boards in practice however seems to be the exception rather than the rule (Andriole, 2009; Bart & Turel, 2010; Valentine & Stewart, 2015).

[5]Acknowledgment: This section is based on the doctoral research of Laura Caluwe, and more specifically on an article that was developed in the context of this doctoral research, i.e., Caluwe and De Haes (2019).

The following subsections summarize existing board-level IT governance research. More specifically, the first subsection deals with the antecedents of board-level IT governance. The second subsection addresses the issue of implementing or effectuating board-level IT governance (i.e., the structures, processes, and relational mechanisms that can be used to deploy IT governance at the level of the board of directors). Finally, the third subsection provides an overview of the consequences of board-level IT governance.

2.5.1.1 The Antecedents of Board-Level IT Governance

Extant literature has empirically validated or suggested numerous factors that (potentially) influence board-level involvement in IT governance. An overview of these antecedents is provided in Table 2.6. The first part of this list summarizes the empirically validated antecedents (i.e., the factors of which the effect on board-level IT governance has been proven). The second part of this list summarizes the suggested antecedents (i.e., the factors that potentially influence board-level IT governance). The antecedent that has received the most attention when it comes to empirical validation is the role of IT in the organization. The IT strategic impact grid (Nolan & McFarlan, 2005) is the most frequently used framework by board-level IT governance researchers to operationalize the role of IT (Bart & Turel, 2010; Parent & Reich, 2009; Posthumus et al., 2010; Turel & Bart, 2014). According to the IT strategic impact grid, board involvement in IT governance is driven by two important factors: (1) the need for reliable IT (low or high) and (2) the need for new IT (low or high). The combination of these two factors results in four modes of IT use (i.e., support mode, factory mode, turnaround mode, and strategic mode) as visualized in Fig. 2.11. Firms in "support mode" are not very dependent on IT. In such firms, IT is primarily used to support routine employee activities. Firms in "factory mode" are much more operationally dependent on IT, while remaining rather unambitious about strategic IT initiatives. In such firms, most of the core business processes are heavily supported by IT. Firms in "turnaround mode" are currently not very operationally dependent on IT, but are in the process of a strategic transformation. They thus anticipate that future strategic IT will fundamentally change their way of doing business. Turnaround mode is hence almost always a "transition mode" (i.e., moving from turnaround mode to factory mode or strategic mode). Finally, firms in "strategic mode" are operationally as well as strategically very dependent on IT. In summary, the degree and nature of the involvement of the board of directors in IT governance (should) depend(s) on the position of the organization in the IT strategic impact grid (Nolan & McFarlan, 2005).

Other studies examining the influence of the role of IT in the organization on the level of involvement of the board in IT governance operationalize the role of IT somewhat differently. Jewer and McKay (2012) consider an organization's operational or strategic reliance on IT. From their operationalization of these constructs, it can be concluded that operational reliance on IT relates to *the need for reliable IT*

Table 2.6 Antecedents of board-level IT governance

	Antecedent		Effect on board-level ITG	Reference(s)
Empirically validated antecedents	Proportion of insiders		Negative	Jewer and McKay (2012)
	Board size		Negative	Jewer and McKay (2012)
	IT competency		Positive	Jewer and McKay (2012), Kambil and Lucas (2002)
	Organization age		Negative	Jewer and McKay (2012)
	Role of IT in the organization	Overall role of IT (i.e., operational and/or strategic reliance on IT)	Positive	Jewer and McKay (2012)
		Need for new IT	Positive	Turel and Bart (2014)
		Need for reliable IT	Positive	Turel and Bart (2014)
		Strategic importance of IT	Positive	Kuruzovich, Bassellier, and Sambamurthy (2012)
		IT intensity	Positive	Benaroch and Chernobai (2017)
	Firm performance		Positive	Benaroch and Chernobai (2017), Premuroso and Bhattacharya (2007)
	Corporate governance		Positive	Premuroso and Bhattacharya (2007)
Suggested antecedents	Lack of IT expertise		Negative	Andriole (2009), Bart and Turel (2010), Buckby and Best (2007), Coertze and von Solms (2013, 2014), Nolan and McFarlan (2005), Parent and Reich (2009), Turel and Bart (2014), Valentine and Stewart (2013a, 2013b, 2015), Yayla and Hu (2014)
	Motivational factors		Negative	Andriole (2009), Kritzinger-von Solms and Strous (2003), Parent and Reich (2009), Posthumus and von Solms (2008), Valentine and Stewart (2013b)
	Director age		Negative	Andriole (2009), Mähring (2006), Valentine and Stewart (2013b)
	Lack of understanding of the role of IT in the organization		Negative	Posthumus and von Solms (2008), Posthumus, Von Solms, and King (2010), Valentine and Stewart (2013b), Yayla and Hu (2014)
	Lack of guidance on board-level IT governance		Negative	Parent and Reich (2009), Posthumus and von Solms (2008)
	Lack of IT information at board level		Negative	Oliver and Walker (2006), Posthumus and von Solms (2008)
	Guidance and regulations		Positive	Bart and Turel (2010), Mähring (2006), Trautman and Altenbaumer-Price (2010)

Fig. 2.11 IT strategic impact
grid (Nolan & McFarlan,
2005)

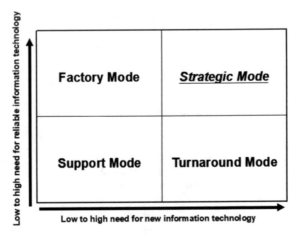

from the IT strategic impact grid, while strategic reliance on IT relates to *the need for new IT*. Benaroch and Chernobai (2017) consider the IT intensity of the firm and argue this parallels the role of IT as defined by Jewer and McKay (2012). The IT intensity is measured as the industry-level IT intensity based on the share of IT capital in total capital for an industry segment, weighted by the percentage of the firm's sales within that segment. Kuruzovich et al. (2012) refer to the strategic importance of IT, which is described as *"the degree to which IT has the potential to have a transformational impact on the associated business of the organization."* Hence, they mainly focus on *the need for new IT*. All studies confirm that the role of IT is related to board-level IT governance. Figure 2.12 summarizes the different perspectives on the role of IT in an organization as well as an overview of board-level IT governance studies based on the IT strategic impact grid, indicating its popularity and application potential.

Numerous other antecedents have been suggested that (potentially) influence board-level involvement in IT governance, like a lack of IT expertise and motivational factors (see "suggested antecedents" in Table 2.6). However, those factors and their hypothesized effects on board-level IT governance have not yet been validated. As such, there are numerous opportunities for further research in this area.

2.5.1.2 Board-Level IT Governance Mechanisms

Extant research also provides insights on the issue of implementing or effectuating board-level IT governance. In line with overall EGIT, board involvement in IT governance can be effectuated through implementing a mix of structures, processes, and relational mechanisms. A summary of these mechanisms as proposed in extant literature is provided in Table 2.7.

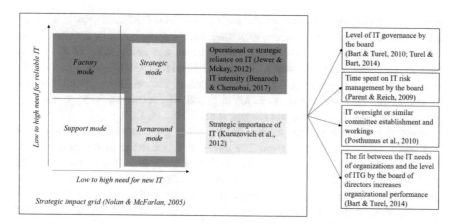

Fig. 2.12 Role of IT in an organization as an antecedent to board-level IT governance

Table 2.7 Board-level IT governance mechanisms (i.e., structures, processes, and relational mechanisms)

Board-level IT governance mechanisms	
Structures	*Reference(s)*
IT oversight or similar committee at the level of the board	Coertze and von Solms (2014), Higgs, Pinsker, Smith, and Young (2016), Nolan and McFarlan (2005), Oliver and Walker (2006), Posthumus et al. (2010), Premuroso and Bhattacharya (2007), Read (2004), Turel and Bart (2014)
IT expertise at the board	Mohamad, Hendrick, O'Leary, and Best (2014), Valentine and Stewart (2013a, 2015)
CIO reporting to the CEO	Valentine and Stewart (2013b)
CIO part of the (executive) board	Benaroch and Chernobai (2017), Coertze and von Solms (2014), Posthumus et al. (2010)
Processes	*Reference(s)*
Asking IT-related questions	Bart and Turel (2010), Nolan and McFarlan (2005), Turel and Bart (2014)
Relational mechanisms	*Reference(s)*
Effective communication about IT from and to the board	Andriole (2009), Coertze and von Solms (2014), Kuruzovich et al. (2012), Oliver and Walker (2006), Yayla and Hu (2014)
CIO regularly meeting with the board	Butler and Butler (2010), Kuruzovich et al. (2012)

Board-Level Structures

Table 2.7 indicates that board-level IT governance structures are widely examined in extant literature. The most-frequently mentioned board-level structure is an *IT oversight or similar committee at the level of the board*. Multiple responsibilities are attributed to such a committee, including: assisting the board in keeping an eye out for what competitors and other organizations are doing with IT (Nolan & McFarlan, 2005); ensuring that IT-related issues is an established topic on the board's agenda and ensuring that the board has all the necessary information for IT-related decision-making (Posthumus et al., 2010); and identifying, mitigating, and reporting on IT-related risks (Higgs et al., 2016).

Another structural mechanism for board-level IT governance is the *IT expertise of directors* (i.e., board members). The value of IT expertise of independent and dependent directors is slightly different. While independent directors with IT expertise enable the board to provide advice to management, to facilitate access to external IT parties, to attract qualified IT management, and to advocate for more IT budgets; internal directors with IT expertise are important to make sure the board understands the business costs of IT risks and enables the swift allocation of resources and priority setting to adjust IT weaknesses (Benaroch & Chernobai, 2017). In order to better understand the IT expertise needed at the level of the board to adequately perform their IT oversight role, Valentine and Stewart (2015) suggested three main IT-related competencies for directors: (1) Direct and govern technology-enabled strategy and planning to maximize the advantages of technology and enhance performance at all levels of the organization, (2) lead and govern business technology investment and risk, and (3) direct and govern technology-enabled innovation and value creation.

The other two IT governance structures deal with the position of the CIO in the organization. Valentine and Stewart (2013b) argue that the CIO should report directly to the CEO. Other approaches (e.g., when the CIO reports to the COO or the CFO) might result in treating IT as a cost, not as a strategic asset. This might then affect the communication of these executives about IT to the board (Valentine & Stewart, 2013b). Other scholars even argue that the CIO can be added to the board of directors, in case IT is a strategic business asset or IT becomes the business itself (Coertze & von Solms, 2014).

Board-Level Processes

Table 2.7 shows that there is a dearth of research on board-level IT governance processes. One such process mechanism that is mentioned in a few studies is that the board should ask themselves and management the right IT-related questions to effectuate their control and advise responsibilities (Bart & Turel, 2010; Nolan & McFarlan, 2005; Turel & Bart, 2014). Extant literature furthermore provides hands-on guidance for boards of directors under the form of question sets (Nolan & McFarlan, 2005).

Board-Level Relational Mechanisms

Table 2.7 indicates that, similar to processes, little academic research is available about board-level IT governance relational mechanisms. A first relational mechanism that is mentioned in extant literature as being essential for boards to become involved in IT-related strategic decision-making and control is effective communication about IT from and to the board. Regarding communication *from* the board, Coertze and von Solms (2014) propose that boards with limited IT expertise should communicate the business strategy to the IT organization in business terms (implying that the CIO is in charge of translating this strategy into IT objectives). On the other hands, boards with considerable IT expertise are able to translate the business strategy in IT terms themselves, resulting in IT-oriented board directives. Regarding communication *to* the board, scholars suggested that it is the responsibility of the CIO to effectively communicate with the board regarding IT-related matters (Andriole, 2009; Yayla & Hu, 2014). This is an important attention point, as the quality of IT-related information that reaches the board contributes to their decision-making (Kuruzovich et al., 2012). Another relational mechanism mentioned in the literature is that the CIO should be able to access the board and frequently meet with them (Butler & Butler, 2010).

Assignment Box 2.5: Board-Level EGIT Mechanisms for Different IT Use Modes

The 'IT strategic impact grid' (Nolan & McFarlan, 2005) was introduced above as a tool to determine the role of IT in the organization (refer back to Fig. 2.11). It was also asserted that organizations with a different role of IT (i.e. a different 'IT use mode') require different ways of implementing board-level IT governance.

Using the table below, map some board-level IT governance structures, processes, and relational mechanisms to the four IT use modes as defined in the IT strategic impact grid.

	Support	Factory	Turnaround	Strategic
Structures				
Processes				
Relational mechanisms				

2.5.1.3   The Consequences of Board-Level IT Governance

Higher levels of board-level IT governance have been found to result in increased organizational performance in multiple studies (Turel & Bart, 2014; Turel, Liu, & Bart, 2017). Jewer and McKay (2012) showed that more board involvement in IT governance leads to a higher contribution of IT to organizational performance. A slightly more specific view is provided by Yayla and Hu (2014), who demonstrated that the IT awareness, defined as "*the extent to which the board is conscious of IT as a business function and able to formulate appropriate conceptions of what IT entails to their firm and industry*" has a positive effect on organizational performance.

Besides value creation as a consequence of board-level IT governance, value protection (i.e., counteracting value destruction) is also investigated as a consequence of board-level IT governance. For instance, Higgs et al. (2016) analyzed the link between board-level technology committees and reported security breaches. As opposed to what might be expected, it was found that, initially, organizations with a technology committee at the level of the board are more likely to report breaches in a given year than those without such a committee. However, as these committees mature, the organization is less likely to be breached. An explanation for this somewhat surprising result is that organizations without a board-level technology committee might not even detect or report security breaches. Young committees might increase the detection and reporting rate, while more established committees might also prevent security breaches.

In summary, studies dealing with the consequences of board-level IT governance are exposing multiple advantages of board-level involvement in IT governance.

2.5.2 *IT Governance Transparency*

IT governance transparency, or IT-related disclosure, pertains to external-oriented communication about the way in which the organization is leveraging and controlling its (current and future) IT (Joshi, Bollen, & Hassink, 2013). Prior research in this area has asserted that transparency and disclosure are critical in the context of IT governance for stakeholder confidence and the creation of a positive image in general (Raghupathi, 2007). Chatterjee, Richardson, and Zmud (2001) found that the incidence of announcements of newly created CIO positions steadily increased, leading them to the conclusion that firms seemed to be aware of the desirability of disclosing IT governance-related information with (potential) investors. Joshi et al. (2013) found that on average, European banks disclose more on IT (governance)-related matters than US banks. While there are multiple possible sources where IT-related publicly disclosed information can be found, the preferred medium for firms to effectuate IT governance transparency appeared to be the annual report (Joshi et al., 2013). While IT (governance)-related disclosure is essentially voluntary in nature (Joshi et al., 2013), some firms are required by law to disclose IT-related failures affecting the quality of their financial reporting (Masli, Richardson, Watson, & Zmud, 2016).

Joshi et al. (2013) presented an IT governance disclosure framework based on the IT governance focus areas as defined by the IT governance institute (2003). This framework can be used to assess a firm's transparency about its IT governance and, from the firm's point of view, to identify potential areas of being transparent about IT governance (i.e., the contents of the disclosure). Specifically, this IT governance disclosure framework contains 39 disclosure items distributed over the following domains: IT strategic alignment, IT value delivery, IT risk management, and IT performance measurement. "IT strategic alignment" deals with the fact that IT investments need to support the strategic goals and objectives of an organization to enable the creation of current and future business value. "IT value delivery" is concerned with the optimization of IT-enabled value creation, where value is broader than strictly monetary (e.g., competitive advantage, higher employee productivity). "IT risk management" is concerned with the protection of IT assets and recovery from IT-related disasters. Finally, "IT performance measurement" is related to the IT budget and IT investments. It is specifically concerned with the expenditure on IT resources and its association to business value. The full disclosure framework, together with a description of each item, is presented in Table 2.8.

Drawing on this IT governance disclosure framework, we have performed research with the objective of analyzing a selection of national corporate governance codes with respect to guidance on how boards should approach IT governance. The findings show that only the South African corporate governance code (i.e., King III) contains a significant amount of such guidance (De Haes, Huygh, Joshi, & Caluwe, 2019). Building on this insight, we further explored the influence of the national corporate governance code on a firm's IT governance transparency by comparing the IT governance transparency of South African and Belgian listed financial services firms. The findings show that South African firms tend to be more concerned with IT governance transparency in their annual reports than Belgian firms, given a comparable IT use intensity and ownership structure (i.e., listed financial services organizations) (De Haes et al., 2019). In another study, we focused on Belgian firms, thereby controlling for the applicable corporate governance code, and put forward two research objectives: (1) to investigate the effect of IT use intensity on IT governance disclosure and (2) to investigate the relationship between ownership structure and IT governance disclosure. The findings offer some preliminary evidence indicating that (1) IT governance disclosure is related to IT use intensity, and (2) that listed firms tend to be more concerned with disclosing on their IT governance compared to firms that are not listed, given a comparable level of IT use intensity (De Haes, Huygh, & Joshi, 2017).

2.5.3   Inter-organizational Governance of IT

Inter-organizational IT governance (or "network IT governance") has similar objectives as intra-organizational IT governance, i.e., aligning IT functionality with the needs of the inter-organizational network (King, 2013). Networks represent

Table 2.8 IT governance disclosure framework (Joshi et al., 2013)

IT strategic alignment items	Description
IT expert on the board	One or more board of directors who is/are independent or non-independent with sufficient knowledge regarding IT and information assets
IT expert with experience on the board	One or more board of directors who is/are with sufficient knowledge as well as work experience regarding IT and information assets
A CIO or an equivalent position in the firm	Firm has a special CIO or an equivalent position with respect to IT and information assets at an executive level
IT committee	A committee looking after IT and information assets at the board level
IT risk is part of audit committee or risk committee	IT and information asset-related risk are on the agenda of the audit or risk committee
IT is part of audit committee	IT and information assets' auditing are part of the audit committee at the board level
IT steering committee	Firm has an IT steering committee which monitors IT management, IT spending, and related cost allocations
IT planning committee	Firm has an IT planning committee which looks after strategic planning and investment decisions on IT and information assets
Technology committee	A special committee which looks after IT and related technology architecture, projects, and governance issue at an executive level
IT committee at an executive level	In some countries, there is a two-tier structure of corporate governance, and in this situation, an IT committee may be formed at an executive level. This committee reports to the supervisory board
CIO or equivalent is on the board	A CIO or an equivalent position is represented at the board-level committee
IT value delivery items	Description
IT governance framework/standard: ITIL/COBIT/ISO, etc.	These are best practices and frameworks for IT governance. The firm has adopted or mentioned to adopt any IT governance framework
IT as an issue in the board meeting	IT and information assets' issues are explicitly discussed at the various board-level meeting
Suggestion/decision/advise by the board on IT	IT and related technology decisions, suggestions at the board level
Special report/section on IT/IT projects in annual report	A special report or a section dedicated to provide information about IT and information assets
IT mentioned as a strategic business issue	IT is mentioned as a strategic business issue to accomplish the business mission and goals
IT projected as strength	IT and information assets are mentioned as the organizational strength to achieve the business objectives, goals, etc.
IT projected as opportunity	IT and information assets are referred to as the key assets to achieve the future opportunities

(continued)

Table 2.8 (continued)

IT value delivery items	Description
Project updates or comments	Updates or comment about ongoing and/or finished (successfully or unsuccessfully) IT and related projects
IT is explicitly mentioned for achieving specific business objectives	IT has been deployed to achieve one or more specific business objectives
Comments/updates on IT performance	There is/are comments about good or bad performance of IT
IT training	Information on IT and related training program for human resource
Green IT	Efficient and environment-friendly use of is termed as Green IT. A firm has reported on such initiative
Direction and status about IT outsourcing and in-sourcing	Information regarding in-sourcing or outsourcing of IT
IT risk management items	Description
IT is referred to under the operational risk	IT is considered as a potential risk to successful business functioning and being treated as an operational risk
Special IT risk management program	Firm has a special program to mitigate IT and related technology risks
Use of IT for regulation and compliance	IT is used to address the regulations and compliance requirements by the legal institutions
IT/electronic data processing (EDP) audit	Firm has explicitly reported regarding IT audit
Information and security policy/plan (IT security)	Firm has a clear information and security policy for its stakeholders (e.g., customers, employee)
The role of IT in accounting and the reporting standards (IAS)	IT support for the accounting and to address certain framework (e.g., Basel II)
Operations' continuity plan	IT and related technology continuity plans are mentioned in case of disaster
IT performance measurement items	Description
Explicit information on IT expenditure	Financial and non-financial statements containing information on the overall IT expenditure
IT budget	Financial section of the document has disclosed the budget on IT and information assets
IT hardware cost	Specific IT hardware cost is mentioned under the IT expenditure
IT software cost	Specific IT software cost is mentioned under the IT expenditure
Explicit IT manpower cost is mentioned	Specific IT manpower cost is mentioned under the IT expenditure
IT expenses are mentioned under administrative cost	IT and information asset-related expenses are mentioned under the administrative cost
IT-related assets are mentioned under intangible assets	IT and related asset are referred as intangible assets and financial are provided as intangible assets
Direct cost on IT is mentioned in currency or percentage	The information on IT spending is given in the percentage of the total revenue or in other accounting ratios

"consciously created forms of social organization whose members strive to achieve common goals" (Raab & Kenis, 2009, p. 205). Many contemporary organizations are increasingly operating in complex networked systems, often facilitated by IT-related innovations (e.g., e-business). Jones, Hesterly, and Borgatti (1997, p. 914) define network governance as *"[involving] a select, persistent, and structured set of autonomous firms (as well as non-profit agencies) engaged in creating products or services based on implicit and open-ended contracts to adapt to environmental contingencies and to coordinate and safeguard exchanges."* This network governance perspective poses new challenges for the governance of IT (Croteau & Bergeron, 2009), more specifically challenges related to allocating accountability, responsibility, and decision rights in network arrangements where there is distributed ownership of IT (Grant & Tan, 2013). The inter-organizational governance of IT can be seen as the authority and accountability framework put in place to encourage the efficient and effective use of IT when sustaining electronic exchanges among business partners. An inter-organizational IT governance arrangement will consist of a mix of structures, processes, and participants (i.e., relational mechanisms) (Croteau & Bergeron, 2009).

Coordination mechanisms (e.g., standards) are very important to regulate such a network, as the possibility for top-down authority (i.e., traditional agency-based control) is limited. Therefore, control mechanisms proposed for intra-organizational IT governance may not be readily applicable to inter-organizational IT governance. In inter-organizational IT governance as opposed to intra-organizational IT governance, the primary concern shifts from decision rights for resource allocations and accountability for the resulting IT projects to decision rights and accountability for inter-organizational IT and information sharing among the organizations involved (Xiao et al., 2013).

According to Croteau and Bergeron (2009, p. 1), the need for inter-organizational IT governance *"is also observed within large organizations with several business units where each of them has its own mission, strategy, structure, processes and IT infrastructure and architecture. The challenge for such organizations is to create an inter-unit governance of IT that is developed in a similar way to the inter-organizational governance of IT."* As KLM classifies as a large organization with several business units, it is felt that many of the EGIT principles, structures, processes, and relational mechanisms as discussed in the KLM case (see supra) can be of value for any IT governance arrangement, both intra- as inter-organizational. Some specific recommendations based on the KLM case for the inter-organizational IT governance context are:

- *An approach toward sourcing decisions in a global economy*: Many organizations move toward networked arrangements to (out)source commoditized IT resources. KLM also operates in such a networked environment and developed selective sourcing criteria regarding choosing between allocating work in-house for customized development or through external IT providers for standardized solutions. Based on the "Stay on the Surfboard" principle, generic business processes that do not result in competitive advantage are supported by generic (i.e., low development cost, off-the-shelf) application packages. Business processes that do have the potential to create competitive advantage can and will be supported by in-house custom-built applications. In a networked and global environment, this principle can support the discussions on what, and what not, to outsource toward other partners in a networked environment.

- *An innovative process to allocate resources across multiple business units*: KLM is a multi-business-unit environment with distributed ownership over IT resources, systems, and processes. As such, these business units operate in a very similar environment as a network of organizations with shared IT resources. An important challenge for such an environment is to find a way to allocate IT (investment) budgets to business units and/or organizations in line with their specific strategies. KLM uses an innovative and inclusive process to capture and prioritize the, often diverse, business drivers of different business units. The design of this process can be inspirational for other multi-unit or inter-organizational environments, as a way to engage—potentially diverse—business units in the decision-making process regarding shared IT resources.

- *The need for an overarching function*: When building a governance model for an inter-organizational or multi-business-unit environment, the focus should be on the optimal value creation of the network (of organizations or business units) as a whole. At KLM, the individual business units drive the portfolio management processes and there is no real aggregation at KLM corporate level. However, the executive committee plays a crucial role in the optimization at group level, as they are responsible for ensuring that the bottom-up portfolio management process ultimately leads to optimal value creation for the KLM group (of business units) as whole. The existence of such overarching function, taking accountability for the governance of IT, appears to be crucial in guarding the value creation of the network as a whole.

- *An approach to manage multi-unit infrastructure investments*: It is often difficult to build the business case for infrastructure investments as benefits are typically hard to articulate and spread across multiple units or organizations. At KLM, the CIO office manages a specific budget which is oriented toward such cross-unit (or cross-organization) infrastructure investments. The CIO office develops business cases that can apply for this budget, which are derived from the emerging business cases of the business units (to understand future infrastructure needs). This approach ensures that future infrastructure investments will be done as required to support the network of business units (or organizations). To build a solid infrastructure in a networked environment, such role of a CIO office that is managing the future infrastructure needs and investments can be a powerful mechanism.

> **Assignment Box 2.6: Mechanisms for Inter-organizational IT Governance**
> Refer back to the list of EGIT mechanisms (i.e. structures, processes, and
> relational mechanisms) displayed in Table 2.3. Judge which of these mech-
> anisms may also be applicable for governing IT in an inter-organizational
> context. Be prepared to defend your suggestions.

2.5.4 Ambidextrous EGIT

While a lot of startups are very successful in leveraging IT for growth and innovation
(e.g., fintech companies), *established* firms (also referred to as *incumbent* firms)
often face challenges in both exploring and exploiting the opportunities that arise
from digitization in a sustainable way. On the one hand, established firms often need
to operate within the constraints of existing legacy information systems and with IT
governance arrangements which are focused on, or at least have the perception of
being solely focused on, "keeping the lights on" and therefore "putting the brakes on
innovation." Also, established firms are often organized around inflexible organizational silos in business and IT, inhibiting the required agility for digital transformation (Horlach, Drews, & Schirmer, 2016). As a well-known example, the collapse
of Eastman Kodak was primarily induced by their inability to keep up with technology change and digital disruption (Valentine & Stewart, 2013b). On the other
hand, there are established firms or business units that blindly follow the technology
hypes and trends (e.g., blockchain, Internet of things), but at the end struggle with
getting these new innovations integrated into the existing operating model of the
firm. Such a hype-driven approach then leads to increasing complexity, security
concerns, etc., often ultimately resulting in a situation where the anticipated benefits
are never realized. This problem primarily occurs when firms only focus on the
technology part, without building the necessary capabilities or revamping their
business model (Swaminathan & Meffert, 2017). For instance, in 2013 the BBC shut
down a £100 million digital transformation. PwC, who was asked to audit the
failure, pointed to a crippling lack of focus on business change (du Preez, 2013).

As a result, established firms are frequently at risk of missing out on digital
transformations that may present strategic opportunities. Recent work in both
academic- and practice-oriented literature, as well as consultancy practice, labels
this challenge as the requirement for *ambidextrous IT*,[6] or *bimodal IT*. This concept

---

[6]The notion of *ambidexterity* is based on the generic recognition that a focus on both exploitation
and exploration is required (Duncan, 1976; Markides & Chu, 2008; O'Reilly & Tushman, 2013;
Tushman & O'Reilly, 2007). Specifically, O'Reilly and Tushman (2013) refer to "organizational
ambidexterity" as the ability of an organization to both compete in mature technologies and
markets where efficiency, control, and incremental improvement are prized (i.e., exploit) and to
also compete in new technologies and markets where flexibility, autonomy, and experimentation
are needed (i.e., explore).

is summarized as the need to simultaneously combine and integrate "exploitation of IT," focused on using IT to run and grow efficiency, stability, and safety, and "exploration of IT," focused on leveraging IT for new (disruptive) innovations (Jöhnk, Röglinger, Thimmel, & Urbach, 2017; Lee, Sambamurthy, Lim, & Wei, 2015). Both the exploitative and the explorative use of IT is said to have a positive impact on downstream firm performance, with the explorative use of IT having the largest impact (Schmitz, Teng, & Webb, 2016). Therefore, an EGIT arrangement that is solely focused on IT exploitation is inherently sub-optimal, keeping this downstream firm performance in mind. It is our premise that building a solid EGIT capability which recognizes the need for both IT exploitation and IT exploration will help established firms to avoid the problems mentioned above. Therefore, the organizational EGIT capability should enable the *ambidextrous use of IT*; i.e., it should be designed to enable both IT exploitation and IT exploration.

In their recent literature review, Horlach et al. (2016) conclude that there are many research gaps and opportunities in this area, related to better understanding how organizations can design and implement IT governance approaches to enable such an ambidextrous use of IT. This includes a better understanding of the required IT governance structures (e.g., the function of Chief Digital Officer and how this role relates to both exploitation and exploration), IT governance processes (e.g., how does the innovation process integrate toward the requirements of the existing operating model), and people aspects—or relational mechanisms (e.g., what type of e-leadership skills do we require to enable ambidextrous IT governance).

Recently, Haffke et al. (2017) have identified four different archetypes for ambidextrous IT. One of these archetypes, the so-called reintegrated bimodal IT approach, is put forward by these authors as the desired end state if the firm wants their IT to be ambidextrous. In their findings, they conclude that this approach: *"[...] allows a company to fully focus on its digital business transformation mission while moving traditional back-end systems operations to outsourcing partners or to a smaller subdivision that operates in the background."* Other archetypes can be considered as intermediate states when transforming the organization's traditional IT function toward this desired end state. Possible pathways for this transformation journey are displayed in Fig. 2.13.

While the first interesting steps in this research journey of ambidextrous EGIT are made, we conclude by acknowledging that further research is needed to find out which IT governance arrangements can be used, and what the containing IT governance mechanisms should look like, when the goal is the ambidextrous use of IT. Allowing for an effective ambidextrous IT use, an ambidextrous EGIT approach will enable firms to be successful in a digitally transforming business environment.

Assignment Box 2.7: EGIT Mechanisms for Ambidextrous IT Use
Refer back to the list of EGIT mechanisms (i.e., structures, processes, and relational mechanisms) displayed in Table 2.3. Judge which of these mechanisms are primarily oriented towards controlling the 'current use of IT' (i.e., IT exploitation), and which ones are primarily oriented toward controlling the

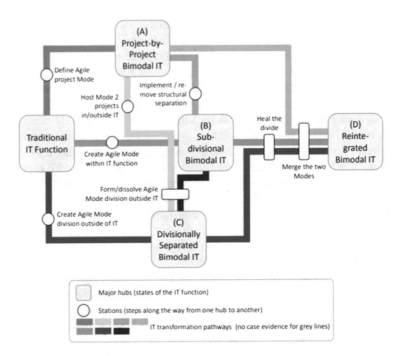

Fig. 2.13 Pathways for transforming the IT function toward bimodal IT (Haffke, Kalgovas, & Benlian, 2017)

'future use of IT' (i.e., IT exploitation). Also judge which of these mechanisms may be leveraged to control both IT exploitation and IT exploration, but may require specific attention/tailoring to establish an appropriate balance between IT exploitation and IT exploration. Be prepared to defend your suggestions.

2.5.5 Viable EGIT

Many studies have been published that provided descriptive accounts of IT governance arrangements (e.g., Ali & Green, 2012; De Haes & Van Grembergen, 2009; Prasad, Green, & Heales, 2012; Weill & Ross, 2004). While such studies often draw on established typologies of IT governance mechanisms, such as the EGIT structures, processes, and relational mechanisms typology as discussed earlier in this chapter, they can be criticized for not leveraging strong established theoretical lenses that would allow to explain from a theoretical point of view *how* EGIT should be organized for it to be effective and *why*. Moreover, while IT governance-related practitioner frameworks and guidelines often provide helpful advice, they are generally very limited in their rigor (Buchwald, Urbach, & Ahlemann, 2014). As such, the IT governance discipline is somewhat hampered by the lack of theoretical underpinnings for IT governance implementations (De Haes & Van Grembergen, 2009).

In response, we proposed a holistic[7] organizing logic[8] for IT governance that is based on the strong interdisciplinary perspective of the Viable System Model (VSM) (which is theoretically grounded in management cybernetics)[9] and informed by extant IT governance literature (Huygh & De Haes, 2019). As such, the VSM-based organizing logic for IT governance aims to provide strong theoretical underpinnings for IT governance arrangements by providing insights on *why* IT governance can continue to fulfill its general purpose of creating and protecting IT business value. Furthermore, by drawing on the essential elements of "organization" identified by the VSM, strong theoretical underpinnings are provided for the required functions of an IT governance arrangement, which directly contributes to the practical perspective of *how* to organize effective IT governance.

Figure 2.14 shows how the essence of a viable system applies to an organizational system of controlling the current and future IT use. The growing pervasiveness of IT in the contemporary business environment represents a changing environmental complexity that is relevant in the context of an organizational system of controlling the current and future IT use. Through leveraging (circle) and controlling (square) current and future IT, "requisite variety" is sought. Requisite variety is achieved when IT governance has an appropriate capacity to be able to effectively control the current and future IT use, and this current and future IT use remains sustainable in the (changing) environment. Only when requisite variety is maintained, the capacity to continue fulfilling the general purpose of creating and protecting IT business value (i.e., viability) is ensured. To maintain viability, the viable system has the capacity of adaptation. Indeed, any (relevant) (IT-related) change in the external environment may require a change at the level of the (current and future) IT use (i.e., to ensure that it remains sustainable in the (changing) environment), which may then also require a change at the level of IT governance (i.e., to ensure that it has the capacity to effectively control this (changing) current

---

[7]It is holistic in the sense that it is aimed at avoiding the "trap of reductionism," i.e., missing the interconnectedness between parts (Reynolds & Holwell, 2010).

[8]Organizing logic can be defined as *"the managerial rationale for designing and evolving specific organizational arrangements"* (Sambamurthy & Zmud, 2000, p. 107).

[9]Stafford Beer developed and described the VSM in his seminal trilogy, under the general heading of *"The managerial cybernetics of organization"* (Beer, 1972, 1979, 1981, 1985). The VSM is theoretically grounded in "management cybernetics," which is about applying cybernetic principles to the management of organizations (Beer, 1959). Beer (1985, p. ix) states that: *"cybernetics is the science of effective organization."* As a result, the VSM can be referred to as *"a theory of organization"* (Anderton, 1989, p. 40).

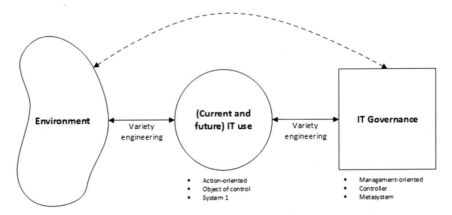

Fig. 2.14 Establishing requisite variety between the environment, the (current and future) IT use, and IT governance (based on Beer 1985)

and future IT use). In short, leveraging the VSM as a theoretical lens for organizational systems of controlling the current and future IT use allows us to incorporate the *evolutionary dynamics* of such a system (both at the level of the object of control—i.e., the current and future IT use—and at the level of the controller—i.e., IT governance—of such a system).

The dashed connection between IT governance and the environment represents the communication between the metasystem—or controller—(i.e., IT governance) and the external environment. Prior IT governance (-related) research has identified issues like IT governance transparency or disclosure (Joshi et al., 2013) and sensing/anticipating environmental change (Overby, Bharadwaj, & Sambamurthy, 2006) in that context.

To illustrate the above, consider the following example. The widespread adoption of the Internet (technological advancement) leads to the introduction of online banking services, which represented a change of (IT-related) environmental complexity for the banking industry. If a bank would then be unable to deliver this (IT-enabled) service, in spite of the changing market demand, its service offerings (i.e., its current and future IT use) would no longer be sustainable in its changed external environment. Indeed, banks would need to match environmental complexity with an adequate operational response to cope with this changing market demand. Simultaneously, the change in operational complexity (i.e., developing and offering the (IT-enabled) online banking service) demands an appropriate response at the level of the managerial complexity, which in this case is the capacity of IT governance (e.g., ensuring that the risks of this (IT-enabled) service are under control). Indeed, insufficient operational complexity results in failure to deliver on market demand and insufficient managerial complexity results in failure to manage effectively (Hoverstadt, 2010).

Drawing on the VSM and its theoretical underpinnings in management cybernetics, the following two fundamental principles underlying the VSM-based
organizing logic for IT governance are articulated. These principles are grounded in
the law of requisite variety and explain *why* IT governance can continue to fulfill its
general purpose of creating and protecting IT business value.

- The variety of the (current and future) IT use should be appropriate so that it
  remains sustainable in the (changing) external environment.
- The IT governance arrangement should have sufficient variety to be able to
  control the (current and future) IT use effectively.

Further building on the VSM, an organizational system of controlling the current
and future IT use will have the capacity to continue fulfilling its general purpose of
creating and protecting IT business value (i.e., viability) if the five interconnected[10]
functions that are necessary and sufficient structural preconditions for system viability (i.e., systems 1 through 5) are accounted for in such a system. As such, the
key elements are identified that allow an organizational system of controlling the
current and future IT use to be effective over time. This insight contributes to the
practical perspective of *how* to organize effective IT governance (as a metasystem).
To substantiate this, the articulation of the VSM-based organizing logic for IT
governance was guided by drawing parallels between the VSM and IT governance
(building on the (sub)systems or functions and communication channels or variety
loops of the VSM). These parallels are summarized in Table 2.9.

Through the identification of the five interconnected functions that are necessary
and sufficient structural preconditions for system viability (Beer, 1979), the VSM
emphasizes the essential elements of "organization" rather than the specific roles or
structures through which this act of "organization" can be realized (i.e., instantiation) (Jackson, 2003). The extant IT governance knowledge base nevertheless
provides insights on how this act of "organization" of IT governance can be realized
in practice (i.e., instantiation). Indeed, the typology of EGIT mechanisms
(i.e., structures, processes, and relational mechanisms), and descriptive studies of
IT governance arrangements can be leveraged for this purpose.

Drawing on the two fundamental principles articulated above, a specific instantiation of the five interconnected functions that are necessary and sufficient structural
preconditions for system viability ultimately depends on the environmental complexity to which the organizational system of controlling the (current and future) IT
use is exposed. This is in line with the widespread agreement that "*a universal best IT
governance [arrangement] does not exist*" (Brown & Grant, 2005, p. 703). Instead,
determining a specific instantiation of the essential elements of "organization" by

---

[10]The five necessary and sufficient structural functions are interconnected through communication
channels or variety loops, together enabling the system to be effective over time (Beer, 1979, 1985;
Jackson, 2003).

Table 2.9 Parallels between the VSM and IT governance (building on the (sub)systems or functions, and communication channels or variety loops of the VSM)

	VSM theory[a]	Parallels to IT governance[b]
VSM (sub)systems or functions		
System 1	The system 1 function is the "action-oriented" component of the viable system, referred to as "operation," while all other functions of organization (i.e., systems 2 through 5, or the metasystem of the system-in-focus) are controlling/managerial, referred to as "management." As such, system 1 essentially represents the reason for the existence of the viable system, while the metasystem is concerned with ensuring that system 1 continues to fulfill the purpose of the system-in-focus. System 1 of the system -in-focus is the combination of all of its embedded viable systems, which together implement the purpose of the system-in-focus	The object of control of IT governance is twofold: (1) the current use of IT and (2) the future use of IT. As such, the "current and future IT use" is the action-oriented component, or that which is controlled, while all other functions of "organization" (i.e., systems 2 through 5—or the metasystem) represent aspects of the controller, in this case IT governance. The unfolding of complexity is about defining system 1 throughout various levels of "recursion" (i.e., granularity). In the context of an organizational system of controlling the current and future IT use, this reflects specific choices regarding how the current and future IT use will be controlled throughout various levels of granularity
System 2	The system 2 function coordinates the activities of the embedded viable systems of the system-in-focus. System 2 mechanisms are geared toward anticipating and avoiding problems at the level of system 1's operational units, rather than solving them	Coordination has been identified as a feasible approach to IT governance, besides the imposition of controls (i.e., through using the command axis). In the context of IT governance, a lack of coordinated action may lead to problems like the duplication of IT projects across business units; the implementation of incompatible technology architectures, infrastructures, and business applications by different business units; and not achieving the full value potential of IT investments
System 3 and 3*	The system 3 function integrates the embedded viable systems into a cohesive whole (i.e., system 1), ensuring that this cohesive whole achieves the purpose of the system-in-focus. To effectuate this integration, system 3 can use the command axis, establish appropriate system 2 mechanisms, and establish and use system 3* mechanisms. System 3*enables system 3 to obtain information directly from system 1's operational units (i.e., bypassing the respective local management units). As such, an accurate view of the actual state of the action-oriented component of the viable system can be obtained when deemed necessary	The system 3 function is responsible for ensuring that the current and future IT use is a cohesive whole which achieves the general purpose of creating and protecting IT business value. Besides senior IT executives (e.g., CIO), the involvement of (senior) business stakeholders in IT governance (including IT strategic planning) is of paramount importance as the value of the current and future IT use will primarily be realized at the business side. Consequently, sufficient IT-related competence needs to be established at executive management level. System 3* mechanisms can be used to get an accurate view of the actual state of (aspects of) the current and future IT use when deemed necessary

(continued)

Table 2.9 (continued)

	VSM theory[a]	Parallels to IT governance[b]
System 4	The system 4 function provides the viable system with the capacity of adaptation. To effectuate this, system 4 is responsible for sensing the current state of the environment (through the alpha communication channel) and anticipating its future states (through the beta communication channel). Armed with this important information, system 4 is actively involved in strategic decision-making (i.e., decision-making about (the path to) desired future states of the system) which happens through the system 3–system 4 variety loop. Other responsibilities of the system 4 function are projecting the system's identity onto its environment and building and maintaining a model of the system-in-focus itself (i.e., enabling self-awareness of the system)	The system 4 function is crucial in providing the organizational system of controlling the current and future IT use with the capacity of "agility" (i.e., the ability to quickly and continually sense and anticipate environmental change (opportunities and threats) and respond readily). The "sensing" component maps to the alpha and beta communication channels which system 4 leverages to sense the current state of the environment and anticipate its future states, respectively. The "responding" component is initiated through the actual decision-making about (the path to) desired future states of the system, which happens through the system 3–system 4 variety loop. The system 4 function is furthermore concerned with communicating about the way in which the organization is leveraging and controlling its (current and future) IT, i.e., IT governance transparency or IT-related disclosure. Finally, being responsible for building and maintaining a model of the system-in-focus itself, system 4 is concerned with enterprise architecture modeling in the context of an organizational system for controlling the current and future IT use
System 5	The system 5 function expresses and represents the identity of the system-in-focus, which is effectuated as its overall direction, values, and purpose. System 5 uses this information to effectively monitor the system 3–system 4 variety loop (i.e., strategic decision-making). System 5 also maintains an understanding of the relation of the system-in-focus with its "containing systems" (e.g., regulatory, industrial, societal)	The system 5 function is related to issues of board-level IT governance. Indeed, the board of directors is an important stakeholder in the context of IT governance. The board has a crucial "monitoring function" to perform in an organizational system of controlling the current and future IT use. A first aspect of this is ensuring that the organization's current and future IT use (and the decision-making related to this) sustains and extends the organization's strategy and objectives. Additionally, from an "IT business value protection" point of view, the board of directors needs to ensure that the IT-related risks do not exceed the organization's overall risk appetite. These activities map to system 5's responsibility of monitoring the system 3–system 4 variety loop (i.e., IT-related strategic decision-making) The activities of the organization in general, and its (current and future) IT use in specific, are required to comply with the constraints and obligations (e.g., regulatory and legal requirements) imposed upon by its containing systems (e.g., regulatory system). This is an important attention point, as the amount of IT-related regulatory and legal requirements with which an organization needs to ensure compliance is increasing

(continued)

Table 2.9 (continued)

	VSM theory[a]	Parallels to IT governance[b]
VSM communication channels or variety loops		
System 3–system 4 variety loop	The system 3–system 4 variety loop concerns decision-making about (the path to) desired future states of the system, i.e., strategic decision-making or planning. The process is mutual between system 3 and system 4, as good strategic decision-making relies heavily on balancing the current capabilities and needs of the organization with the strategic threats and opportunities driven by the external environment. The variety of the system 3–system 4 variety loop determines the responsiveness of the system-in-focus to environmental change	In the context of an organizational system of controlling the current and future IT use, the system 3–system 4 variety loop maps to IT-related strategic decision-making or planning (e.g., strategic information systems' planning). The information that is fed into the strategic decision-making process is a large determinant of the quality of the resulting strategic decisions. The system 3 function must provide accurate information about the actual state (e.g., current capabilities and needs) of system 1 (i.e., the current and future IT use). System 4, related to its responsibility of sensing the current state of the environment and anticipating its potential future states, must provide accurate information about (potential) changes in the system's external environment. The variety of the system 3–system 4 variety loop determines the responsiveness of the system-in-focus to environmental change (i.e., an important aspect of (IT-related) agility)
Communication with the environment	The system-in-focus is linked with its environment through system 1 (i.e., through its embedded viable systems linked to their corresponding embedded environments) and through system 4. System 4 has two important channels available to communicate with the environment: an alpha and a beta channel. Through the alpha channel, the system-in-focus communicates with its current environment (i.e., through projecting its direction, values, and purpose; and to monitor its current environment). Through the beta channel, the system-in-focus anticipates possible futures of the system's environment	The organization's total external environment consists of its current competitors, new market entrants, customers, suppliers, governments, industry associations, and other social and economic forces. These elements (and their activities) determine the environmental uncertainty that the organization has to deal with and can possibly influence the way in which an organization leverages and controls its (current and future) IT. The system's purpose is used as a filter to separate noise from relevant information when interacting with its environment. As such, for an organizational system of controlling the current and future IT use, information is relevant if it is useful to support decision-making related to IT business value creation or IT business value protection (i.e., counteract IT business value destruction)

The alpha channel and the beta channel are used by system 4 to sense the current state of the environment and anticipate its future states, respectively. The ability to quickly and continually sense and anticipate environmental change (opportunities and threats) is a critical enabler of organizational agility in general and IT strategic agility in specific. There is however a difference between (1) a more proactive stance to environmental change (i.e., anticipating and possibly creating future states of the environment heavily drawing on the beta channel) and (2) a more reactive stance to environmental change (i.e., predominantly sensing the current state of the environment using the alpha channel)

In the context of an organizational system of controlling the current and future IT use, the alpha communication channel is also used to inform the organization's environment about the way in which the organization is leveraging and controlling its (current and future) IT, i.e., IT governance transparency or IT-related disclosure |

(continued)

Table 2.9 (continued)

	VSM theory[a]	Parallels to IT governance[b]
Command axis	The command axis consists of (1) a resource bargaining channel, (2) an accountability channel, and (3) an intervention channel. The resource bargaining channel is used to negotiate the activities that will be tackled at the level of system 1 and the performance targets that should be met, as well as negotiating the resources (e.g., financial, human) required for this. The accountability channel is used to provide summarized reporting on the state of operation, regarding the agreed-upon performance targets and using the agreed-upon performance metrics. Finally, the intervention channel is used to communicate and enforce, e.g., legal and corporate requirements	In the context of an organizational system of controlling the current and future IT use, the command axis provides the stakeholders involved in IT governance with the power to command and make decisions. The first thread of the command axis is the bargaining channel. In the context of the future use of IT, resource bargaining is primarily concerned with IT project portfolio management. In the context of the current use of IT, resource bargaining is for instance concerned with agreeing upon SLAs, which specify the service level targets and the responsibilities (of both the service provider and the client). The outcome of the debate at the level of the system 3–system 4 variety loop reflects the "planned IT strategy," while the actual (current and future) IT use at the level of system 1 (i.e., the implementation of the planned IT strategy) reflects the "realized IT strategy." As such, the bargaining channel is the link in-between. IT performance measurement (which is about monitoring and evaluating IT projects, and monitoring IT services, based on appropriate performance measures) effectuates the accountability channel in the context of an organizational system of controlling the current and future IT use. In the context of an organizational system of controlling the current and future IT use, the intervention channel is used to communicate IT-related policies (and an obligation to comply). IT-related policies might be sourced in voluntary internal actions (e.g., password requirements as part of overall IT security policies) or might be formulated based on legal and regulatory requirements that are externally imposed. In the latter case, such policies are formulated and enforced to ensure compliance with these external legal and regulatory requirements
Algedonic channel	The algedonic channel is used to transfer "algedonic signals," which is critical information that requires the immediate attention of the metasystem. The information is critical in the sense that there is a direct and considerable impact related to the purpose of the system, as such possibly impacting its viability	As organizations are becoming increasingly dependent on IT, IT-related disruptions or incidents have increasingly adverse effects for organizations. It is therefore important that for instance operational IT failures (e.g., technical glitches, service outages, and security breaches) are detected quickly, so that immediate remedial action can take place. Indeed, such a failure of operational IT systems (i.e., current use of IT) has a negative impact on shareholder wealth, thereby effectively resulting in IT value destruction. IT value destruction can evidently result from IT investment failure (i.e., future use of IT) as well

[a]Substantiation can be found in Chap. 2 of the doctoral dissertation of Huygh (2019)
[b]Substantiation can be found in Chap. 4 of the doctoral dissertation of Huygh (2019)

means of implementing a specific IT governance arrangement (consisting of specific IT governance mechanisms) is considered a complex endeavor, as what works for one organization will not necessarily work for another (ISACA, 2018).

Assignment Box 2.8: Investigating KLM's EGIT Through the Viable System Model

Revisit the KLM case discussed earlier in this chapter. Categorize KLM's EGIT mechanisms according to the essential elements of 'organization' as identified by the Viable System Model (VSM) (see template). Be prepared to justify your mapping. Also discuss where there are potential areas for improvement in the KLM case, based on your diagnosis of KLM's EGIT using the VSM as a theoretical lens.

VSM (sub)system or function	KLM EGIT mechanisms
System 5	
System 4	
System 3 and 3*	
System 2	
System 1	

2.6   Summary

This second chapter discussed the genesis and evolution of EGIT, both in academic research and practice. Then, this chapter introduced mechanisms that can be used to implement EGIT in practice. Indeed, developing a high-level model for the Enterprise Governance of IT is the first step, deploying it throughout all levels of the organization is the next challenging step. To effectuate this, EGIT can be deployed using a mixture of various structures, processes, and relational mechanisms. These EGIT mechanisms were discussed in this chapter, including a demonstration of how such mechanisms were leveraged in the context of KLM, a large international airline company. Finally, specific EGIT-related topics were discussed such as the role of the board in EGIT, IT governance transparency, the inter-organizational governance of IT, ambidextrous EGIT, and a more theoretical view on EGIT by drawing on the lens of the Viable System Model (VSM).

Study Questions

1. Discuss and illustrate an EGIT structure.
2. Discuss and illustrate an EGIT process.
3. Discuss and illustrate an EGIT relational mechanism.

4. Discuss and illustrate EGIT mechanisms that are relevant to effectuate board involvement.
5. Explain why organizations should voluntarily report on IT (governance)-related matters and what are potential topics that can be disclosed.
6. Discuss some of the specific challenges in the context of the inter-organizational governance of IT.
7. Explain what is meant by "ambidextrous IT use" and why this is a relevant attention point in the context of EGIT.
8. Discuss how the Viable System Model (VSM) can be used as a theoretical lens to diagnose an EGIT arrangement.

References

Ailon, G. (2011). Mapping the cultural grammar of reflexivity: The case of the Enron scandal. *Economy and Society, 40*(1), 141–166.

Ali, S., & Green, P. (2012). Effective information technology (IT) governance mechanisms: An IT outsourcing perspective. *Information Systems Frontiers, 14*(2), 179–193.

Anderton, R. (1989). The need for formal development of the VSM. In R. Espejo & R. Harnden (Eds.), *The viable system model: Interpretations and applications of Stafford Beer's VSM* (pp. 39–50). New York: Wiley.

Andriole, S. (2009). Boards of directors and technology governance: The surprising state of the practice. *Communications of the Association for Information Systems, 24*(1), 373–394.

Bart, C., & Turel, O. (2010). IT and the board of directors: An empirical investigation into the "governance questions" Canadian board members ask about IT. *Journal of Information Systems, 24*(2), 147–172.

Beer, S. (1959). *Cybernetics and management.* London: The English Universities Press.

Beer, S. (1972). *Brain of the firm.* London: Allen Lane.

Beer, S. (1979). *The heart of enterprise.* New York: Wiley.

Beer, S. (1981). *Brain of the firm* (2nd ed.). Chichester: Wiley.

Beer, S. (1985). *Diagnosing the system for organizations.* West Sussex: Wiley.

Benaroch, M., & Chernobai, A. (2017). Operational IT failures, IT value destruction, and board-level IT governance changes. *MIS Quarterly, 41*(3), 729–762.

Brown, A. E., & Grant, G. G. (2005). Framing the frameworks: A review of IT governance research. *Communications of the Association for Information Systems, 15*(1), 696–712.

Brown, C. (1999). Horizontal mechanisms under differing is organization contexts. *MIS Quarterly, 23*(3), 421–454.

Brown, C. V. (1997). Examining the emergence of hybrid IS governance solutions: Evidence from a single case site. *Information Systems Research, 8*(1), 69–94.

Brown, C. V., & Magill, S. L. (1998). Reconceptualizing the context-design issue for the information systems function. *Organization Science, 9*(2), 176–194.

Buchwald, A., Urbach, N., & Ahlemann, F. (2014). Business value through controlled IT: Toward an integrated model of IT governance success and its impact. *Journal of Information Technology, 29*(2), 128–147.

Buckby, S., & Best, P. J. (2007, July 1). Development of a board IT governance (ITG) review model. In *Proceedings of the 2007 AFAANZ Conference.* Accounting & Finance Association of Australia and New Zealand.

Butler, R., & Butler, M. J. (2010). Beyond King III: Assigning accountability for IT governance in South African enterprises. *South African Journal of Business Management, 41*(3), 33–45.

Caluwe, L., & De Haes, S. (2019). Board Level IT Governance: A Scoping Review to Set the Research Agenda. *Information Systems Management, 36*(3), 262–283.

Chatterjee, D., Richardson, V. J., & Zmud, R. W. (2001). Examining the shareholder wealth effects of announcements of newly created CIO positions. *MIS Quarterly, 25*(1), 43–70.

Choudhary, V., & Vithayathil, J. (2013). The impact of cloud computing: should the IT department be organized as a cost center or a profit center? *Journal of Management Information Systems, 30*(2), 67–100.

Coertze, J., & von Solms, R. (2013). The board and IT governance: A replicative study. *African Journal of Business Management, 7*(35), 3358–3373.

Coertze, J., & von Solms, R. (2014). The board and CIO: The IT alignment challenge. In *HICSS 2014 Proceedings*.

Croteau, A.-M., & Bergeron, F. (2009). Interorganizational governance of information technology. In *Proceedings of the 42nd Hawaii International Conference on System Sciences*.

De Haes, S., Gemke, D., Thorp, J., & Van Grembergen, W. (2011). KLM's enterprise governance of IT journey: From managing costs to managing business value. *MIS Quarterly Executive, 10* (3), 109–120.

De Haes, S., Huygh, T., & Joshi, A. (2017). Exploring the contemporary state of information technology governance transparency in Belgian firms. *Information Systems Management, 34* (1), 20–37.

De Haes, S., Huygh, T., Joshi, A., & Caluwe, L. (2019). National corporate governance codes and IT governance transparency in annual reports. *Journal of Global Information Management, 27*(4).

De Haes, S., & Van Grembergen, W. (2009). An exploratory study into IT governance implementations and its impact on business/IT alignment. *Information Systems Management, 26*(2), 123–137.

De Haes, S., Van Grembergen, W., & Debreceny, R. S. (2013). COBIT 5 and enterprise governance of information technology: Building blocks and research opportunities. *Journal of Information Systems, 27*(1), 307–324.

Duncan, R. B. (1976). The ambidextrous organization: Designing dual structures for innovation. *The Management of Organization, 1*, 167–188.

du Preez, D. (2013). *PwC slams BBC for failed £100 m digital transformation project*. Retrieved from http://www.computerworlduk.com/it-management/pwc-slams-bbc-for-failed-100m-digital-transformation-project-3494357/.

Garrity, J. T. (1963). Top management and computer profits. *Harvard Business Review, 41*(4), 6–12.

Grant, G., & Tan, F. B. (2013). Governing IT in inter-organizational relationships: Issues and future research. *European Journal of Information Systems, 22*(5), 493–497.

Haffke, I., Kalgovas, B., & Benlian, A. (2017). Options for transforming the IT function using bimodal IT. *MIS Quarterly Executive, 16*(2), 101–120.

Henderson, J. C., & Venkatraman, N. (1993). Strategic alignment: Leveraging information technology for transforming organizations. *IBM Systems Journal, 32*(1), 4–16.

Higgs, J. L., Pinsker, R. E., Smith, T. J., & Young, G. R. (2016). The relationship between board-level technology committees and reported security breaches. *Journal of Information Systems, 30*(3), 79–98.

Horlach, B., Drews, P., & Schirmer, I. (2016). Bimodal IT: Business-IT alignment in the age of digital transformation. In *Multikonferenz Wirtschaftsinformatik (MKWI)* (pp. 1417–1428).

Hoverstadt, P. (2010). The viable system model. In M. Reynolds & S. Holwell (Eds.), *Systems approaches to managing change: A practical guide* (pp. 87–133). London: Springer.

Huang, R., Zmud, R. W., & Price, R. L. (2010). Influencing the effectiveness of IT governance practices through steering committees and communication policies. *European Journal of Information Systems, 19*(3), 288–302.

Huygh, T. (2019). *Investigating IT governance through the viable system model* (doctoral dissertation). University of Antwerp, Antwerp, Belgium.

Huygh, T., & De Haes, S. (2019). Investigating IT governance through the viable system model. *Information Systems Management, 36*(2), 168–192.

Institute of Directors in Southern Africa. (2009). *King III code of corporate governance for South Africa*. Retrieved from https://jutalaw.co.za/uploads/King_III_Report/.

ISACA. (2018). *COBIT 2019 Framework: Introduction & methodology*.

ISO/IEC. (2008). *ISO/IEC Standard 38500: Corporate governance of information technology*.

ISO/IEC. (2015). *ISO/IEC Standard 38500: Information technology—Governance of IT for the organization*.

IT Governance Institute (ITGI). (2003). *Board briefing on IT governance, 2nd edition*. Retrieved from http://www.isaca.org/knowledge-center/research/researchdeliverables/pages/board-briefing-on-it-governance-2nd-edition.aspx.

Jackson, M. C. (2003). *Systems thinking: Creative holism for managers*. New York: Wiley.

Jewer, J., & McKay, K. (2012). Antecedents and consequences of board IT governance: Institutional and strategic choice perspectives. *Journal of the Association for Information Systems, 13*(7), 581–617.

Joachim, N., Beimborn, D., & Weitzel, T. (2013). The influence of SOA governance mechanisms on IT flexibility and service reuse. *The Journal of Strategic Information Systems, 22*(1), 86–101.

Jöhnk, J., Röglinger, M., Thimmel, M., & Urbach, N. (2017). How to implement agile IT setups: A taxonomy of design options. In *Proceedings of the 25th European Conference on Information Systems (ECIS), Guimarães, Portugal, June 5–10, 2017* (pp. 1521–1535). Retrieved from http://aisel.aisnet.org/ecis2017_rp/98.

Jones, C., Hesterly, W. S., & Borgatti, S. P. (1997). A general theory of network governance: Exchange conditions and social mechanisms. *Academy of Management Review, 22*(4), 911–945.

Joshi, A., Bollen, L., & Hassink, H. (2013). An empirical assessment of IT governance transparency: Evidence from commercial banking. *Information Systems Management, 30*(2), 116–136.

Kambil, A., & Lucas, H. C. (2002). The board of directors and the management of information technology. *Communications of the Association for Information Systems, 8*(1).

Kerr, D. S., & Murthy, U. S. (2013). The importance of the CobiT framework IT processes for effective internal control over financial reporting in organizations: An international survey. *Information & Management, 50*(7), 590–597.

King, J. L. (1983). Centralized versus decentralized computing: Organizational considerations and management options. *ACM Computing Surveys, 15*(4), 319–349.

King, N. (2013). Exploring the impact of operating model choice on the governance of inter-organizational workflow: The U.S. e-prescribing network. *European Journal of Information Systems, 22*(5), 548–568.

Kritzinger-von Solms, E., & Strous, L. (2003). Information security: A corporate governance issue. In *Integrity and internal control in information systems V* (Vol. 124, pp. 115–133). Kluwer Academic Publishers.

Kuruzovich, J., Bassellier, G., & Sambamurthy, V. (2012). IT governance processes and IT alignment: Viewpoints from the board of directors. In *2012 45th Hawaii International Conference on System Sciences* (pp. 5043–5052). IEEE. https://doi.org/10.1109/HICSS.2012.394.

Lawrence, P. R., & Lorsch, J. W. (1967). *Organization and environment*. Boston, MA: Harvard Business School, Division of Research.

Lee, O.-K. (Daniel), Sambamurthy, V., Lim, K. H., & Wei, K. K. (2015). How does IT ambidexterity impact organizational agility? *Information Systems Research, 26*(2), 398–417.

Loh, L., & Venkatraman, N. (1992). Diffusion of information technology outsourcing: Influence sources and the Kodak effect. *Information Systems Research, 3*(4), 334–358.

Mähring, M. (2006). The role of the board of directors in IT governance: A review and agenda for research. In *AMCIS 2006 Proceedings*.

Markides, C., & Chu, W. (2008). Innovation through ambidexterity: How to achieve the ambidextrous organization. In L. Costanzo & B. MacKay (Eds.), *Handbook of research on strategy and foresight*. London: Elgar.

Masli, A., Richardson, V., Watson, M., & Zmud, R. W. (2016). Senior executives' IT management responsibilities: Serious IT-related deficiencies and CEO/CFO turnover. *Management Information Systems Quarterly, 40*(3), 687–708.

Mintzberg, H. (1979). *The structuring of organizations*. Englewood Cliffs, NJ: Prentice-Hall.

Mohamad, S., Hendrick, M., O'Leary, C., & Best, P. (2014). Developing a model to evaluate the information technology competence of boards of directors. *Corporate Ownership & Control, 12*(1), 64–74.

Nolan, R., & McFarlan, F. (2005). Information technology and the board of directors. *Harvard Business Review, 83*(10), 96–106.

Oliver, G. R., & Walker, R. G. (2006). Reporting on software development projects to senior managers and the board. *Abacus, 42*(1), 43–65. https://doi.org/10.1111/j.1467-6281.2006.00188.x.

Olson, M. H., & Chervany, N. L. (1980). The relationship between organizational characteristics and the structure of the information services function. *MIS Quarterly, 4*(2), 57.

O'Reilly, C. A., & Tushman, M. L. (2013). Organizational ambidexterity: Past, present, and future. *Academy of Management Perspectives, 27*(4), 324–338.

Overby, E., Bharadwaj, A., & Sambamurthy, V. (2006). Enterprise agility and the enabling role of information technology. *European Journal of Information Systems, 15*(2), 120–131.

Parent, M., & Reich, B. H. (2009). Governing information technology risk. *California Management Review, 51*(3), 134–152.

Peterson, R. R. (2004). Crafting information technology governance. *Information Systems Management, 21*(4), 7–22.

Posthumus, S., & von Solms, R. (2008). Agency theory: Can it be used to strengthen IT governance? In *Proceedings of The IFIP TC 11 23rd International Information Security Conference*. Springer US.

Posthumus, S., Von Solms, R., & King, M. (2010). The board and IT governance: The what, who and how. *South African Journal of Business Management, 41*(3), 23–32.

Prasad, A., Green, P., & Heales, J. (2012). On IT governance structures and their effectiveness in collaborative organizational structures. *International Journal of Accounting Information Systems, 13*(3), 199–220.

Premuroso, R. F., & Bhattacharya, S. (2007). Is there a relationship between firm performance, corporate governance, and a firm's decision to form a technology committee? *Corporate Governance: An International Review, 15*(6), 1260–1276.

Raab, J., & Kenis, P. (2009). Heading toward a society of networks. *Journal of Management Inquiry, 18*(3), 198–210.

Raghupathi, W. (2007). Corporate governance of IT: A framework for development. *Communications of the ACM, 50*(8), 94–99.

Read, T. J. (2004). Discussion of director responsibility for IT governance. *International Journal of Accounting Information Systems, 5*(2), 105–107. https://doi.org/10.1016/j.accinf.2004.01.003.

Reynolds, M., & Holwell, S. (2010). Introducing systems approaches. In M. Reynolds & S. Holwell (Eds.), *Systems approaches to managing change: A practical guide* (pp. 1–23). Berlin: Springer.

Ross, J. W., & Weill, P. (2002). Six IT decisions your IT people shouldn't make. *Harvard Business Review, 80*(11), 84–95.

Sambamurthy, V., & Zmud, R. (1999). Arrangements for information technology governance: A theory of multiple contingencies. *Management Information Systems Quarterly, 23*(2), 261–290.

Sambamurthy, V., & Zmud, R. W. (2000). Research commentary: The organizing logic for an enterprise's IT activities in the digital era—A prognosis of practice and a call for research. *Information Systems Research, 11*(2), 105–114.

Schlosser, F., Beimborn, D., Weitzel, T., & Wagner, H.-T. (2015). Achieving social alignment between business and IT—An empirical evaluation of the efficacy of IT governance mechanisms. *Journal of Information Technology, 30*(2), 119–135.

Schmitz, K., Teng, J. T. C., & Webb, K. (2016). Capturing the complexity of malleable IT use: Adaptive structuration theory for individuals. *Management Information Systems Quarterly, 40* (3). Retrieved from http://aisel.aisnet.org/misq/vol40/iss3/9.

Schwarz, A., & Hirschheim, R. (2003). An extended platform logic perspective of IT governance: Managing perceptions and activities of IT. *The Journal of Strategic Information Systems, 12* (2), 129–166.

Standards Australia. (2005). *AS 8015-2005.*

Swaminathan, A., & Meffert, J. (2017). *Digital @ scale.* Hoboken, New Jersey: Wiley.

Tallon, P. P., Ramirez, R. V., & Short, J. E. (2013). The information artifact in IT governance: Toward a theory of information governance. *Journal of Management Information Systems, 30* (3), 141–178.

Tavakolian, H. (1989). Linking the information technology structure with organizational competitive strategy: A survey. *MIS Quarterly, 13*(3), 309.

The Committee on the Financial Aspects of Corporate Governance. (1992). *Financial aspects of corporate governance* (The Cadbury Report).

Trautman, L. J., & Altenbaumer-Price, K. (2010). *The board's responsibility for information technology governance.*

Trites, G. (2004). Director responsibility for IT governance. *International Journal of Accounting Information Systems, 5*(2), 89–99.

Turel, O., & Bart, C. (2014). Board-level IT governance and organizational performance. *European Journal of Information Systems, 23*(2), 223–239.

Turel, O., Liu, P., & Bart, C. (2017). Board-level information technology governance effects on organizational performance: The roles of strategic alignment and authoritarian governance style. *Information Systems Management, 34*(2), 117–136.

Tushman, M. L., & O'Reilly, C. (2007). Research and relevance: Implications of Pasteur's quadrant for doctoral programsand faculty development. *Academy of Management Journal, 50* (4), 769–774.

Valentine, E., & Stewart, G. (2013a). Director competencies for effective enterprise technology governance. In *24th Australasian Conference on Information Systems (ACIS)* (pp. 1–11). RMIT University.

Valentine, E., & Stewart, G. (2013b). The emerging role of the board of directors in enterprise business technology governance. *International Journal of Disclosure and Governance, 10*(4), 346–362.

Valentine, E., & Stewart, G. (2015). Enterprise business technology governance: Three competencies to build board digital leadership capability. In *HICSS 2015 Proceedings.*

Vithayathil, J. (2018). Will cloud computing make the Information Technology (IT) department obsolete? *Information Systems Journal, 28*(4), 634–649.

Weill, P., & Ross, J. (2004). *IT governance: How top performers manage IT decision rights for superior results.* Harvard Business Press.

Wilkin, C. L., Campbell, J., & Moore, S. (2013). Creating value through governing IT deployment in a public/private-sector inter-organisational context: A human agency perspective. *European Journal of Information Systems, 22*(5), 498–511.

Wilkin, C. L., & Chenhall, R. H. (2010). A review of IT governance: A taxonomy to inform accounting information systems. *Journal of Information Systems, 24*(2), 107–146.

Williams, C. K., & Karahanna, E. (2013). Causal explanation in the coordinating process: A critical realist case study of federated IT governance structures. *MIS Quarterly, 37*(3), 933–964.

Winkler, T. J., & Brown, C. V. (2013). Horizontal allocation of decision rights for on-premise applications and software-as-a-service. *Journal of Management Information Systems, 30*(3), 13–48.

Wu, S. P.-J., Straub, D. W., & Liang, T.-P. (2015). How information technology governance mechanisms and strategic alignment influence organizational performance: Insights from a matched survey of business and IT managers. *MIS Quarterly, 39*(2), 497–518.

Xiao, J., Xie, K., & Hu, Q. (2013). Inter-firm IT governance in power-imbalanced buyer–supplier dyads: Exploring how it works and why it lasts. *European Journal of Information Systems, 22*(5), 512–528.

Yayla, A. A., & Hu, Q. (2014). The effect of board of directors' IT awareness on CIO compensation and firm performance. *Decision Sciences, 45*(3), 401–436. https://doi.org/10.1111/deci.12077.

Zmud, R. W. (1984). Design alternatives for organizing information systems activities. *MIS Quarterly, 8*(2), 79–93.

Zmud, R. W., Boynton, A. C., & Jacobs, G. C. (1986). The information economy: A new perspective for effective information systems management. *Data Base, 18*(1), 17–23.

Chapter 3
Business/IT Alignment

Abstract This chapter discusses the impact of Enterprise Governance of IT on business/IT alignment. The first question that is answered in this chapter is how an organization can measure and evaluate its current state of business/IT alignment. This discussion is supplemented by providing insights on the relationship between Enterprise Governance of IT and business/IT alignment. The chapter ends with a section on the contextualization of business/IT alignment (i.e., a multidimensional perspective on business/IT alignment, and social (business/IT) alignment).

3.1 Measuring Business/IT Alignment

The concept of business/IT alignment was already introduced in the first chapter. More specifically, the introductory chapter briefly explained that business/IT alignment is about aligning business strategy, IT strategy, business operations, and IT operations, and as such, it was concluded that alignment is a complex challenge for organizations.

Extant literature does not agree on a universal way to measure business/IT alignment. Many researchers have developed models that attempt to capture the complex alignment construct as complete as possible. Each measurement model has its own approach, and as a result, it is very difficult to compare the results of alignment studies leveraging different approaches. Some established approaches are discussed below, each having their strengths and weaknesses. In the end, it is important to select the approach that is suited best for the type of activity or research one is trying to do.

3.1.1 The Matching and Moderation Approach

The matching approach looks at the difference in ratings between two pairs of related items. When there is a high difference between the ratings of related items,

© Springer Nature Switzerland AG 2020
S. De Haes et al., *Enterprise Governance of Information Technology*,
Management for Professionals, https://doi.org/10.1007/978-3-030-25918-1_3

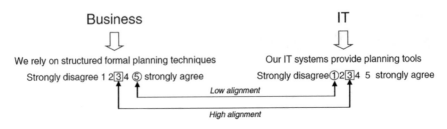

Fig. 3.1 Matching approach

alignment is low, and conversely, when there is a low difference, alignment is high. Figure 3.1 illustrates the matching approach.

Leveraging the matching approach, researchers look for parallelism between business and IT. If the difference in scores between business and IT is high, alignment is low (in Fig. 3.1, difference in scores for low alignment is 4), and conversely, if the difference between the scores in low, alignment is high (in Fig. 3.1, difference in scores of high alignment is 0). Applying this approach, using a set of questions can lead to an alignment score for the organization. One of the shortcomings of this method is the question whether the scores necessarily need to be at the same level to indicate high degrees of alignment. Take the example in Fig. 3.1: it is clear that if the business scores 5 on formal planning techniques and IT scores 1 on providing planning tools that alignment is low as IT is not supporting business needs. However, if the business does not rely on structured formal planning techniques (score 1 on left-hand side) but IT scores a better rate of 2 or 3 on providing planning tools, IT might be outperforming the business slightly, but does that really imply low alignment? However, this method is clearly an intuitive and simple approach to undertake and therefore often used in practice and research.

A related technique is the moderation approach. In this approach, alignment is seen as an interaction rather than a parallelism and as such quite often leads to different outcomes than the moderation approach. It is the combination or synergy between business and IT, rather than the difference, which is important. The moderation approach does not calculate the difference but the product terms. In the example of Fig. 3.1, this implies that the business score of 1 and the IT score of 5 results in an alignment score of 5 and the business score of 3 and the IT score of 3 in an alignment score of 9. It is clear that this approach differs from the matching approach as two low scores are now seen as "low alignment" where in the matching approach; two (equal) low scores result in "high alignment". The basic assumption in the moderation approach is that the interactive relationship (moderation) between business and IT, and not the difference, will impact business performance. For example, two 3's would lead to an alignment score of 9 and two 5's would lead to an alignment score of 25 using the moderation approach. In the matching approach, both scenarios would lead to an alignment score of 0, i.e., high alignment. In the moderation approach, the higher score of 25 (two 5's) is assigned as this represents a higher interaction effect between business and IT which will impact firm performance.

Whatever method is chosen, matching or moderation, it should be clear that both approaches are valuable, but that they can lead to different conclusions regarding the state of business/IT alignment in an organization.

3.1.2 The Profile Deviation Approach

Measuring alignment based on the profile deviation approach is based on two steps. First, an "ideal alignment scenario" has to be deducted (from theory) and next, deviations from this ideal state are calculated.

A well-known example can be found in the study of Sabherwal and Chan (2001). These authors tried to define IT strategies that map best to specific business strategies. Those business strategies were defined based on the Miles and Snow (1978) typology, which identifies different types of business strategies: defenders (aiming to reduce costs, maximizing efficiency, and effectiveness of production, avoiding organizational change), prospectors (seen as leading innovators, reacting first on signals of change in their market) and analyzers (closely watching competitor's activities and carefully evaluating organizational changes). Table 3.1 demonstrates which IT strategies align best with specific business strategies, according to their insights. "IT for efficiency" is oriented toward internal and inter-organizational efficiencies and long-term decision-making and maps well to the defenders' business strategy. "IT for flexibility" focuses on market flexibility and quick strategic decisions which maps to the prospectors' business strategy. "IT for comprehensiveness" enables comprehensive decisions and quick responses through knowledge of other organizations which is in line with the analyzers' business strategy.

Based on this model, organizations can be classified against each of the categories and the distance against the ideal state can be determined. It is clear that the value of this type of measurement stands or falls with the validity of the theorized "ideal alignment scenario".

Table 3.1 Mapping IT and business strategies (Sabherwal & Chan, 2001)

IT strategy	Business strategy		
	Defenders	Prospectors	Analysers
IT for efficiency	High	Low	Low
IT for flexibility	Low	High	Low
IT for comprehensiveness	Low	Low	High

3.1.3   The Scoring Approach

A typical example of the scoring approach is the information economics method developed by Parker and Benson (1989). This method can be used as an alignment measurement whereby both business and IT people score major IT investments to verify the degree of alignment against a set of (business and IT) criteria. The method typically departs from the return on investment (ROI) of a project and different non-tangibles such as "strategic match of the project" (business evaluation) and "match with the strategic IT architecture" (IT evaluation). In essence, information economics is a scoring technique for projects, resulting in a weighted total score based on the scores for the ROI and the non-tangibles. Typically, scores from 0 to 5 are attributed whereby 0 means no contribution and 5 refers to a high contribution; the values obtain a positive score and the risks a negative score (see Table 3.2).

A limitation of the information economics approach to assessing alignment is that it is focused only on one major IT project. To counter such limitations, alternative scoring instruments were developed. Weill and Broadbent (1998) developed a "diagnostic to assess alignment" (see Table 3.3). This approach requires the respondents to assess ten statements that relate to the degree of alignment, on a scale from 1 to 5 (1 = always true, 5 = never true). The average of the assessments on all the ten statements provides the alignment score.

Weill and Ross (2005) proposed a governance performance measure (see Fig. 3.2) which is based on the scores regarding perceived governance outcomes. Respondents have to score on a scale from 1 (not important) to 5 (very important)

Table 3.2 Information economics (Van Grembergen & Van Bruggen, 1997)

Traditional ROI (+)		
+ value linking (+) + value acceleration (+)		
+ value restructuring (+) + innovation (+)		
= *Adjusted ROI*	+ Business *Value*	+ *IT Value*
	• Strategic match (+)	• Strategic IT architecture (+)
	• Competitive advantage (+)	
	• Competitive response (+)	
	• Management information (+)	
	• Service and quality (+)	
	• Environmental quality (+)	
	• Empowerment (+)	
	• Cycle time (+)	
	• Mass customization (+)	
	− *Business Risk*	− *IT Risk*
	• Business strategy risk (−)	• IT Strategy risk (−)
	• Business organization risk (−)	• Definitional uncertainty (−)
		• Technical risk (−)
		• IT service delivery risk (−)
= *VALUE (business contribution)*		

Table 3.3 Diagnostic to assess alignment (Weill & Broadbent, 1998)

	Always true				Never true
1. Senior management has no vision for the role of IT	1	2	3	4	5
2. The IT group drives IT projects	1	2	3	4	5
3. There is no IT component in the division's strategy	1	2	3	4	5
4. Vital information necessary to make decisions is often missing	1	2	3	4	5
5. Islands of automation exist	1	2	3	4	5
6. Management perceives little value from computing	1	2	3	4	5
7. A "them and us" mentality prevails	1	2	3	4	5
8. IT doens't help for the hard tasks	1	2	3	4	5
9. It's hard to get financial approval for IT projects	1	2	3	4	5
10. Senior management sees outsourcing as a way to control IT	1	2	3	4	5
	Average:				

how important a particular governance outcome is (question 1), and on a scale from 1 (not successful) to 5 (very successful) how well IT governance contributed to meeting that outcome (question 2). The outcomes that are to be scored are cost-effective use of IT, effective use of IT for growth, effective use of IT for asset utilization, and effective use of IT for business flexibility. Based on these answers, a weighted governance performance score can be calculated. Since not all firms rank the outcomes with the same importance, the answers to the first question are used as a weighting factor.

3.1.4   The Maturity Model Approach

Organizations can also use a maturity model to assess the state of alignment. This is a method of scoring that enables the organization to grade itself from non-existent (0) to optimized (5). This tool offers an easy-to-understand way to determine the "as-is" and the "to-be" (according to enterprise strategy) state and enables the organization to benchmark itself against best practices and standard guidelines. This way, gaps can be identified, and specific actions can be defined to move toward the desired level of strategic alignment maturity.

A good example of strategic alignment maturity models was developed by Luftman (2000), who defined five maturity levels around six alignment-related domains (e.g., communication and partnership), using the attributes described in the first column of Table 3.4. The other two columns indicate the characteristics or values of each attribute to obtain a level 1 and level 5 strategic alignment maturities, respectively.

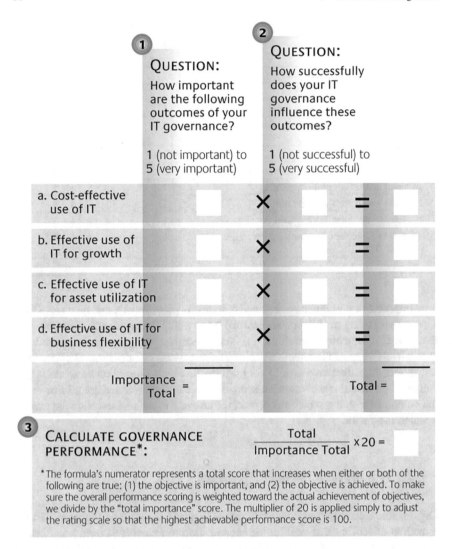

Fig. 3.2 Governance performance measurement (Weill & Ross, 2005)

Based on this maturity model, Luftman reports on international business/IT alignment benchmarks. One example is given in Fig. 3.3, which shows that the retail and transportation sectors are leading the benchmark and, surprisingly, the financial sector achieves merely an averages outcome.

Table 3.4 Strategic alignment maturity levels (Luftman, 2000)

Attribute	Characteristics level 1	Characteristic level 5
Communications maturity		
• Understanding of business by IT	Minimum	Pervasive
• Understanding of IT by business	Minimum	Pervasive
• Inter/intra-organizational learning	Casual, ad hoc	Strong and structured
• Protocol rigidity	Command and control	Informal
• Knowledge sharing	Ad hoc	Extra-enterprise
• Liaison(s) breath/effectiveness	None or ad hoc	Extra-enterprise
Competency/value measurements maturity		
• IT metrics	Technical	Extended to external partners
• Business metrics	Ad hoc	Extended to external partners
• Balanced metrics	Ad hoc, unlinked	Business, partner and IT metrics
• Service level agreements	Sporadically present	Extended to external partners
• Benchmarking	Not generally practiced	Routinely performed with partners
• Formal assessments/reviews	None	Routinely performed
• continuous improvement	None	Routinely performed
Governance maturity		
• Business strategic planning	Ad hoc	Integrated across and external
• IT strategic planning	Ad hoc	Integrated across and external
• Reporting/organization structure	CIO reports to CFO	CIO reports to CEO
	Central/decentral	Federated
• Budgetary/control	Cost center, erratic	Investment center, profit center
• IT investment management	Cost based, erratic	Business value
• Steering committee(s)	Not formal, regular	Partnership
• Prioritization process	Reactive	Value added partner
Partnership maturity		
• Business perception of IT value	IT perceived as a cost	IT co-adapts with business
• Role of IT in strategic business planning	No seat at business table	Co-adaptive with business
• Shared goals, risk, rewards/penalties	IT takes risk	Risks and rewards shared
• IT program management	Ad hoc	Continuous improvement
• relationship/trust style	Conflict/minimum	Valued partnership
• business sponsor/champion	None	At the CEO level
Scope & architecture maturity		
• Traditional, enabler/driver	Traditional systems	Business strategy driver/enabler
• Standards articulation	None or ad hoc	Inter-enterprise standards
• Architectural integration:	No formal integration	Evolve with partners

(continued)

Table 3.4 (continued)

Attribute	Characteristics level 1	Characteristic level 5
− Functional organization		Integrated
− Enterprise		Standard enterprise architecture
− Inter-enterprise		with all partners
• Architectural transparency, flexibility	None	Across the infrastructure
Skills maturity		
• Innovation, entrepreneurship	Discouraged	The norm
• Locus of power	In the business	All executives, including CIO
• Management style	Command and control	Relationship based
• Change readiness	Resistant to change	High, focused
• Career crossover	None	Across the enterprise
• Education, cross-training	None	Across the enterprise
• Attract & retain best talent	No program	Effective program for
		Hiring and retaining

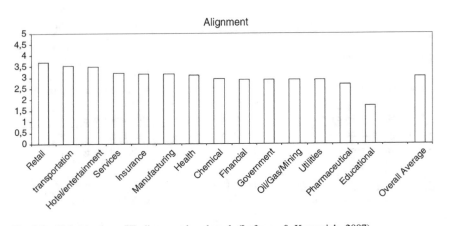

Fig. 3.3 Global business/IT alignment benchmark (Luftman & Kempaiah, 2007)

Assignment Box 3.1: Business/IT Alignment Benchmarking
Compare the international business/IT alignment results as presented in
Fig. 3.3 and try to explain the differences between sectors.

3.2 The Relationship Between Enterprise Governance of IT and Business/IT Alignment

As discussed in the first chapter, business/IT alignment is a crucial outcome of Enterprise Governance of IT and an essential link in the chain to enable IT business value. In this section, we illustrate the relationship between Enterprise Governance of IT and business/IT alignment based on the results of analyzing "extreme cases" (De Haes & Van Grembergen, 2009). This research started with creating a business/IT alignment benchmark for the Belgian financial services sector based on a sample of ten Belgian financial services organizations. In each organization, five to ten senior business and IT managers completed a questionnaire measuring business/IT alignment maturity (on a scale from 0 to 5), based on the Luftman (2000) maturity model as discussed in the previous section (refer back to Table 3.4). Based on the results of this benchmark, four extreme case organizations were selected (i.e., two high performers and two low performers in terms of business/IT alignment), in which a workshop was organized to measure the EGIT maturity based on a generic maturity scale from 0 (non-existent) to 5 (optimized). This maturity assessment was based on the IT governance institute's generic maturity model (IT Governance Institute (ITGI), 2003), which is visualized in Table 3.5. The collected data allowed for detailed cross-case analysis, looking for causes that could explain why some organizations achieved a higher business/IT alignment score than other organizations.

After measuring business/IT alignment in ten Belgian financial services organizations, it appeared that the overall business/IT alignment maturity is 2.69 on a scale of 5 in the Belgian financial services sector (Fig. 3.4). The benchmark contained two organizations with a relatively high business/IT alignment maturity

Table 3.5 Generic maturity model (IT Governance Institute (ITGI), 2003)

■ 0 Non-existent.
Complete lack of any recognisable processes. The enterprise has not even recognised that there is an issue to be addressed.
■ 1 Initial/Ad Hoc.
There is evidence that the enterprise has recognised that the issues exist and need to be addressed. There are, however, no standardised processes; instead there are ad hoc approaches that tend to be applied on an individual or case-by-case basis. The overall approach to management is disorganised.
■ 2 Repeatable but Intuitive.
Processes have developed to the stage where similar procedures are followed by different people undertaking the same task. There is no formal training or communication of standard procedures, and responsibility is left to the individual. There is a high degree of reliance on the knowledge of individuals and, therefore, errors are likely.
■ 3 Defined Process.
Procedures have been standardised and documented, and communicated through training. It is mandated that these processes should be followed; however, it is unlikely that deviations will be detected. The procedures themselves are not sophisticated but are the formalisation of existing practices.
■ 4 Managed and Measurable.
Management monitors and measures compliance with procedures and to take action where processes appear not to be working effectively. Processes are under constant improvement and provide good practice. Automation and tools are used in a limited or fragmented way.
■ 5 Optimised.
Processes have been refined to a level of good practice, based on the results of continuous improvement and maturity modelling with other enterprises. IT is used in an integrated way to automate the workflow, providing tools to improve quality and effectiveness, making the enterprise quick to adapt.

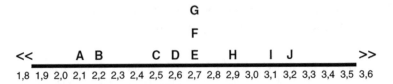

Fig. 3.4 Business/IT alignment maturity benchmark in ten Belgian financial services organizations (De Haes & Van Grembergen, 2009)

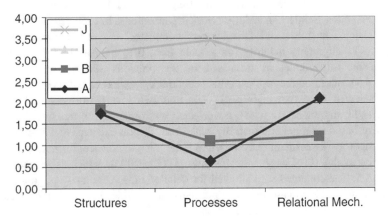

Fig. 3.5 Comparing extreme cases (1) (De Haes & Van Grembergen, 2009)

compared to the overall average (high performers I and J) and two organizations with a relatively low business/IT alignment maturity compared to the benchmark (low performers A and B). The other six organizations were all situated around the overall average. An interesting consideration here is what the desired target or to be situation would be for the financial services sector. While there is no literature available in this domain, taking the high dependency on IT into account, one could argue that at least a maturity level 3 would be required, which implies standardized and documented processes and procedures.

In each of these four "extreme cases", it was assessed in which maturity the organization was applying each of the 33 EGIT mechanisms as discussed in chap. 2 . When comparing the average maturity of the EGIT mechanisms (i.e., structures, processes, and relational mechanisms) in those extreme cases, it appears that in general the high performers have more mature EGIT structures and processes, as shown in Fig. 3.5. This figure also shows that that processes on average were less mature compared to structures, indicating that it is more difficult to implement processes than structures.

The analysis of the "extreme cases" furthermore indicated that the organizations with low business/alignment maturity did have a lot of EGIT mechanisms in place, but the average maturity of these mechanisms was below maturity level 2, as shown

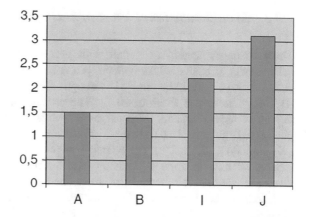

Fig. 3.6 Comparing extreme cases (2) (De Haes & Van Grembergen, 2009)

in Fig. 3.6. This might indicate that the impact on business/IT alignment of EGIT mechanisms that have a maturity level lower than 2 is rather limited.

The impact of relational mechanisms on business/IT alignment maturity was not clearly demonstrated in this research. However, a finding was that the two high performers had started their EGIT implementation many years ago and came to a point where many structures and processes were embedded in day-to-day practice. At that time, the importance of relational mechanisms becomes less important. The relational mechanisms are likely very important in the initiating phase of EGIT, in which the two low performers were situated.

An interesting EGIT structure that was not used by any of the organizations, although being promoted by scholars as very important, is the "IT strategy committee at the level of the board of directors" (Turel & Bart, 2014). This mechanism is promoted as a structure to ensure that the board gets involved in the Enterprise Governance of IT. During the interviews, three out of four "extreme case" organizations stated that board involvement in IT governance is not feasible and probably not required. The latter is of course in great contrast with the arguments provided in the section on board-level EGIT in Chap. 2.

3.3 Contextualizing Business/IT Alignment

This section explores and presents some new perspectives on business/IT alignment. Especially, some new academic studies suggest that business/IT alignment can be conceptualized at a multidimensional level. In this section, we will discuss the importance of the multilevel view in the conceptualization of business/IT alignment. Next, the section will also introduce the notion of "social alignment" between business and IT. Although social alignment between business and IT is not a new topic in information systems literature, in recent years, it has drawn considerable attention of many scholars in the area of business/IT alignment.

3.3.1 Multidimensional View of Business/IT Alignment

Many academic scholars together with business executives consider that the achievement of business/IT alignment is a complex process, which requires interaction between business and IT through multiple organizational dimensions (Benbya, Leidner, & Preston, 2019). The current information systems literature provides three dominant dimensions to understand the dynamic nature of business/IT alignment: (i) strategic dimension, (ii) operational dimension, and (iii) individual dimension. The strategic alignment dimension, which essentially focuses on how to align IT strategy with business strategy, is so far the most discussed perspective in extant literature. The assumption is that such strategic fit will facilitate the efficient use of IT resources to create and protect IT business value (Benbya et al., 2019; Wu, Straub, & Liang, 2015). The operational alignment dimension focuses on the ability of management to align IT infrastructure with the business processes in the organization (Benbya et al., 2019). The assumption here is that an organization needs to carefully design and align IT organizational structure with various organizational units. The key objective of the operational dimension is to achieve efficient alignment between IT and organizational structures to avoid misalignment between business and IT. Lastly, the individual dimension mainly looks into how IT infrastructure and individual user needs can be integrated seamlessly. This is particularly important for those organizations where individual discretion is almost undermined in the selection and use of IT.

Table 3.6 summarizes the three business/IT alignment dimensions based on the study of Benbya and McKelvey (2006). This provides a brief overview of the components that establish the focus of each alignment dimension. For example, the strategic alignment dimension is more structural in nature. That is, it provides specific components in the form of IT strategy, business strategy, strategic IT planning, and types of IT strategy configurations. For example, an organization's attempt to achieve business/IT alignment, and thereby a higher impact on IT business value, can be realized through three distinct ways of aligning IT strategy to business strategy (Chen, Mocker, Preston, & Teubner, 2010). First, IT strategy is developed as an integral part of the business strategy. In other words, IT strategy is not a strategy on its own. The assumption here is that the IT strategy is developed to support the existing business strategy. This as such is a business-centric approach to develop IT strategy. Second, an organization might show an IT function-centric approach to develop IT strategy. In such an approach, IT strategy is developed in an isolated manner and with a focus on a functional-level role of IT assets. In other words, IT strategy is primarily considered as a functional-level strategy for the organization and focuses on planning of IT assets. Third, IT strategy can be developed separately from the business strategy. However, IT strategy is considered as an organizational-level strategy. This approach is more organization-centric and exhibits a managerial attitude toward IT.

Following Chen et al. (2010), we can infer that organizations can select one of the three approaches to align IT and business strategy primarily based on the desired impact of the IT strategy. If the organization's key focus is to ensure successful implementation and realization of business strategy, then this confirms a business-centric approach of the organization and requires addressing the key question: "how can IT be used to achieve business strategy?" This will require that the IT strategy should support the business strategy to achieve business/IT alignment. However, if an organization is facing the challenge of identifying and allocating IT assets (e.g., IT staff, IT infrastructure, IT applications IT processes, and IT budget) efficiently, then it is desired to opt for a functional-level IT strategy. Lastly, if senior management wants to promote a shared understanding across the whole organization about the role of IT between business and IT functions, an organization-centric approach to develop the IT strategy will be adopted. The organization-centric approach is essentially a higher-order approach when compared to business-centric and IT function-centric approaches.

The operational dimension of alignment is concerned with the transformation of strategy into daily business. This dimension seeks alignment of IT structure with organizational structure and also ensures the integration of organizational infrastructure with IT infrastructure. The term IT structure in this context refers to the set of rules, which are outlined in the form of written documents or by establishing formal positions in the organization (Benbya & McKelvey, 2006). The key components of operational alignment, like locus of responsibility and decision-making rights, provide a formal authority to translate IT strategy into action and reduce the possibility of the misalignment between business and IT.

Lastly, the individual dimension of alignment focuses on the fit between IT infrastructure and user needs. The individual dimension challenges the view that IT infrastructure, once well aligned with other organizational structure(s), remains static. Instead, this dimension suggests that IT infrastructure should co-evolve with user needs (Benbya & McKelvey, 2006). In other words, user needs are constantly evolving as the internal and external technology landscape is constantly changing because of new emerging technologies (e.g., use of social media or smartphones for work activities) or organizational contingencies (e.g., change in technology platform because of mergers and acquisitions). This results in the fact that organizations need to constantly adapt to ever-changing user needs and understand the IT infrastructure needs of different actors (e.g. user, vendors etc.)

3.3.2 Social Business/IT Alignment

In the previous section, we broadly discussed several alignment dimensions. Many information systems scholars group these dimensions (i.e., mainly the strategic and operational dimensions) under the heading of the "intellectual dimension" of alignment (Wu et al., 2015). This term essentially captures the fact that there is an explicit nature to recognize and achieve business/IT alignment. This explicitness is mainly expressed through IT strategy, IT planning, and IT structures (e.g., documentation, CIO position, and IT planning committee). However, business/IT

Table 3.6 Alignment dimensions and components (Benbya & McKelvey, 2006)

Business/IT alignment dimension	Definition	Components
Strategic dimension	Alignment of IT strategy with business strategy	IT strategy, business strategy strategic planning
Operational dimension	Alignment between organizational structure and IT structure Alignment between actor's communication and degree of involvement with IT strategy domains	Locus of responsibility Decision-making rights Deployment of IT personnel Organizational actors' values Communication with each other
Individual dimension	Alignment between IT infrastructure and user's needs	Understanding of each other IT infrastructure Users' expectations and needs

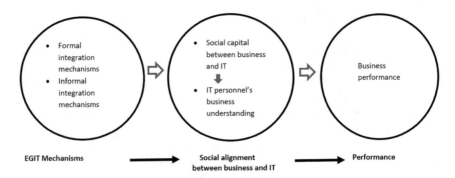

Fig. 3.7 Social alignment between business and IT

alignment also exhibits so-called social alignment, which focuses on values, communication, and shared understanding between business and IT executives (Reich & Benbasat, 1996). Social alignment can be achieved through formal and informal EGIT mechanisms. The study of Schlosser, Beimborn, Weitzel, and Wagner (2015) provides an overview of how to conceptualize and measure social alignment between business and IT.

As shown in Fig. 3.7, formal integration (e.g., regular meetings, and liaison unit) and informal integration (e.g., top management support and joint trainings) (EGIT) mechanisms can positively influence social alignment between business and IT. Social alignment can be conceptualized as social capital between business and IT, and IT personnel's business understanding. Social capital between business and IT is mostly about mutual trust and respect, interaction, and equal participation in change management processes. IT personnel's business understanding is considered to be the outcome of the social capital between business and IT. That is, social capital between business and IT will positively influence IT personnel's business understanding. Schlosser et al. (2015) confirm that both formal and informal EGIT mechanisms positively impact social alignment between business and IT. Both types of mechanisms have a strong impact on creating social capital between business and IT, which in turn impacts IT personnel's business understanding. There is also a direct effect of informal integration mechanisms on IT personnel's business understanding. The impact of social alignment between business and IT on business performance is further discussed in Chap. 4, which is about IT business value.

3.4   Summary

Extant literature does not agree on a universal way to measure business/IT alignment. Many researchers have developed models that attempt to capture the complex alignment construct as complete as possible. Each measurement model has its own approach, and as a result, it is very difficult to compare the results of alignment studies leveraging different measurement models or approaches. Some potential approaches were described in this chapter, all having their strengths and weaknesses. In the end, it is important to select the approach that is suited best for the type of activity or research one is trying to do.

This chapter also reported on the results of a study that illustrates the relationship between business/IT alignment and Enterprise Governance of IT, using Luftman's maturity model as an instrument to measure business/IT alignment. Based on this study, it is concluded that well-aligned organizations clearly adopted more mature EGIT mechanisms when compared to poorly aligned organizations. Finally, the multidimensional perspective on alignment was discussed, which provides some key insights on understanding the complex nature of the business/IT alignment concept.

Study Questions

1. Discuss how business/IT alignment can be measured and determine which is the most practical approach.
2. Explain how business/IT alignment can be measured using Luftman's maturity model.
3. Explain the relationship between Enterprise Governance of IT and business/IT alignment.
4. Explain the multidimensional view of business/IT alignment.
5. What is social alignment between business and IT?

References

Benbya, H., Leidner, D., & Preston, D. (2019). *MIS quarterly research CUration on information systems alignment.* Retrieved from https://www.misqresearchcurations.org/blog/2019/3/14/information-systems-alignment.

Benbya, H., & McKelvey, B. (2006). Using coevolutionary and complexity theories to improve is alignment: A multi–Level approach. *Journal of Information Technology, 21*(4), 284–298.

Chen, D., Mocker, M., Preston, D., & Teubner, A. (2010). Information systems strategy: Reconceptualization, measurement, and implications. *Management Information Systems Quarterly, 34*(2), 233–259.

De Haes, S., & Van Grembergen, W. (2009). An exploratory study into IT governance implementations and its impact on business/IT alignment. *Information Systems Management, 26*(2), 123–137.

IT Governance Institute (ITGI). (2003). *Board briefing on IT governance,* (2nd ed.). Retrieved from http://www.isaca.org/knowledge-center/research/researchdeliverables/pages/board-briefing-on-it-governance-2nd-edition.aspx.

Luftman, J. (2000). Assessing business-IT alignment maturity. *Communications of the Association for Information Systems, 4*.

Luftman, J., & Kempaiah, R. (2007). An update on business-IT alignment: "a line" has been drawn. *MIS Quarterly Executive, 6*(3), 165–177.

Miles, R. E., & Snow, C. C. (1978). *Organizational strategy, structure, and process.* New York: Mcgraw-Hill.

Parker, M. M., & Benson, R. J. (1989). Enterprisewide information economics: Latest concepts. *Journal of Information Systems Management, 6*(4), 7–13.

Reich, B. H., & Benbasat, I. (1996). Measuring the linkage between business and information technology objectives. *MIS Quarterly, 20*(1), 55.

Sabherwal, R., & Chan, Y. E. (2001). Alignment between business and IS strategies: A study of prospectors, analyzers, and defenders. *Information Systems Research.* Retrieved from http://pubsonline.informs.org/doi/abs/10.1287/isre.12.1.11.9714.

Schlosser, F., Beimborn, D., Weitzel, T., & Wagner, H.-T. (2015). Achieving social alignment between business and IT—An empirical evaluation of the efficacy of IT governance mechanisms. *Journal of Information Technology, 30*(2), 119–135.

Turel, O., & Bart, C. (2014). Board-level IT governance and organizational performance. *European Journal of Information Systems, 23*(2), 223–239.

Van Grembergen, W., & Van Bruggen, R. (1997). Measuring and improving corporate information technology through the balanced scorecard technique. In *Proceedings of the European Conference on the Evaluation of Information Technology.* The Netherlands: Delft.

Weill, P., & Broadbent, M. (1998). *Leveraging the new infrastructure - How market leaders capitalize on Information technology.* Boston: Harvard Business School Press.

Weill, P., & Ross, J. (2005). A matrixed approach to designing IT governance. *MIT Sloan Management Review, 46*(2), 26–34.

Wu, S. P.-J., Straub, D. W., & Liang, T.-P. (2015). How information technology governance mechanisms and strategic alignment influence organizational performance: Insights from a matched survey of business and IT managers. *MIS Quarterly, 39*(2), 497–518.

Chapter 4
IT Business Value

Abstract Previous chapters described the concepts of Enterprise Governance of IT and business/IT alignment, as well as the relationship between them. The first chapter explained that the ultimate outcome of Enterprise Governance of IT is (the creation and protection of) IT business value. More specifically, Enterprise Governance of IT enables IT business value, through the mediating mechanism of business/IT alignment. The concept of IT business value deals with the contribution of the (current and future) use of IT to organizational performance. In other words, it deals with the question "are we getting the benefits out of our IT (operations and investments)?" This chapter starts with a brief discussion about the IT productivity paradox and the IT productivity cycle. Then, two important management instruments are introduced that are helpful in managing and realizing IT business value: the business case (process) and the IT balanced scorecard. Lastly, this chapter draws on recent EGIT-related literature to facilitate a discussion in line with the conceptual model underlying this book: i.e., EGIT enables IT business value, through the mediating mechanism of business/IT alignment.

4.1 To Value or not to Value

Investments in IT are growing extensively, and business managers often worry that the benefits of IT investments might not be as high as expected. The same worry accounts for the perceived ever-increasing total cost of the IT department, without clear evidence of the value derived from it. Getting IT business value and especially measuring that value is therefore an important attention point in the context of enterprise governance of IT. These responsibilities are to be shared by both business and IT and should take both tangible and intangible costs, benefits, and risks into account. Measuring and managing IT business value should provide answers to questions such as:

- If I spend a dollar/euro extra on IT, what do I get back?
- How does my IT benchmark against competitors?
- Do I get back from IT what was promised?

© Springer Nature Switzerland AG 2020
S. De Haes et al., *Enterprise Governance of Information Technology*,
Management for Professionals, https://doi.org/10.1007/978-3-030-25918-1_4

- How do I learn from past performance to optimize my organization?
- Is my IT implementing its strategy, in line with the business strategy?
- ...

The second section of this chapter deals with the productivity of IT. More specifically, this section outlines the fundamental issue of the IT productivity paradox and the IT productivity cycle. In the third section of this chapter, we look at how to demonstrate, measure, and manage the value of a single IT(-enabled) investment through the business case process. In the fourth section of this chapter, we will discuss how to demonstrate, measure, and manage the performance and value of the IT function or department using the balanced scorecard as an instrument. The fifth and final section of this chapter is dedicated to recent EGIT-related research findings, which validate the premise that EGIT enables IT business value, through the mediating mechanism of business/IT alignment.

In support of this chapter (and by extension the whole book), some definitions from the area of IT value management are provided, as organizations often have different interpretations regarding what is meant by an IT "project", a "program" and a "portfolio." We propose definitions for these concepts as visualized in Fig. 4.1.

A *project* is a structured set of activities concerned with the delivery of a defined technical capability based on an agreed schedule and budget. Projects are defined at the level of the delivery of IT applications and solutions, such as a CRM application or a new Web site, which are necessary but not sufficient to achieve a required business outcome. A *program* is a structured grouping of projects that are both necessary and sufficient to achieve a business outcome and deliver value. A program therefore is the combination of the "IT project" and all other business-related projects such as defining new business processes, providing training, and managing change. Finally, the suite of investment programs, including also those with no IT involvement, is to be managed as a *portfolio* in order to optimize the overall value for the organization.

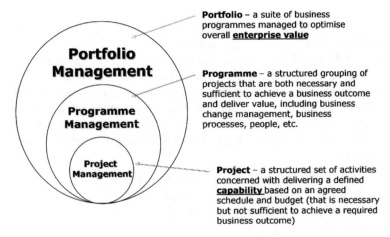

Portfolio – a suite of business programmes managed to optimise overall **enterprise value**

Programme – a structured grouping of projects that are both necessary and sufficient to achieve a business outcome and deliver value, including business change management, business processes, people, etc.

Project – a structured set of activities concerned with delivering a defined **capability** based on an agreed schedule and budget (that is necessary but not sufficient to achieve a required business outcome)

Fig. 4.1 Project (management), program (management) and portfolio (management) (ISACA, 2008)

4.2   The IT Productivity Paradox and the IT Productivity Cycle

At its core, the term IT business value attempts to capture how (current and future) IT can bring about business benefits. There is a long history and debate on the topic of IT business value, most commonly in the context of the so-called IT black hole or IT productivity paradox. The main argument in the context of the *IT productivity paradox* debate is that, despite large investments in IT, there are no (observable) productivity gains. Over the past three decades, many academic scholars have tried to understand and assess this paradox. The outcomes of IT-enabled initiatives were linked to different productivity measures. These measures mainly included firm profitability, revenue, return on investment on individual projects, and stock returns (Oz, 2005). Using these types of productivity measures, researchers found mixed evidence. That is, in some cases, studies have found a significant impact of IT investments on productivity, whereas other studies did not find any association between IT investments and productivity. This suggested that the measurement of benefits essentially is the most challenging task in examining IT business value. The term "value" in the context of IT-enabled initiatives therefore is a very intricate notion. Value can be assessed in various ways. For example, value can manifest through improved decision making, customer loyalty, employee satisfaction, improved customer relationship, etc., leading to productivity gains (in terms of increases in profit and revenue growth). It is necessary to understand that some value outcomes might indirectly contribute to productivity gains, some may not, and some even cannot be measured to examine the link to productivity (Oz, 2005). The value assessment of IT-enabled initiatives through directly measuring the relationship between IT expenditure and net income or revenue growth (as a measure of productivity) might result in flawed inferences. Indeed, profit does not qualify as an apt surrogate to measure productivity (Oz, 2005). In the fourth section of this chapter, we will discuss the IT balanced scorecard. This will contribute to understanding the multi-dimensionality of IT business value.

While acknowledging the complex nature of IT business value, Oz (2005) provides a simple theory in the form of the *IT productivity cycle*. The purpose of the IT productivity cycle essentially is to gain insights on value creation and protection from IT investments, and more importantly understand the cyclic nature of IT-enabled initiatives. Senior executives responsible for IT investments can also draw some meaningful conclusions to benchmark and set expectations about IT-enabled initiatives drawing on this IT productivity cycle. Especially, the cycle helps to explain why at the *organizational level* we see the benefits of IT-enabled investments, but such benefits are often missing at the *industry level*. As shown in Fig. 4.2, the IT productivity cycle is composed of five phases: (1) adoption of new IT, (2) increased profit, (3) new IT becomes standard, (4) competition pushes prices down, and (5) productivity gains in dollars (i.e., monetary terms) decrease.

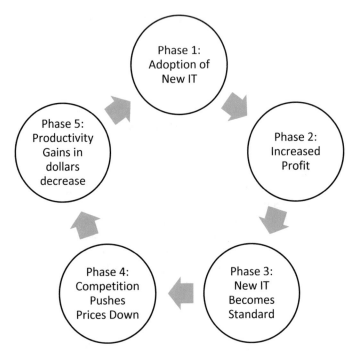

Fig. 4.2 IT productivity cycle (Oz, 2005)

In *phase 1*, one (or a limited number of) organization(s) undertake(s) IT-enabled initiatives like the development of new IT systems or new hardware to support existing IT infrastructure or to create entirely new IT solutions for new products or services. The assumption is that the investment in this new IT will result into productivity. Also, if the new IT is developed by a (or some) specific organization (s), then the productivity gains will be higher and specific to that (or those) organization(s) in the long term.

In *phase 2*, those organizations who successfully implement the new IT achieve higher productivity gains, which then translate into increased profit in monetary terms. This profit will be even higher if the new IT is proprietary to the organization and cannot be copied easily by competitors. Interestingly, many organizations struggle to implement new IT successfully, which can result in losses. The risk of failure is higher for those organizations who want to seek first-mover advantage with the deployment of new emerging technologies. Of course, these organizations are also the ones who will achieve higher market share and thereby higher profit as a risk payoff if the new IT is implemented successfully.

In *phase 3*, the market competition recognizes the need for the new IT to remain competitive. That is, organizations who have not adopted the new IT in the first wave of adoption seek it as a competitive necessity for their productivity. For example, in the commercial banking sector, some banks invested heavily in ATMs in the early 1970s to increase market share, but today it is seen a competitive necessity (rather than a competitive asset) by any commercial bank. This informs us that over a certain period of time a new IT becomes the norm (or standard) for business operations. For example, e-mail, Internet banking, and e-commerce platforms classify as such basic technologies for almost every contemporary organization to perform day-to-day business operations.

In *phase 4*, market competition is impacted because of the standardization of the new IT. That is, the majority of organizations are adopting this (now mature) technology and gain productivity benefits. This ultimately pushes the firms to cut the prices of the relevant products and services. This is possible because the mature technology helps organizations to reduce the production costs, and thus, benefits can be passed on to the customers.

In *phase 5*, we often find claims of drops in productivity gains, which are not necessarily correct. For instance, if the organization measures the productivity in terms of firm profitability or sales in monetary value, then it might arrive at a wrong conclusion. This is because the mature IT will push the unit price of the product or service down, although the actual productivity has gone up. And obliviously, it will not reflect in monetary value. This conclusion holds for both organizational- and industry-level analysis (more often for the industry) of IT business value.

In earlier chapters of this book, the concepts of EGIT and business/IT alignment were introduced and discussed. Interestingly, both EGIT and business/IT alignment can influence most of the phases of the IT productivity cycle, if we study this cycle at the organizational level. The adoption of new IT, which is the initial phase of the cycle, does suggest that value creation is contingent upon the successful adoption of the new IT. Many organizations need to find a right mix of EGIT structures, processes, and relational mechanisms while implementing and/or updating IT. Therefore, EGIT can play a pivotal role during the first two phases of the IT productivity cycle. In the next section of this chapter, the business case process is introduced to explain how IT investment decisions in new (or existing) IT can be made while improving the success rate of IT adoptions. The discussion on the IT balanced scorecard in the fourth section of this chapter predominantly assumes that IT business value is multi-faceted. Specifically, the IT balanced scorecard provides a profound approach to monitor and evaluate IT business value with the help of financial and non-financial measures. This is not only important during phase 2 of the IT productivity cycle, but also applicable to phases 3 and 4. In the scenario of higher competition (i.e., phases 3 and 4), the IT balanced scorecard (together with other EGIT mechanisms) can help executives to evaluate, direct, and monitor digital assets efficiently. In the next chapter of this book, we will introduce the COBIT 2019 framework, to specify key principles, design factors, governance and management objectives, alignment goals, and enterprise goals to assist the design and implementation of effective EGIT. This is as such relevant to all five phases of the IT productivity cycle.

4.3 The Business Case Process[1]

Academic scholars seem to agree that a business case is a formal document that provides a structured overview of information about a potential investment. All useful information is bundled in the business case, and relevant calculations are described to provide a rationale and justification for the potential investment (Krell & Matook, 2009). The overall goal of a business case is consistently described as to enable well-founded business decisions to make, let proceed, or stop the investment (ISACA, 2008; Post, 1992). As a result, we define a business case as a formal investment document with a structured overview of relevant information that provides a rationale and justification of an investment with the intent to enable well-founded investment decision-making (Maes, De Haes, & Van Grembergen, 2013).

Many business cases which are developed to support the investment approval gather dust on a shelf afterward (Franken, Edwards, & Lambert, 2009). Nonetheless, continuously using a business case throughout an entire investment life cycle can increase the adoption of the information system (IS) and is fundamental to benefit realization (Al-Mudimigh, Zairi, & Al-Mashari, 2001; Law & Ngai, 2007). Moreover, it is one of the major success factors for an investment and a source of a competitive advantage (Altinkemer, Ozcelik, & Ozdemir, 2014; Krell & Matook, 2009). Therefore, organizations should start to approach a business as a process instead of as a document. A process approach on business cases can be conceived as a business process which attempts to transform the formal business case document into a living document (Franken et al., 2009). We therefore define such a business case process as a set of logically related tasks that affect a business case and supports continuous business case usage with the intent to enable well-founded investment decision-making and to ultimately increase investment success (Maes, De Haes, & Van Grembergen, 2015).

A business case process runs in parallel with an investment life cycle, presented through a simplified three-phase perspective: before, during, and after implementation. The conceptual model, displayed in Fig. 4.3, is developed based on a literature review and presents a business case process consisting of three distinct but consecutive phases supported by an accommodating layer. These four components constitute together the business case process model and each component is defined in Table 4.1.

For each component, a set of practices was identified. These practices are presented in Table 4.2 (for business case development), in Table 4.3 (for business case maintenance), in Table 4.4 (for business case review), and in Table 4.5 (for business case process accommodation).

---

[1]Acknowledgment: This section is based on the doctoral research of Kim Maes. Additional substantiation can hence be found in the doctoral dissertation (see Maes 2014).

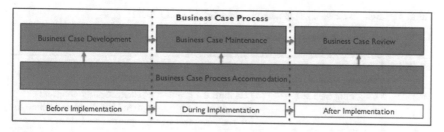

Fig. 4.3 Business case process conceptual model (aligned with an investment life cycle) (Maes et al., 2015)

Table 4.1 Components of the business case process model (Maes et al., 2015)

Component	Definition: A set of logically related practices to…
Business Case Development (BCD)	Identify relevant investment information that is integrated in a structured way with adequate and objective argumentation, in order to provide a rationale and justification of the initial investment idea
Business Case Maintenance (BCM)	Monitor whether the investment is implemented in accordance with the business case (e.g., objectives, changes and costs) and to update the business case with the prevailing reality (e.g., assumptions and risks)
Business Case Review (BCR)	Monitor benefit realization resulting from the utilization of products and services and to facilitate the evaluation of the overall investment success
Business Case Process Accommodation (BCPA)	Facilitate an adequate execution of the business case process adjusted to the investment and organizational context

In our research, we asked experts to give their opinion on the perceived effectiveness and perceived ease of implementation of each business case (process) practice.

Stakeholder attention is found to be very effective: both identifying their expectations (BCD03) and ensuring their active involvement (BCPA07) is positioned within the top three of highly effective practices. Indeed, stakeholders should be invited to participate in the development of a business case, and no investment should be approved without their active involvement (Matthews, 2004; Smith, McKeen, Cranston, & Benson, 2010). Communicating the business case to stakeholders is believed to be crucial in order to achieve their support and involvement (Luna-Reyes, Zhang, Ramón Gil-García, & Cresswell, 2005). They must be able to understand the business case, so it should be presented and communicated to them in an appropriate business language (Davenport, Harris, & Shapiro, 2010; Sherif & Vinze, 2002). One expert concluded: *"it is clear that personally, based on experience, I value the importance of stakeholder information, consultation, and commitment very high. It is a critical success factor for business case realization."*

Table 4.2 Business case development practices (Maes et al., 2015)

Code	A business case is developed by…	Definition
BCD01	Capturing investment vision	Capture the investment vision and establish the appropriate investment context
BCD02	Capturing business drivers	Capture the business challenges and opportunities that drive the investment and how they contribute to the achievement of the organizational strategy
BCD03	Identifying stakeholder expectations	Identify the stakeholders' expectations, needs, and requirements in terms of delivered benefits
BCD04	Identifying technology opportunities	Identify proven and emerging technologies that support the business drivers and may realize the investment objectives
BCD05	Identifying investment scope	Identify what will be done in the investment and what not, and explain why
BCD06	Identifying investment assumptions	Identify realistic assumptions and their logic for business drivers, investment objectives, investment solution(s), benefits, and costs
BCD07	Identifying investment objectives	Identify and categorize what objectives the investment should achieve
BCD08	Identifying investment solution(s)	Identify what organizational and technological changes are required, design one or more alternative investment solutions and implementation scenarios, and assign change owners
BCD09	Identifying investment benefits	Identify and categorize what benefits will be created by the investment based on relevant evidence, define their explicit measures, and assign benefit owners
BCD10	Identifying investment costs	Identify and categorize what costs will be created by the investment based on relevant evidence and define their explicit measures
BCD11	Identifying investment risks	Identify and evaluate the impact and probability of investment risks and critical success factors and determine preferred solutions to take a proactive approach
BCD12	Developing benefits realization plan	Develop a structured plan on when each benefit will be realized, in relevant phases and with appropriate consideration of organizational factors
BCD13	Evaluating investment feasibility and viability	Evaluate the feasibility and viability of each alternative investment solution
BCD14	Evaluating cost/benefit analysis	Capture identified investment costs and benefits with measures and values and evaluate cost/benefit analysis to support the financial argumentation

Another set of practices that are perceived to be highly effective deals with what the investment wants to realize. One expert clarifies: "*It is of utmost importance to (1) know exactly what problem you want to solve, (2) understand how this will be solved, and (3) obtain and maintain the desire to achieve this.*" Although the latter

Table 4.3 Business case maintenance practices (Maes et al., 2015)

Code	A business case is maintained by…	Definition
BCM01	Monitoring business case relevance	Monitor the business drivers, objectives and assumptions, and control whether they are still relevant and realistic
BCM02	Monitoring investment scope	Monitor the investment scope and realization of changes, and control whether it is still in line with the business case relevance
BCM03	Monitoring investment costs	Monitor whether the investment costs are consumed according to the scope and identified changes
BCM04	Monitoring investment risks	Monitor the investment risks and evaluate their impact on the business case
BCM05	Updating business case to react adequately	Update the business case frequently based on business case monitoring and identify adequate actions

Table 4.4 Business case review practices (Maes et al., 2015)

Code	A business case is reviewed by…	Definition
BCR01	Identifying objective evaluation criteria	Identify and communicate objective criteria with predefined weighting that help to evaluate the investment effectiveness and efficiency
BCR02	Evaluating investment effectiveness	Monitor benefits realization and evaluate the contribution of investment objectives and changes
BCR03	Evaluating investment efficiency	Evaluate the effort and costs that were consumed to realize the investment

refers mostly to the importance of stakeholder attention and involvement, the other two can directly be linked to BCD01, BCD02, BCD05, and BCD07. These four practices focus on the identification of the investment vision and what business drivers will be tackled, what will be included in the investment scope or not, and which objectives should be realized. The development of a business case should start from these fundamental questions (Ward, Daniel, & Peppard, 2008). The business drivers explain the current internal and external issues that the organization is facing, which directly influence the investment vision. In one exploratory case study, we discovered that market circumstances demanded fast decision-making for investing, divesting, and restructuring business divisions. As the company's daily operations and supporting ERP system were too inflexible to enable this, they initiated a new worldwide ERP investment.

The consensus levels on perceived ease of implementation scores are much lower, and many experts attributed a score of 3 to several practices (i.e., moderate easiness). This demonstrates that experts find it much more difficult to agree on their ease of implementation. We observe two outliers that are perceived to be easy to implement (>70% of experts): BCPA02 and BCM03. As BCPA02 deals with the

Table 4.5 Business case process accommodation practices (Maes et al., 2015)

Code	A business case process is accommodated by...	Definition
BCPA01	Establishing adaptable business case approach	Establish an adaptable business case approach according to investment and accept a growing maturation and granularity through its development and usage
BCPA02	Establishing business case templates, training, and guidance	Establish standard business case templates and tools and accommodate training and guidance on what constitute business case practices and how to employ them adequately
BCPA03	Establishing maximum objectivity in business case usage	Maximize objectivity to support well-founded and comparable decision-making without influence from politics, lobbying or institutional powers
BCPA04	Establishing simple and dynamic business case usage	Describe and employ business case practices and its content in a simple, straightforward and dynamic manner to encourage their usage
BCPA05	Establishing business case practices as standard approach	Establish and evangelize business case practices as a standard way of working
BCPA06	Ensuring business case practice improvements	Ensure business case practice improvements further through experience and continuous learning
BCPA07	Ensuring communication and involvement with stakeholders	Ensure clear communication and active involvement with all stakeholders in order to gain insight, commitment, and ownership
BCPA08	Ensuring stakeholder confirmation	Ensure formal confirmation from relevant stakeholders on the (updated) business case to increase their commitment
BCPA09	Evaluating business case regularly	Evaluate all business case documents in order to make well-founded decisions to approve, let proceed, or stop the investment

establishment of business case templates, training and guidance (BCPA02), experts perceive that such documents are easy to be created and distributed among stakeholders. The fact that this practice has not received high consensus on its perceived effectiveness contradicts with Smith et al. (2010). In one case study, the authors found that "the creation of a standard business case template was a big early win" for the investments. Next, the monitoring of investment costs (BCM03) is perceived as easy to implement by 83% of the experts (same score as effectiveness). Identifying costs (BCD10), which could be seen as the foundation of BCM03, was also perceived as easy to implement but did not reach high consensus on perceived effectiveness. It is found hard to comprehensively identify, forecast, and quantify costs (Goldschmidt, 2005; Powell, 1993), while we found in case studies that investment costs are relatively easy to be monitored on a frequent basis. This finding is somewhat surprising and contradictive, because the monitoring of costs is largely dependent upon a solid identification of what costs the investment will generate, and as such what costs should be monitored. We claim that not effectively performing the identification of costs will undoubtedly impact the effectiveness of the monitoring practice.

Very low consensus levels on ease of implementation were obtained for 25 practices. This finding should not come as a surprise as many organizations still struggle with business case usage (Jeffery & Leliveld, 2004; Taudes, Feurstein, & Mild, 2000). Business cases are often developed on the IT side although the responsibility should be positioned on the business side (Beatty & Williams, 2006). IT people are less able to perform this job as they have difficulties to estimate the added value that comes from strategic and tactical business opportunities such as flexibility, service, and market innovation (Taudes et al., 2000). We conclude that a great discrepancy can be found between how effective most business case practices are perceived and the perception of their ease of implementation. This contrast signals to us an important urge to investigate how these practices can be better implemented in the future.

If the consensus level for perceived effectiveness and ease of implementation is averaged for the different process model components (see Fig. 4.4), we discern that most consensus is achieved for effectiveness on practices in the Business Case Maintenance component, closely followed by those in the Business Case Development component. The consensus rate for Business Case Process Accommodation practices is still within the high consensus cut-off level (>70%), while only 64% of the experts perceive Business Case Review practices as effective. Practices from this component are also perceived lowest on ease of implementation. Although all four components receive a low to very low consensus rate on perceived ease of implementation, again practices from the Business Case Maintenance component achieve the highest rate. Hence, we might reason that organizations will achieve the highest return on effort when they implement the practices from the Business Case Maintenance component. Following up on the relevance of the business case is certainly important, as the business drivers and objectives can be impacted by a shift in market, organizational or technological issues (Al-Mudimigh et al., 2001). If an organization wants to understand how it needs to react to these changes, this impact should be investigated. This might require an update of the business case (Brown & Lockett, 2004). If a dramatic change threatens the business case relevance, one should re-assess the fundamental assumptions and perform a new cost–benefit analysis (Flynn, Pan, Keil, & Mähring, 2009). We think experts perceive the effectiveness of these Business Case Maintenance practices as high as they possess the ability to have a direct impact on last-minute changes and to contribute greatly to the effects of ongoing investment decision-making. After all, a continuous reflection on an update of the business case throughout the entire investment life cycle is important for ultimate benefit realization (Al-Mudimigh et al., 2001).

The lowest return might be expected from practices in the Business Case Review component, as they score lowest on both effectiveness and ease of implementation. Potentially, experts have reasoned that the job is done by then and that these

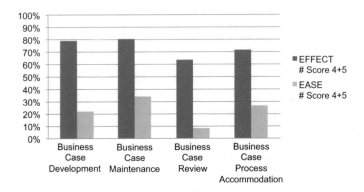

Fig. 4.4 Consensus levels on perceived effectiveness and perceived ease of implementation of business case practices per process model component (based on score 4 and 5 on five-point ordinal scale)

practices have no direct impact anymore on the final result. This is however not entirely true, because monitoring benefit realization is included in BCR02. Most probably, the practice has therefore achieved the highest consensus rate on effectiveness in its process model component. Together with the identification of objective evaluation criteria, it is the only practice that realizes the high consensus cut-off level of 70%. Indeed, a set of evaluation criteria should be established in an objective manner and with prior agreement by the stakeholders (Ashurst, Doherty, & Peppard, 2008). After the resulting products and services from the investment have officially been launched, benefit realization should be frequently monitored against the objective evaluation criteria (Fonstad & Robertson, 2006). In one case study, we found that the organization updated its benefit realization plan after the launch to be most in line with reality (including additional changes requested during the project).

> **Assignment Box 4.1: Assessment of the Business Case Process in Practice**
> In case you have access to an organization: for a recently finalized IT-enabled investment, or a running investment, assess how the investment is being managed through the lens of the business case process. For each of the identified business case (process) practices presented in this section, assess (for example on a scale from 0 to 5), whether or not the organization is applying each of these practices. If possible, discuss your results in the context of the realized (or unrealized) benefits of the investment under review.

4.4 The (IT) Balanced Scorecard

The IT balanced Scorecard (IT BSC) is becoming a popular tool to measure and manage the value of IT, with its concepts widely supported and dispersed by international consultant groups such as Gartner and others. As a result of this interest, many real-life applications have been developed and are supported by software tools.

4.4.1 IT BSC Core Concepts

In the early nineties, Kaplan and Norton (1992) introduced the BSC at the enterprise level (see Fig. 4.5). Their fundamental premise is that the evaluation of a firm should not be restricted to a traditional financial evaluation but should be supplemented with objectives and measures concerning customer satisfaction, internal processes, and the ability to innovate. Results achieved within these additional perspective areas should ensure future financial results and drive the organization towards its strategic goals while keeping all four perspectives in balance. For each of the four perspectives of the business BSC, a three-layered structure was proposed:

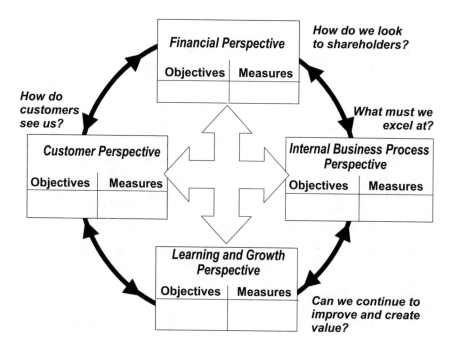

Fig. 4.5 Generic business balanced scorecard (Kaplan & Norton, 1996)

- Mission (e.g., to become the customers' most preferred supplier);
- Objectives (e.g., to provide the customers with new products);
- Measures (e.g., percentage of turnover generated by new products).

The BSC can be applied to the IT function, its processes, and projects (Van Grembergen, Saull, & De Haes, 2003). To achieve that, the focus of the four perspectives of the business BSC needs to be translated, as shown in Table 4.6. The User Orientation perspective represents the users' (internal or external) evaluation of IT. The Operational Excellence perspective represents the IT processes employed to develop and deliver the applications. The Future Orientation perspective represents the human and technology resources needed by IT to deliver its services over time. The Business Contribution perspective captures the IT business value.

Again, each of these perspectives has to be translated into corresponding objectives and measures that assess the current situation. These assessments need to be repeated periodically and aligned with pre-established objectives and measures. Example measures for the four perspectives are provided in Table 4.7.

To leverage the IT BSC as a management (and business/IT alignment) instrument, it should be enhanced with cause-and-effect relationships between measures. These relationships are articulated by two types of measures: outcome measures (or lag indicators) and performance drivers (or lead indicators). A well-developed scorecard should contain a good mix of these two types of measures. Outcome measures without performance drivers do not communicate how they are to be

Table 4.6 Generic IT balanced scorecard (Van Grembergen et al., 2003)

User orientation How do the users view the IT department?	Corporate contribution How does management view t he IT department?
Mission To be the preferred supplier of information systems	Mission To obtain a reasonable business contribution of IT investments
Objectives • Preferred IT supplier • Partnership with users • User satisfaction	Objectives • Control of IT expenses • Business value of the IT function • Business value of new IT projects
Operational excellence How effective and efficient are the IT processes?	Future orientation How well is IT positioned to answer future challenges?
Mission To deliver effective and efficient deliver IT applications and services	Mission To develop opportunities to answer future challenges
Objectives • Efficient software development • Efficient computer operations • Efficient help desk function	Objectives • Training and education of IT staff • Expertise of IT staff • Research into emerging information technologies

Table 4.7 Example measures for IT balanced scorecard

Corporate contribution

- Control of IT Expenses
  - Percentage over or under IT budget
  - Allocation to different budget items
  - IT budget as a percentage of turnover
  - IT expenses per staff member
- Business value of the IT function
  - Percentage of the development capacity engaged in strategic projects
  - Relationship between new developments/infrastructure investments/replacement investments
- Business value of new IT Projects
  - Financial evaluation based on ROI, NPV, IRR, and PB
  - Business evaluation based on information economics

User orientation

- Preferred IT Supplier
  - Percentage of applications managed by IT
  - Percentage of applications delivered by IT
- Partnership with users
  - Index of user involvement in generating applications
  - Index of user involvement in developing new applications
- User satisfaction
  - Index of user-friendliness of applications
  - Index of user satisfaction

Operational excellence

- Efficient software development
  - Average days late in delivering software
  - Average unexpected budget increase
  - Percentage of projects performed within SLA
  - Percentage of maintenance activities
- Efficient computer operations
  - Percentage unavailability of network
  - Response times per category of users
  - Percentage of jobs done within time
- Efficient help desk function
  - Average answer time of help desk
  - Percentage of questions answered within time

Future orientation

- Training and education of staff
  - Number of educational days per person
  - Education budget as a % of total IT budget
- Expertise of the IT staff
  - Number of years of IT experience per staff member
  - Age pyramid of the IT staff
- Research into emerging technologies
  - % of budget spent on IT research

---

achieved. And performance drivers without outcome measures may lead to significant investment without a measurement indicating whether the chosen strategy is effective. A good example of a cause-and-effect relationship, defined throughout the whole scorecard, is shown in Fig. 4.6: more and better education of IT staff (future perspective) is an enabler (performance driver) for a better quality of developed systems (operational excellence perspective) which in turn is an enabler for increased user satisfaction (user perspective) which eventually must lead to a higher business value of IT (business contribution perspective).

The proposed IT BSC links with the business, mainly through the business contribution perspective. The relationship between IT and business can be more explicitly expressed through a cascade of scorecards. In Fig. 4.7, the relationship between IT scorecards and the business scorecard is illustrated. The IT development BSC and the IT operational BSC both are enablers of the IT Strategic BSC which in turn is the enabler of the Business BSC. This cascade of scorecards becomes a linked set of measures which will be instrumental in aligning IT and business strategy and which will help to determine how IT business value is created.

Fig. 4.6 Cause-and-effect relationships within the IT strategic balanced scorecard

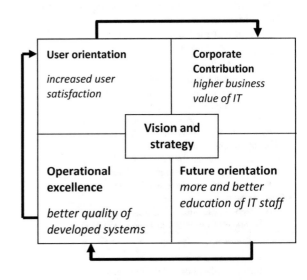

Fig. 4.7 Cascade of balanced scorecards

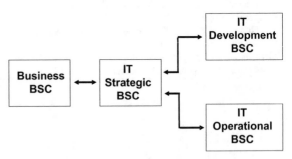

4.4.2 Mini-case

In this section, the development and implementation of an IT BSC within the Information Services Division (ISD) of a Canadian tri-company financial group consisting of Great-West Life, London Life, and Investors Group (hereafter named "The Group") is described and discussed.

4.4.2.1 Company Introduction

The Great-West Life Assurance Company, London Life, and Investors Group are members of the Power Financial Corporation group of companies, with London Life as a wholly owned subsidiary of The Great-West Life Assurance Company. In 2001, MacKenzie Financial was also acquired by the Power Financial Corporation Group, but as the IT balanced scorecard project does not cover this company, MacKenzie's organization and IT division will not be considered in this mini-case.

The Great-West Life Assurance Company is an international corporation offering life insurance, health insurance, retirement savings, specialty reinsurance, and general insurance, primarily in Canada and the USA. Great-West serves the financial security needs of more than 13 million people in Canada and the USA. Great-West has more than $86.9 billion (all figures in this mini-case are in Canadian dollars) in assets under administration and $477 billion of life insurance in force. Founded in Winnipeg in 1891, Great-West is now a leading life and health insurer in the Canadian market in terms of market share.

London Life was founded in Ontario in 1874 and has the leading market share of individual life insurance in Canada. London Life markets life insurance, disability insurance and retirement savings, and investment products through its exclusive sales force. The company is a supplier of reinsurance primarily in the USA and Europe and is a 39% participant in a joint venture life insurance company Shin Fu in Taiwan. London Life has more than $30 billion assets under administration and $142.6 billion of life insurance in force.

Investors Group, with its corporate headquarters in Winnipeg, was founded more than 70 years ago. Investors Group is Canada's leading provider of mutual funds, offering a wide spectrum of funds, including those created through strategic partnerships with some of the best known Canadian and international investment management firms. It also offers a wide range of insurance and mortgage options, and currently has $17.1 billion of life insurance coverage in force through three different carriers, and administers with more than $7.6 billion of primarily residential mortgages. Investors Group manages assets of $40.5 billion.

The trend in financial services industry consolidation was a motivating factor behind the acquisition of London Life by Great-West Life and the merger of the IT divisions of the three companies in November 1997. At that time, the tri-company IT expenditures had exceeded $200 million. The ability to reduce these costs and to achieve true synergies and economies of scale within the IT operations was clearly a driver and opportunity for the companies to realize. The merger enabled single systems solutions across all three companies to be explored and implemented as well as single operational processes. Forming a tri-company-shared services organization positioned management to:

- Achieve world-class status as an information services group,
- Maximize purchasing power and operating efficiency,
- Leverage technology investments, and
- Optimize technical infrastructure and application support costs.

Figure 4.8 depicts the current IT organizational structure of the merged IT division, which employed 812 full-time/part-time employees in 2002. Also, the position of the IT division relative to the higher reporting levels is indicated. Application delivery and technology services are, respectively, the traditional IT department's systems development and operations of the combined organizations. Application delivery is separated from account management and people management in order to focus on continuous improvement of delivery performance. Account management is the linkage with the clients/users. This component ensures

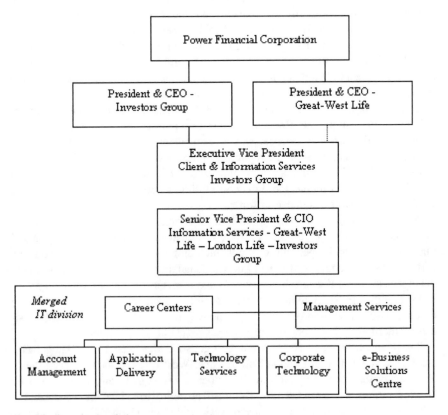

Fig. 4.8 Organizational chart

effective communication and translation of business needs into IT processes and educates users on the IT corporate agendas. Account management employs IT generalists who provide IT insights into business strategy and decision-making. Career centers are focused on the professional development of IT people and ensure attention to people issues in order to reduce turnover of talented IT employees. Corporate technology enables the development of a common architecture and provides technology directions. The eBusiness Solution Center works on the introduction of new technologies that enable eBusiness solutions for "The Group." Management services focus on running IT as a business and ensure effective financial management and management reporting including IT scorecard reporting.

4.4.3 IT BSC Project and Its Organization

Before the merger, the CIO of Great-West Life (who is the present CIO of the merged IT division) began focusing on the scorecard as a (potentially) effective measurement tool. His objective was to ensure that IT was fairly evaluated. In his own words: *"Through the balanced scorecard I would know what was important to the business and I would not fall victim to the early termination syndrome. Or at least I would have a better chance of survival."*

However, once the three companies came together through the acquisition and merger of the IT groups, the stakes were raised considerably. Now, the IT division had exposures on multiple fronts with stakeholders who were concerned about the perceived loss of control over their vital IT services. This prompted an executive request for a formal measure of factors to measure IT success. The response of the merged IT division was to formalize the criteria into a new and extended IT scorecard based on the experiences gained within Great-West Life.

Senior management of all the three companies questioned the benefits of huge investments in IT and how more value might be achieved through better alignment of business strategy and IT strategy. Within "The Group", the specific concerns for the different stakeholders were the following (see Table 4.8).

It was believed that the IT balanced scorecard could provide an answer to the key questions of the different stakeholders. The formal development of the IT balanced scorecard began in 1998. From the start, the objectives were clearly stated:

- Align IT plans and activities with business goals and needs.
- Align employees' efforts toward IT objectives.
- Establish measures for evaluating the effectiveness of the IT organization.
- Stimulate and sustain improved IT performance.
- Achieve balanced results across stakeholder groups

At the beginning of the implementation period (December 1999), the scorecard effort was not yet approached as a formal project, and as a result, progress had been somewhat limited. In 2000, the formality of the project was increased, and the CIO

Table 4.8 IT-related concerns of different stakeholders

Stakeholders	Key questions
Board of directors and executive management committee	• Does IT support the achievement of business objectives? • What value does the expenditure on IT deliver? • Are IT costs being managed effectively? • Are IT risks being identified and managed? • Are targeted inter-company IT synergies being achieved?
Business unit executives	• Does IT deliver its services at a competitive cost? • Does IT deliver on its service-level commitments? • Do IT investments positively affect business productivity or the customer experience? • Does IT contribute to the achievement of our business strategies?
Corporate compliance and internal audit	• Are the organization's assets and operations protected? • Are the key business and technology risks being managed? • Are proper processes, practices, and controls in place?
IT organization	• Are we developing the professional competencies needed for successful service delivery? • Are we creating a positive workplace environment? • Do we effectively measure and reward individual and team performance? • Do we capture organizational knowledge to continuously improve performance? • Can we attract/retain the talent we need to support the business?

(Information Services Executive) was appointed as sponsor. In 2001, a project manager/analyst was formally assigned to the IT balanced scorecard project.

4.4.3.1 Building the IT BSC

It was recognized by the CIO that building an IT BSC was meaningful under two conditions, which required (a) a clearly articulated business strategy and (b) the new Information Services Division (ISD) moving from a commodity service provider to a strategic partner. During several meetings between IT and executive management; the vision, strategy, measures of success, and value of IT were jointly created. Typically, pure business objectives were used as the standard to assess IT. The vision and strategy of ISD were defined as:

- ISD is a single IT organization focused on developing world-class capabilities to serve the distinct customer needs of its three sponsoring companies.
- ISD operates as a separate professional services business on a full recovery and nonprofit basis.

- ISD supports the achievement of company strategies and goals through the industry consolidation period.
- ISD becomes the "supplier of choice" of information services.
- ISD establishes a forward-looking enterprise architecture strategy which enables the use of technology as a competitive edge in the financial service market place.
- ISD becomes the "employer of choice" for career-oriented IT professionals in the markets in which ISD and "The Group" operate.

These issues go to the heart of the relationship between IT and the business and will be reflected in the IT strategic balanced scorecard. Table 4.9 shows the perspective questions and mission statements for the four quadrants: corporate contribution, customer orientation, operational excellence, and future orientation. Figure 4.9 displays the objectives for each perspective.

Corporate Contribution Perspective

The corporate contribution perspective evaluates the performance of the IT organization from the viewpoint of executive management, the board of directors and the shareholders, and provides answers to the key questions of these stakeholders concerning IT governance (refer back to Table 4.8). The key issues, as depicted by Fig. 4.9, are business/IT alignment, value delivery, cost management, risk management, and inter-company synergy achievement. Benchmarks have been used where an objective standard was available or could be determined in most cases from external sources.

The main measurement challenges are with the areas of business/IT alignment and value delivery. Currently, *business/IT alignment* is measured by the approval of the IT operational plan and budget. Although not a discrete measure of alignment, the approval process within "The Group" is particularly thorough and as a result is accepted by business executives as a good indicator. All aspects of development, operations, and governance/support services are examined and challenged to ensure they are essential to achieving business objectives or supporting the enabling IT strategy.

In the *value delivery* area, the performance of a specific IT services group delivering to a specific business unit (e.g., "group insurance" services) is measured. For each business unit, specific measures are and/or will be defined. The ultimate responsibility for achieving and measuring IT business value rests with the business and is reflected in the business results of the individual lines of business in different ways, depending on the nature of value being sought.

Cost management is a traditional financial objective and is in the first place measured through the attainment of expense and recovery targets. The expenses refer to the costs that the IT organization has made for the business, and the recovery refers to the allocation of costs to IT services and the internal chargeback to the business. All IT costs are fully loaded (no profit margin) and recovered from the lines of business on a fair and equitable basis as agreed to by the companies' CFOs.

Table 4.9 Perspective questions and mission statements of the IT strategic scorecard

Customer orientation	Corporate contribution
Perspective question How should IT appear to business unit executives to be considered effective in delivering its services? *Mission* To be the supplier of choice for all information services, either directly or indirectly through supplier relationships	*Perspective question* How should IT appear to the company executive and its corporate functions to be considered a significant contributor to company success? *Mission* To enable and contribute to the achievement of business objectives through effective delivery of value-added information services
Operational excellence	Future orientation
Perspective question At which services and processes must IT excel to satisfy the stakeholders and customers? *Mission* To deliver timely and effective IT services at targeted service levels and costs	*Perspective question* How will IT develop the ability to deliver effectively and to continuously learn and improve its performance? *Mission* To develop the internal capabilities to continuously improve performance through innovation, learning and personal organizational growth

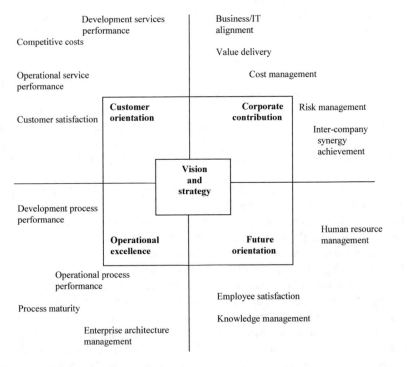

Fig. 4.9 Objectives of the IT strategic scorecard

Comparisons with similar industries will be drawn to benchmark these measures. Besides this, IT unit costs (e.g., application development) will be measured and compared to the "top performing levels" benchmark provided by compass.

The development of the *risk management* measures is the priority for the upcoming year. Currently, the results of the internal audits are used and benchmarked against criteria provided by OSFI, the Canadian federal regulator in the financial services sector. The execution of the Security Initiative and the delivery of a disaster recovery assessment need to be accomplished in the upcoming year. This will enable the business to get insights on how well they are prepared to respond to different disaster scenarios.

Inter-company synergy achievement is measured through the achievement of single-system solutions, targeted cost reductions, and the integration of the IT organizations. This measure is very crucial in the context of the merger of the three IT organizations in the sense that it enables a post-evaluation of this merger and demonstrates to management whether the new IT organization is effective and efficient. The selection of single-system solutions was a cooperative effort between business leaders and IT staff, resulting in a "target state architecture" depicting the target applications architecture. The synergy targets were heavily influenced by the consulting firm (Bain & Co.) that was used to assist in evaluating the London Life acquisition and the tri-company IT merger potential. The consultants suggested specific dollar reduction targets for technology services (IT operations) and application delivery services (IT development) largely based on norms they had developed from their previous merger and acquisition work. The approval of the target state architecture plan and the attainment of the targeted integration cost reductions will be measured. The IT organization integration measure refers to the synergies within the IT organization, e.g., is there one single service desk for the three companies or are there three different ones?

The corporate contribution perspective is summarized in Table 4.10.

Customer Orientation Perspective

The customer orientation perspective evaluates the performance of IT from the viewpoint of internal business users (customers of IT) and, by extension, the customers of the business units. It provides answers to the key questions of these stakeholders concerning IT service quality (refer back to Table 4.8). As shown in Fig. 4.9, the issues in this perspective focuses on are competitive costs, development services performance, operational services performance, and customer satisfaction.

In the *customer satisfaction* area, the IT BSC of the merged IT organization is relying on annual interviews with key business managers. It is the intent to set up one generic survey, which can be reused, with relevant questions that cover the topics mentioned in Fig. 4.9.

The *competitive costs* area can demonstrate to the business how cost competitive the IT organization is compared to other (e.g., external) parties. This insight is

Table 4.10 Corporate contribution perspective

Objective	Measures	Benchmarks
Business/IT alignment	• Operational plan/budget approval	• Not applicable
Value delivery	• Measured in business unit performance	• Not applicable
Cost management	• Attainment of expense and recovery targets • Attainment of unit cost targets	• Industry expenditure comparisons • Compass operational "top performance" levels
Risk management	• Results of internal audits • Execution of Security Initiative • Delivery of disaster recovery assessment	• OSFI sound business practices • Not applicable • Not applicable
Inter-company synergy achievement	• Single-system solutions • Target state architecture approval • Attainment of targeted integration cost reductions • IT organization integration	• Merger and acquisition guidelines • Not applicable • Not applicable • Not applicable

realized by measuring the attainment of IT unit cost targets and the blended labor rate, which provides an overall single rate for any IT professional who is appointed to the business. The competitive cost measures are benchmarked against compass's operational "top performing level" and against the offerings of commercial IT service vendors (market comparisons).

Development services performance measures are project-oriented, using attributes such as goal attainment, sponsor satisfaction, and project governance (i.e., the way the project is managed). These data are mostly captured by interviews with key managers. The most effective time to establish the basis for these (project) development measures is when business cases are being prepared and projects are evaluated. Each IT project initiative will be evaluated by the IS Executive Committee in which IT and business managers determine—based on the business drivers, budget, and state architecture compliance—which projects need to be executed. When a project is approved, the project manager defines clear targets for cost, schedule, quality, scope, and governance. The quantitative data (e.g., budget) are reported throughout the lifecycle of the project. After completion of the project, the quantitative and qualitative data are evaluated during the major project review and the main success drivers, delivery issues, and lessons learned are documented.

In terms of *operational service performance*, IT management measures achievement against targeted service levels. For each operational unit (e.g., data center), average response time, service availability, and resolution time for incidents are rolled-up to these service performance measures in the strategic balanced scorecard. The results are benchmarked against the performance of competitors.

The customer orientation perspective is summarized in Table 4.11.

Table 4.11 Customer orientation perspective

Objective	Measures	Benchmarks
Customer satisfaction	• Business unit survey ratings: 　– Cost transparency and levels 　– Service quality and responsiveness 　– Value of IT advice and support 　– Contribution to business objectives	• Not applicable
Competitive costs	• Attainment of unit cost targets • Blended labor rates	• Compass operational "top-level performing" levels • Market comparison
Development services performance	• Major project success scores: 　– Recorded goal attainment 　– Sponsor satisfaction ratings 　– Project governance rating	• Not applicable
Operational services performance	• Attainment of targeted service levels	• Competitor comparisons

Operational Excellence Perspective

The operational excellence scorecard provides the performance of IT from the viewpoint of IT management (process owners and service delivery managers) and the audit and regulatory bodies. The operational excellence perspective copes with the key questions of these stakeholders and provides answers to questions of maturity, productivity, and reliability of IT processes (refer back to Table 4.8). The issues that are of focus here, as displayed in Fig. 4.9, are development process performance, operational process performance, process maturity, and enterprise architecture management.

In relation to *development process performance*, function point-based measures of productivity, quality, and delivery rate such as number of faults per 100 installed function points and delivery rate of function points per month are defined. Benchmark data on industry performance will be gathered from a third party (e.g., Compass).

In the *operational process performance* area, measures of productivity, responsiveness, change management effectiveness, and incident occurrence level are benchmarked against selected compass studies (e.g., on data centers and client–server.)

The *process maturity* is assessed using the COBIT framework (version 3) and its maturity models. "The Group" has identified 15 out the 34 priority processes that

Table 4.12 Operational excellence perspective

Objective	Measures	Benchmarks

Development process performance	• Function point measures of:
	  – Productivity
	  – Quality
	  – Delivery rate
		• To be determined

Operational process performance	• Benchmark-based measures of:
	  – Productivity
	  – Responsiveness
	  – Change management effectiveness
	  – Incident occurrence levels
		• Selected compass benchmark studies

Process maturity	• Assessed level of maturity of COBIT processes	• To be determined
Enterprise architecture management	• Major project architecture approval • Product acquisition compliance to technology standards • "State of the infrastructure" assessment	• Not applicable

should have a maturity assessment in 2003, and the other processes will be measured later.

Enterprise architecture management deals with the IT responsibility to define an enterprise architecture which supports long-term business strategy and objectives and to act as a steward on behalf of business executives to protect the integrity of that architecture. Major project architecture approval measures the compliance of net new systems as they are proposed, developed, and implemented. Product acquisition compliance technology standards measure the adherence to detailed technology standards which are at the heart of minimizing technology diversity and maximizing inter-company technology synergies. The "State of the Infrastructure" assessment measures the degree to which IT has been able to maintain a robust and reliable infrastructure as required to deliver effectively to business needs. It does so by comparing each platform area against risk-based criteria for potential impact on business continuity, security and/or compliance.

The operational excellence perspective is summarized in Table 4.12.

Future Orientation Perspective

The future orientation perspective shows the performance of IT from the viewpoint of the IT organization itself: i.e., process owners, practitioners, and support professionals. The future orientation perspective provides answers to stakeholder questions regarding IT's readiness for future challenges (refer back to Table 4.8). The issues focused on, as depicted in Fig. 4.9, are human resources management, employee satisfaction, and knowledge management. The measures that will appear in the future orientation quadrant of the IT strategic balanced scorecard are in many cases the aggregated results of measures used in the unit scorecards (e.g., career center).

Table 4.13 Future orientation perspective

Objective	Measures	Benchmarks

Human resource management	• Results compared with targets on:
	  – Staff complement by skill type
	  – Staff turnover
	  – Staff "billable" ratio
	  – Professional development days per staff member
		– Not applicable
		– Market comparison
		– Industry standard
		– Industry standard

Employee satisfaction	• Survey scores on:
	  – Compensation
	  – Work climate
	  – Feedback
	  – Personal growth
	  – Vision and purpose
		• North American technology dependent companies

Knowledge management	• Delivery of internal process improvements to "Cybrary" • Implementation of "lessons learned" sharing process	• Not applicable • Not applicable

Human resource management is an objective that is measured through: the staff complement by skill type (number of people with a certain profile, e.g., systems analyst), staff turnover, staff "billable" ratio (i.e., hours billed/total hours salary paid; if this ratio can be increased, the IT organization can charge lower rates to the business for the IT assigned people), and professional development days per staff member. Each of these measures is then compared against targets that were set in advance.

Employee satisfaction is measured by using surveys with questions relating to compensation, work climate, feedback, personal growth, and vision and purpose. Benchmark data of North American technology dependent companies are provided by a third party.

In the *knowledge management* area, the delivery of internal process improvements to the "Cybrary" is very important. The "Cybrary" refers to the intranet that all employees can assess for seeking and sharing knowledge. To measure improvements, measures (e.g., number of hits per day on the "Cybrary") still need to be developed. Closely linked to this, knowledge management is also measured by the implementation of the "lessons learned" sharing process. Here too, specific measures still need to be developed.

The future orientation perspective is summarized in Table 4.13.

4.4.3.2 Maturity of the Developed IT BSC

At the beginning of the project, the IT BSC was primarily focused on the operational level of the IT department. It was acknowledged from the beginning that this could not be the end result. Therefore, actions were started to go beyond the operational IT BSC and to measure the true value of IT at the business level. The Vice President Information Services emphasized: *"The Balanced Scorecard gives a balanced view of the total value delivery of IT to the business. It provides a snapshot of where your IS organization is at a certain point in time. Most executives, like me, do not have the time to drill down into the large amount of information."*

The organization established two ways to demonstrate the business value, one at service delivery level and one at the IT strategy level. As will be illustrated hereafter, the goal is to evolve to an IT strategic BSC that shows how the business objectives are enabled by IT.

A cascade of balanced scorecards has been established to create a link between the scorecards at the unit level and the overall business objectives (see Fig. 4.10). A link between the IT BSC and the Business BSC is not yet implemented as there is currently no formal business BSC for "The Group." The scorecards at the unit level are classified into three groups: operational services scorecards (e.g., IT service desk scorecard), governance services scorecards (e.g., career center scorecard), and development services scorecards (e.g., application development scorecard). The measures of these unit scorecards are rolled-up or aggregated in the IT strategic balanced scorecard. This in turn is fed into, and evaluated against, the business objectives. This way, the service (and value) delivered by IT is directly measured against the objectives of the overall business. Moreover, on an annual basis, the IT strategic BSC is reviewed by business and IT management and the result is fed back into the next annual planning cycle. This planning cycle defines what the business needs are and what IT must do to accomplish those needs.

For example, from the IT service desk scorecard (i.e., a unit scorecard, which is situated in the operational services scorecard group), measures such as average speed of answer, overall resolution rate at initial call, and call abandonment rate (all three customer orientation measures) are rolled-up to service-level performance measures in the IT strategic balanced scorecard. Other measures of this unit scorecard, such as expense management (corporate contribution perspective), client

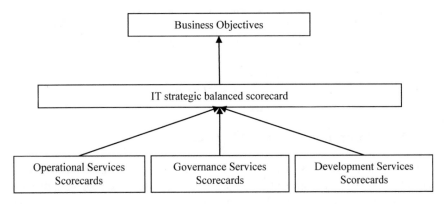

Fig. 4.10 Cascade of scorecards

satisfaction (customer orientation perspective), process maturity of incident management (operational excellence perspective), and staff turnover (future orientation perspective), will aggregate as part of the IT strategic scorecard. The overall view of the IT strategic balanced scorecard is then fed into and evaluated against the defined business objectives.

The second way to demonstrate business value is situated within the IT strategic balanced scorecard. The cause-and-effect relationships between performance drivers and outcome measures of the four quadrants are established as indicated in Fig. 4.11. These connections help to understand how the contribution of IT toward the business will be realized: building the foundation for delivery and continuous learning and growth (future orientation perspective) is an enabler for carrying out the roles of the IT division's mission (operational excellence perspective) which is in turn an enabler for measuring up to business expectations (customer expectations perspective) which eventually must lead to ensuring effective IT governance (corporate contribution perspective). The construction of cause-and-effect relationships is a critical issue in the further development of the IT strategic BSC. These relationships are not yet been explicitly defined although they are implicit in the existing scorecard. For instance, the "professional development days per staff member" measure can be identified as a performance driver for the outcome measures "development process performance."

The corporate contribution perspective of Fig. 4.11 is an enabler (performance driver) of the (generic) business objectives of "The Group" with its specific measures such as business/IT alignment, value delivery, cost management, risk management, and inter-company synergy achievement. The CIO and its executive management are aware that an explicit articulation of these relationships has to be done and that it may help to improve the IT strategic BSC and its link with the business objectives, and later on with the implementation of a business BSC.

Assignment Box 4.2: Cause-and-Effect Relationships
A major attention point in developing an IT Balanced Scorecard is identifying the cause-and-effect relationships across the whole scorecard. In the case study, these relationships are not described. Identify what you think are outcome measures and what their corresponding performance drivers are.

Assignment Box 4.3: Cascade of Scorecards
At the case company there are, besides the IT strategic balanced scorecard, also scorecards implemented at unit level. The measures of these unit scorecards are rolled-up or aggregated in the IT strategic balanced scorecard. Develop a generic scorecard for the IT development department.

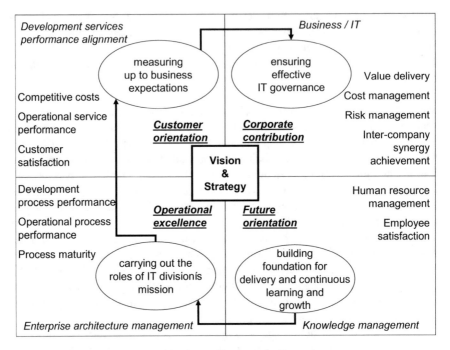

Fig. 4.11 IT strategic scorecard objectives and cause-and-effect

4.5 Validating the EGIT-Alignment-Value Relationship

Prior sections of this chapter have explained the purpose of business cases (for IT(-enabled) projects) and the value of using the IT balanced scorecard to manage and realize IT business value. Interestingly, many recent researches have drawn on the EGIT-Alignment-Value conceptual model that was introduced in the first chapter of this book. Quantitative information has been collected and analyzed to validate the relationships of this conceptual model, and the balanced scorecard perspective has been applied to examine the business value from IT. As such, many of these studies arrive at conclusions that validate the fundamental premise underlying this book: i.e., EGIT enables business/IT alignment, which in turn enables IT business value. For instance, Wu, Straub, and Liang (2015) collected and analyzed data of 131 Taiwanese organizations, which ultimately confirmed these relationships. Another example is the study of Schlosser, Beimborn, Weitzel, and Wagner (2015) on social (business/IT) alignment, which was already introduced in the third chapter. While Wu et al. (2015) confirm that IT governance mechanisms enable the intellectual dimension of business/IT alignment, Schlosser et al. (2015) show that IT governance mechanisms also enable the social dimension of business/IT alignment. Combining the insights of both studies, both the intellectual and the social dimensions of business/IT alignment enable IT business value. This "EGIT value path" is visually presented in Fig. 4.12.

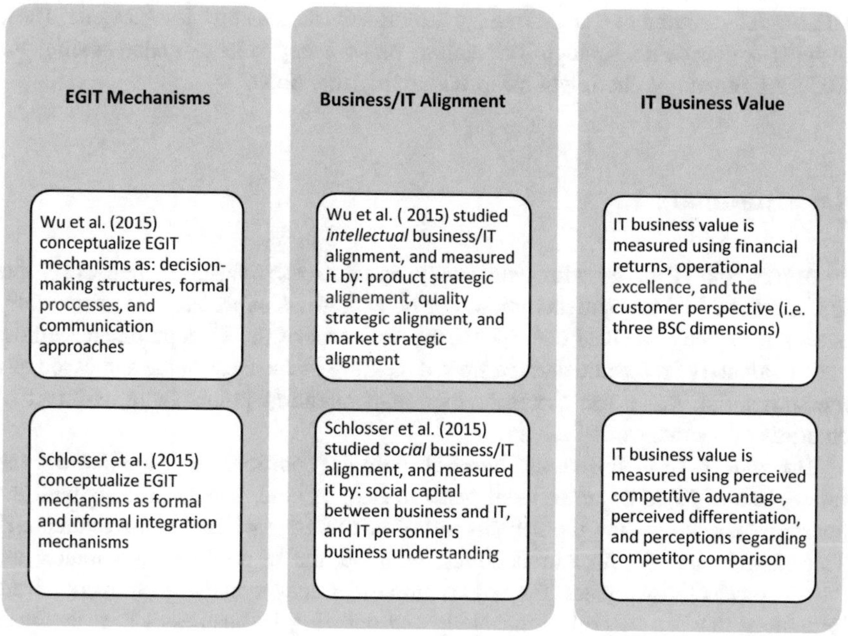

EGIT Mechanisms	Business/IT Alignment	IT Business Value
Wu et al. (2015) conceptualize EGIT mechanisms as: decision-making structures, formal proccesses, and communication approaches	Wu et al. (2015) studied *intellectual* business/IT alignment, and measured it by: product strategic alignement, quality strategic alignment, and market strategic alignment	IT business value is measured using financial returns, operational excellence, and the customer perspective (i.e. three BSC dimensions)
Schlosser et al. (2015) conceptualize EGIT mechanisms as formal and informal integration mechanisms	Schlosser et al. (2015) studied s*ocial* business/IT alignment, and measured it by: social capital between business and IT, and IT personnel's business understanding	IT business value is measured using perceived competitive advantage, perceived differentiation, and perceptions regarding competitor comparison

Fig. 4.12   EGIT value path

We can certainly draw a few conclusions from this increasing stream of IT business value literature. First, the proposed premise that EGIT enables business/IT alignment, which in turn enables IT business value is finding substantial empirical validation. This is not only important for any theory building exercise, but such validation also has important managerial implications. Indeed, executives are provided with evidence that designing appropriate EGIT mechanisms indirectly creates business value. Second, organizations need to focus on business/IT alignment, as it propagates the benefits of EGIT mechanisms. This alignment is multifold. That is, organizations can derive benefits from, and should as such focus on, the intellectual as well as the social dimension of business/IT alignment. Lastly, IT business value is also multidimensional. Executives need to understand that IT(-enabled) initiatives do not uniquely result in financial performance. Indeed, non-financial measures are also key to take into account in the context of IT business value.

Adding to the above discussion, the current business/IT alignment literature also suggests that executives need to be careful in selecting the appropriate level of business/IT alignment while evaluating IT business value. Recent studies, like Queiroz (2017), have shown that firm-level (i.e., strategic alignment dimension) and process-level (i.e., operational alignment dimension) business/IT alignment can lead to different conclusions regarding the effect of alignment on IT business value. If executives select operational excellence as strategic orientation, then both levels (or alignment dimensions) result into similar impacts. However, if the strategic orientation is to achieve product leadership or customer intimacy, only firm-level business/IT alignment (i.e., strategic alignment dimension) is relevant. These insights suggest that strategic orientation plays a key role in understanding the EGIT-Alignment-Value relationship underlying this book.

4.6   Summary

Investments in IT are growing extensively, and business managers often worry that the benefits of IT investments might not be as high as expected. The same worry accounts for the perceived ever-increasing total cost of the IT department, without clear evidence of the value derived from it. Getting IT business value and especially measuring that value are therefore important attention points in the context of enterprise governance of IT.

The concept of IT business value deals with the contribution of the (current and future) use of IT to organizational performance. In other words, it deals with the question "are we getting the benefits out of our IT (operations and investments)?" This chapter started with a brief discussion about the IT productivity paradox and the IT productivity cycle. Then, two important management instruments were introduced that are helpful in managing and realizing IT business value: the business case (process) and the IT balanced scorecard. Lastly, this chapter presented insights from recent EGIT-related literature to facilitate a discussion in line with the conceptual model underlying this book: i.e., EGIT enables IT business value, through the mediating mechanism of business/IT alignment.

Study Questions

1. Describe the concept of the IT productivity paradox. Explain how it relates to the "IT doesn't matter article" (Carr, 2003) discussed in the first chapter of this book.
2. How can the IT productivity cycle explain the IT productivity paradox?
3. How can the EGIT concept be linked to the IT productivity cycle?
4. Explain why and how the business case could be used in the context of an IT-enabled investment.
5. Explain how the balanced scorecard can be applied to the IT function.
6. How can you leverage the IT balanced scorecard as a management and alignment instrument?
7. Explain and illustrate the difference between outcome measures and performance drivers in the context of the IT balanced scorecard.
8. Explain the concept of the "cascade of scorecards".

9. Explain the aggregating and rolling up mechanism of measures and indicate which typical IT measures you think should appear on the business balanced scorecard.
10. How does existing research conceptualize and measure EGIT mechanisms, business/IT alignment, and IT business value?

References

Al-Mudimigh, A., Zairi, M., & Al-Mashari, M. (2001). ERP software implementation: An integrative framework. *European Journal of Information Systems, 10*(4), 216–226.

Altinkemer, K., Ozcelik, Y., & Ozdemir, Z. D. (2014). Productivity and performance effects of business process reengineering: A firm-level analysis. *Journal of Management Information Systems, 27*(4), 129–162.

Ashurst, C., Doherty, N. F., & Peppard, J. (2008). Improving the impact of IT development projects: The benefits realization capability model. *European Journal of Information Systems, 17*(4), 352–370.

Beatty, R. C., & Williams, C. D. (2006). ERP II: Best practices for successfully implementing an ERP upgrade. *Communications of the ACM, 49*(3), 105–109.

Brown, D. H., & Lockett, N. (2004). Potential of critical e-applications for engaging SMEs in e-business: A provider perspective. *European Journal of Information Systems, 13*(1), 21–34.

Carr, N. G. (2003). IT doesn't matter. *Harvard Business Review, 81*(5), 41–49.

Davenport, T. H., Harris, J., & Shapiro, J. (2010). Competing on talent analytics. *Harvard Business Review, 88*(10), 52–58.

Flynn, D., Pan, G., Keil, M., & Mähring, M. (2009). De-escalating IT projects. *Communications of the ACM, 52*(10), 131–134.

Fonstad, N., & Robertson, D. (2006). Transforming a company, project by project: The IT engagement model. *MIS Quarterly Executive, 5*(1), 1–14.

Franken, A., Edwards, C., & Lambert, R. (2009). Executing strategic change: Understanding the critical management elements that lead to success. *California Management Review, 51*(3), 49–73.

Goldschmidt, P. (2005). HIT and MIS: Implications of health information technology and medical information systems. *Communications of the ACM, 48*(10), 68–74.

ISACA. (2008). *The Val IT Framework 2.0.*

Jeffery, M., & Leliveld, I. (2004). Best practices in IT Portfolio Management. *MIT Sloan Management Review, 45*(3), 40–49.

Kaplan, R. S., & Norton, D. P. (1992). The balanced scorecard—Measures that drive performance. *Harvard Business Review, 70*(1), 71–79.

Kaplan, R. S., & Norton, D. P. (1996). *The balanced scorecard: Translating strategy into action.*

Krell, K., & Matook, S. (2009). Competitive advantage from mandatory investments: An empirical study of Australian firms. *The Journal of Strategic Information Systems, 18*(1), 31–45.

Law, C. C. H., & Ngai, E. W. T. (2007). ERP systems adoption: An exploratory study of the organizational factors and impacts of ERP success. *Information & Management, 44*(4), 418–432.

Luna-Reyes, L. F., Zhang, J., Ramón Gil-García, J., & Cresswell, A. M. (2005). Information systems development as emergent socio-technical change: A practice approach. *European Journal of Information Systems, 14*(1), 93–105.

Maes, K. (2014). *The exploration of a process perspective on business cases and its relationship with the perceived success of IT enabled investments* (doctoral dissertation). University of Antwerp, Antwerp, Belgium.

Maes, K., De Haes, S., & Van Grembergen, W. (2013). Using a business case throughout an investment: An exploratory case study on a business case process. In *Proceedings of Americas Conference of Information Systems (AMCIS)*. Chicago.

Maes, K., De Haes, S., & Van Grembergen, W. (2015). Exploring the business case process for IT enabled investments. *International Journal of IT/Business Alignment and Governance, 6*(2), 14–30.

Matthews, H. (2004). Thinking outside 'the box': Designing a Packaging Take-back System. *California Management Review, 46*(2), 105–119.

Oz, E. (2005). Information technology productivity: In search of a definite observation. *Information & Management, 42*(6), 789–798.

Post, B. Q. (1992). A business case framework for group support technology. *Journal of Management Information Systems, 9*(3), 7–26.

Powell, P. (1993). Causality in the alignment of information technology and business strategy. *The Journal of Strategic Information Systems, 2*(4), 320–334.

Queiroz, M. (2017). Mixed results in strategic IT alignment research: A synthesis and empirical study. *European Journal of Information Systems, 26*(1), 21–36.

Schlosser, F., Beimborn, D., Weitzel, T., & Wagner, H.-T. (2015). Achieving social alignment between business and IT—An empirical evaluation of the efficacy of IT governance mechanisms. *Journal of Information Technology, 30*(2), 119–135.

Sherif, K., & Vinze, A. (2002). Domain engineering for developing software repositories: A case study. *Decision Support Systems, 33*(1), 55–69.

Smith, H., McKeen, J., Cranston, C., & Benson, M. (2010). Investment spend optimization: A new approach to IT Investment at BMO financial group. *MIS Quarterly Executive, 9*(2), 65–81.

Taudes, A., Feurstein, M., & Mild, A. (2000). Options analysis of software platform decisions: A case study. *MIS Quarterly, 24*(2), 227.

Van Grembergen, W., Saull, R., & De Haes, S. (2003). Linking the IT balanced scorecard to the business objectives at a major Canadian Financial Group. *Journal for Information Technology Cases and Applications, 5*(1), 23–45.

Ward, J., Daniel, E., & Peppard, J. (2008). Building better business cases for IT investments. *MIS Quarterly Executive, 7*(1), 1–15.

Wu, S. P.-J., Straub, D. W., & Liang, T.-P. (2015). How information technology governance mechanisms and strategic alignment influence organizational performance: Insights from a matched survey of business and IT managers. *MIS Quarterly, 39*(2), 497–518.

Chapter 5
COBIT as a Framework for Enterprise Governance of IT

Abstract This chapter discusses Control Objectives for Information and Related Technology (COBIT) as a framework for enterprise governance of information and technology (EGIT). The chapter starts with a brief overview of COBIT's history. Then, the most recent version of the COBIT framework, i.e., COBIT 2019, is introduced. Next, the six principles that describe the core requirements of an EGIT system as introduced in the COBIT 2019 framework are presented and discussed. This is followed by an overview of the COBIT 2019 core model and its 40 governance and management objectives and the specific guidance contained therein. The COBIT 2019 performance management approach is also introduced. Finally, some insights and examples are provided that demonstrate how the generic guidance contained in COBIT 2019 can be applied to the specific context of an enterprise.

5.1 Cobit History

Control Objectives for Information and Related Technology (COBIT) is developed by Information Systems Audit and Control Association (ISACA), which is an international professional membership association for individuals interested or employed in IT audit, IT risk, and IT governance fields. ISACA was founded in 1967 and has grown into an internationally recognized organization which currently counts more than 150,000 members worldwide. COBIT was initially developed to support (financial) audit professionals who were increasingly confronted with automated environments. ISACA released the first edition of COBIT in 1996 as a framework for executing IT audit assignments. This first edition was quickly succeeded by the second edition in 1998, which was built around a comprehensive set of control objectives for IT processes. In 1998, recognizing an increasing importance of IT for enterprises and with that the growing need for effective control over this IT, ISACA founded the IT Governance Institute (ITGI) as a think tank for IT governance. Insights gathered through the ITGI have greatly contributed to COBIT's evolution toward a mature good-practice framework for IT management

© Springer Nature Switzerland AG 2020
S. De Haes et al., *Enterprise Governance of Information Technology*,
Management for Professionals, https://doi.org/10.1007/978-3-030-25918-1_5

and IT governance (De Haes, Van Grembergen, & Debreceny, 2013). Building on the auditing basis of the first two editions, COBIT was developed further into a broader IT management framework. The third version of the COBIT framework was released in 2000 and incorporated management guidelines (including metrics, critical success factors, and maturity models for IT processes). In 2005, ISACA released COBIT 4.0, which introduced several new management and governance concepts, such as (1) the alignment of business and IT goals and their relationships with the supporting IT processes, (2) roles and responsibilities in the context of the IT processes, and (3) the inter-relationships between IT processes. The purpose of this fourth edition was to further establish COBIT as a generally accepted framework for IT governance.

Resulting from ITGI's (2003) insights that value delivery and risk management are key outcome areas of IT governance,[1] the "Val IT" (first version in 2006 and second version in 2008) and "Risk IT" (in 2009) frameworks were released as complements to COBIT 4, and its direct successor COBIT 4.1 (which was released in 2007). The Val IT and Risk IT frameworks addressed the IT-related business processes and responsibilities in value creation and risk management, respectively. As a next step, ISACA merged COBIT with the Val IT and Risk IT frameworks and released COBIT 5 as an integrated good-practices framework for IT governance and IT management in 2012 (De Haes et al., 2013). COBIT 5 also had stronger ties with established frameworks and standards like ISO/IEC 38500, ITIL, PRINCE2, and TOGAF. Drawing on ISO/IEC 38500, for instance, COBIT 5 explicitly separated IT governance from IT management by introducing an additional process domain containing IT governance processes, i.e., "Evaluate, Direct and Monitor (EDM)".

In November 2018, the successor of COBIT 5, i.e., COBIT 2019, was officially released. This most recent COBIT update is aimed at facilitating a more flexible, tailored implementation of effective "enterprise governance of information and technology (EGIT)" and includes the modification of COBIT principles, an updated goals cascade, the introduction of three new processes, the introduction of focus areas (which is aimed at providing a focus on specific problem-solving situations), and the introduction of design factors (which is aimed at better facilitating a tailored EGIT implementation). In general, the evolution of the COBIT framework is a healthy response to numerous relevant (IT-related) changes that enterprises are confronted with (e.g., a changing role of information and technology, changing sourcing models for IT services, changing business models because of digital transformation, a changing regulatory landscape, etc.) (Steuperaert, 2019). A historical timeline of the evolution of the COBIT framework is presented in Fig. 5.1.

---

[1]ITGI (2003) recognized value delivery and risk management as outcome areas; and strategic alignment, resource management, and performance measurement as drivers.

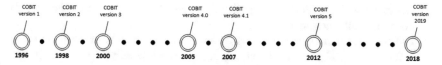

Fig. 5.1   COBIT historical timeline

5.2   Introducing the Cobit 2019 Framework

The most recent update of the COBIT framework, i.e., COBIT 2019, is aimed at facilitating a flexible and tailored EGIT design and implementation. Compared to its predecessor COBIT 5, COBIT 2019 is characterized by the following major changes.

- COBIT 2019 introduces three new **(governance and management) objectives** (i.e., APO14—"managed data"; BAI11—"managed projects"; and MEA04 —"managed assurance"). This implies the introduction of three new processes, as each objective directly maps to a single process. It should be noted that the processes related to BAI11—"managed projects" and MEA04—"managed assurance" were already included in COBIT 5. BAI01 referred to the "manage programs and projects"—process in COBIT 5. In COBIT 2019, this process is now split over two separate management objectives (i.e., BAI01—"managed programs" and BAI11—"managed projects"). Similarly, MEA02 referred to the "monitor, evaluate, and assess the system of internal control"—process in COBIT 5. In COBIT 2019, this process is now split over the following two management objectives: MEA02—"managed system of internal control" and MEA04—"managed assurance". As such, only the APO14—"managed data" management objective and its related process is an entirely new addition to the COBIT framework.
- COBIT 2019 identifies the **components** of an effective EGIT system (which are similar to the COBIT 5 "enablers"): processes; organizational structures; information flows and items; people, skills and competencies; policies and procedures; culture, ethics, and behavior; and services, infrastructure, and applications. To achieve (any of) the governance and management objectives contained in the COBIT 2019 core model, enterprises should implement an EGIT system composed of these key components.
- COBIT 2019 introduces an updated **goals cascade**. The achievement of the governance and management objectives enables the achievement of **alignment goals** (which were called "IT-related goals" in COBIT 5), which in turn enables the achievement of **enterprise goals**. As such, stakeholder value is ultimately provided (i.e., meeting stakeholder needs).
- COBIT 2019 identifies the **design factors** (e.g., role of IT, compliance requirements, threat landscape, etc.) that should be considered in the context of

designing and implementing an EGIT system that is tailored to the specific context of the enterprise.

- COBIT 2019 introduces the concept of **focus areas**, which is aimed at providing a focus on specific problem-solving situations while adhering to the COBIT 2019 core model and its governance and management objectives. A focus area will concern a specific topic or issue that can be addressed by a specific collection of governance and management objectives and their components (or a variant of the generic guidance). Focus area guidance will be available for topics like information security, information and technology risk, and DevOps.

The COBIT 2019 framework is organized into four main publications.

1. *"COBIT 2019 Framework: Introduction and Methodology"* introduces the structure of the overall COBIT 2019 framework, explains its concepts and terminology (e.g., components, design factors, focus areas, goals cascade, etc.), and presents the updated COBIT principles. This publication introduces the COBIT 2019 core model and its 40 governance and management objectives, which provides the platform for establishing an EGIT arrangement. Furthermore, the updated COBIT 2019 performance management system is introduced. Finally, some insights on the design and implementation of an EGIT system are provided.

2. *"COBIT 2019 Framework: Governance and Management Objectives"* contains a detailed description of the COBIT 2019 core model and each of its 40 governance and management objectives. For each governance or management objective, a description and purpose is provided as well as its specific goals cascade (i.e., its contribution to enterprise goals through alignment goals) and example metrics for these goals. Then, the components (i.e., process; organizational structures; information flows and items; people, skills and competencies; policies and procedures; culture, ethics, and behavior; and services, infrastructure, and applications) which are required to achieve the governance or management objective are discussed in turn. This guide also explicitly refers to other standards and frameworks for further guidance. An updated alignment to global standards, frameworks, and best practices guards the relevancy of COBIT and ensures that COBIT maintains its established position as the overarching EGIT framework.

3. *"COBIT 2019 Design Guide: Designing an Information and Technology Governance Solution"* provides prescriptive how-to insights for COBIT users related to the design of an EGIT system. With the new concept of "design factors", COBIT 2019 provides hands-on insights on the factors that can influence an EGIT system. This guide furthermore includes a workflow for designing an EGIT system that is tailored to the enterprise's specific context.

4. *"COBIT 2019 Implementation Guide: Implementing and Optimizing an Information and Technology Governance Solution"* provides a road map for continuous improvement of an EGIT system. This implementation guide logically is strongly linked to the design guide.

5.3 Cobit 2019 Principles

The COBIT 2019 framework introduces the six principles that describe the core requirements of an EGIT system (visualized in Fig. 5.2). Each of these principles is discussed below and related to concepts and insights from the IT governance field. As such, the relevance of these principles is demonstrated.

5.3.1 Provide Stakeholder Value: Strategic Alignment and the Balanced Scorecard

According to ISACA, the purpose of an EGIT system is to satisfy stakeholder needs and to create and protect value from the use of information and technology. The COBIT goals cascade (see Fig. 5.3) shows how the achievement of governance and management objectives (through implementing EGIT) ultimately contributes to satisfying stakeholder needs. Drawing on this cascade, stakeholder needs cascade to prioritized enterprise goals. These prioritized enterprise goals cascade to the alignment goals that are important for achieving those enterprise goals. Finally, these alignment goals cascade to governance and management objectives that should be met to achieve those alignment goals.

As such, this principle of providing stakeholder value corresponds to the *strategic alignment* discussion as initiated by Henderson and Venkatraman (1993).[2] Indeed, the alignment of alignment goals and enterprise goals is of crucial importance to provide stakeholder value (i.e., to satisfy stakeholder needs). However, strategic alignment is often perceived as a very complex challenge, and decision-makers are often unsure about how to achieve this crucial objective (Preston & Karahanna, 2009). To approach this issue in practice, COBIT provides hands-on guidance related to understanding how enterprise goals cascade to alignment goals (or vice versa, how the achievement of alignment goals contributes to the achievement of enterprise goals). More specifically, COBIT 2019 provides a generic list of enterprise goals (EG), alignment goals (AG), and their inter-relationships (i.e., which alignment goals contribute in a "primary (P)" or a "secondary (S)" way to the achievement of the enterprise goals) (as shown in Table 5.1).

As an illustration of this cascade, Table 5.1 shows that the enterprise goal of "Compliance with internal policies" (EG11) requires a primary focus (P) on the alignment goal of "I&T compliance with internal policies" (AG11). Additionally, this enterprise goal requires a secondary focus (S) on the alignment goal of "I&T compliance and support for business compliance with external laws and regulations" (AG01).

---

[2]Refer to Chap. 3 on business/IT alignment for additional substantiation.

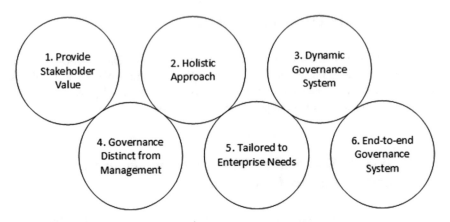

Fig. 5.2 EGIT system principles (ISACA, 2018b)

Fig. 5.3 COBIT goals cascade (ISACA, 2018b)

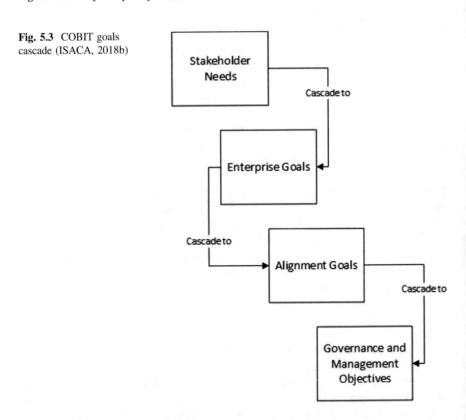

Further drawing on the COBIT goals cascade, the identification of this alignment goal (AG11) that is of primary importance for achieving the enterprise goal EG11 allows for the identification of the governance and management objectives that

Table 5.1 Mapping of enterprise goals (EG) and alignment goals (AG) (ISACA, 2018a)

		EG01 Portfolio of competitive products and services	EG02 Managed business risk	EG03 Compliance with external laws and regulations	EG04 Quality of financial information	EG05 Customer-oriented service culture	EG06 Business service continuity and availability	EG07 Quality of management information	EG08 Optimization of internal business process functionality	EG09 Optimization of business process costs	EG10 Staff skills, motivation and productivity	EG11 Compliance with internal policies	EG12 Managed digital transformation programs	EG13 Product and business innovation
AG01	I&T compliance and support for business compliance with external laws and regulations		S	P								S		
AG02	Managed I&T-related risk		P				S							
AG03	Realized benefits from I&T-enabled investments and services portfolio	S				S			S	S			P	
AG04	Quality of technology-related financial information				P			P		P				
AG05	Delivery of I&T services in line with business requirements	P				S	S		S				S	
AG06	Agility to turn business requirements into operational solutions	P					S		S				S	S
AG07	Security of information, processing infrastructure and applications, and privacy		P				P							
AG08	Enabling and supporting business processes by integrating applications and technology	P				P			S		S		P	S
AG09	Delivering programs on time, on budget and meeting requirements and quality standards	P				S			S	S			P	S
AG10	Quality of I&T management information				P			P		S				
AG11	I&T compliance with internal policies		S	P								P		
AG12	Competent and motivated staff with mutual understanding of technology and business					S					P			
AG13	Knowledge, expertise and initiatives for business innovation	P		S									S	P

should be met in order to achieve this alignment goal AG11. As illustrated in Table 5.2, the management objectives "Managed I&T management framework" (APO01), "Managed system of internal control" (MEA02), and "Managed assurance" (MEA04) are of primary importance (P) for achieving the alignment goal AG11. Additionally, some other governance objectives (i.e., EDM01, EDM03, and EDM05) and management objectives (i.e., DSS05, DSS06, MEA01, and MEA03) are of secondary importance (S) for achieving alignment goal AG11. The achievement of these governance and management objectives can be effectuated through implementing an EGIT system consisting of the appropriate components (i.e., processes and other related components). Specific guidance related to this last point can be found in the *"COBIT 2019 Framework: Governance and Management Objectives"* guide.

To verify whether stakeholder needs are indeed being satisfied, a sound measurement process needs to be established. Traditional performance methods such as return on investment (ROI) capture the financial worth of IT projects and systems but reflect only a limited (tangible) part of the value that can be delivered through the current and future use of IT (Schwarz & Hirschheim, 2003).

To enable a measurement process of broader scope, COBIT draws on the concept of the (IT) balanced scorecard[3] as developed by Kaplan and Norton (1996) and Van Grembergen, Saull, and De Haes (2003). All enterprise goals and alignment goals are grouped in the balanced scorecard (BSC) dimensions (i.e., financial,

---

[3]Refer to Chap. 4 on IT business value for additional substantiation.

Table 5.2 Mapping of governance and management objectives to alignment goals (AG) (ISACA, 2018a)

		AG01 I&T compliance and support for business compliance with external laws and regulations	AG02 Managed I&T-related risk	AG03 Realized benefits from I&T-enabled investments and services portfolio	AG04 Quality of technology-related financial information	AG05 Delivery of I&T services in line with business requirements	AG06 Agility to turn business requirements into operational solutions	AG07 Security of information, processing infrastructure and applications, and privacy	AG08 Enabling and supporting business processes by integrating applications and technology	AG09 Delivering programs on time, on budget and meeting requirements and quality standards	AG10 Quality of I&T management information	AG11 I&T compliance with internal policies	AG12 Competent and motivated staff with mutual understanding of technology and business	AG13 Knowledge, expertise and initiatives for business innovation
EDM01	Ensured governance framework setting and maintenance	P	S	P						S		S		
EDM02	Ensured benefits delivery			P		S	S			S				S
EDM03	Ensured risk optimization	S	P					P				S		
EDM04	Ensured resource optimization			S		S	S			S	P		S	
EDM05	Ensured stakeholder engagement				S						P	S		
APO01	Managed I&T management framework	S	S	P		S		S	S	S	S	P		
APO02	Managed strategy			S		S	S		P				S	S
APO03	Managed enterprise architecture			S		S	P	S	P					
APO04	Managed innovation			S			P		S				S	P
APO05	Managed portfolio			P		P	S		S	S				
APO06	Managed budget and costs			S	P						P	S		
APO07	Managed human resources			S		S				S			P	P
APO08	Managed relationships			S		P	P		S	S			P	P
APO09	Managed service agreements					P			S					
APO10	Managed vendors					P	S			S				
APO11	Managed quality			S	S	S					P	P		
APO12	Managed risk		P					P						
APO13	Managed security	S	S					P						
APO14	Managed data	S	S		S						P			
BAI01	Managed programs			P			S		S	P				
BAI02	Managed requirements definition			S		P	P		S	P			S	
BAI03	Managed solutions identification and build			S		P	P		S	P				
BAI04	Managed availability and capacity					P		S	S					
BAI05	Managed organizational changes			P		S	S		P	P			S	
BAI06	Managed IT changes		S			S	P		S					
BAI07	Managed IT change acceptance and transitioning		S				P			S				
BAI08	Managed knowledge		S				S		S	S			P	P
BAI09	Managed assets				P						S			
BAI10	Managed configuration					S		P						
BAI11	Managed projects			P		S	P			P				
DSS01	Managed operations					P			S					
DSS02	Managed service requests and incidents		S			P		S						
DSS03	Managed problems		S			P		S						
DSS04	Managed continuity		S			P		P						
DSS05	Managed security services	S	P			S		P				S		
DSS06	Managed business process controls		S			S		S	P			S		
MEA01	Managed performance and conformance monitoring	S		S		P				S	P	S		
MEA02	Managed system of internal control	S	S		S	S		S		S	S	P		
MEA03	Managed compliance with external requirements	P											S	
MEA04	Managed assurance	S	S		S	S						S		P

customer, internal, and learning and growth). COBIT also provides example metrics to measure each of those (enterprise and alignment) goals and to instantiate appropriate scorecards accordingly. Tables 5.3 and 5.4 provide examples of this approach for the enterprise goals (i.e., EG11 and EG12) and the alignment goals (i.e., AG11 and AG13), respectively.

Moreover, COBIT 2019 provides example metrics at the level of the governance or management practices that belong to a given governance or management objective. These practices are an integral part of the crucial process component that is (besides other components like organizational structures) required to achieve a given governance or management objective. An example is shown in Table 5.5 for

Table 5.3 Enterprise goals EG11 and EG12 with example metrics (ISACA, 2018b)

Enterprise goal	BSC dimension	Example metrics
Compliance with internal policies (EG11)	Internal	• Number of incidents related to non-compliance with policy • Percent of stakeholders who understand policies • Percent of policies supported by effective standards and working practices
Managed digital transformation programs (EG12)	Learning and growth	• Number of programs on time and within budget • Percent of stakeholders satisfied with program delivery • Percent of business transformation programs stopped • Percent of business transformation programs with regular reported status updates

Table 5.4 Alignment goals AG11 and AG13 with example metrics (ISACA, 2018b)

Alignment goal	BSC dimension	Example metrics
I&T compliance with internal policies (AG11)	Internal	• Number of incidents related to non-compliance with IT-related policies • Number of exceptions to internal policies • Frequency of policy review and update
Knowledge, expertise, and initiatives for business innovation (AG13)	Learning and growth	• Level of business executive awareness and understanding of I&T innovation possibilities • Number of approved initiatives resulting from innovative I&T ideas • Number of innovation champions recognized/awarded

Table 5.5 Management practice BAI02.01 and example metrics (ISACA, 2018a)

Management practice	Example metrics
BAI02.01: Define and maintain business functional and technical requirements	• Percent of requirements reworked due to misalignment with enterprise needs and expectations • Percent of requirements validated through approaches such as peer review, model validation, or operational prototyping

the management objective "Managed requirements definition" (BAI02), providing specific example metrics that can be used to measure the achievement of one of its management practices (in this case, BAI02.01).

Consolidating all of these metrics at different levels of the goals cascade (i.e., enterprise goals level, alignment goals level, and management practice level) enables enterprises to build a comprehensive balanced scorecard for its entire IT-related environment. Such a linked scorecard serves as a comprehensive instrument to verify whether stakeholder needs are being met.

5.3.2   *Holistic Approach: Organizational Systems*

ISACA states that an effective EGIT system is built from a number of components (i.e., processes and other related components) that work together in a holistic way. This is related to what is described in strategic management literature as the need for an "organizational system", i.e., *"the way a firm gets its people to work together to carry out the business"* (De Wit & Meyer, 2014). Such organizational systems require the definition and application, in a holistic whole, of structures (e.g., organizational units and functions) and processes (to ensure tasks are coordinated and integrated), and attention to people and relational aspects (e.g., culture, values, joint beliefs, etc.).

Peterson (2004) and De Haes and Van Grembergen (2009) have applied this organizational system concept to the discussion of EGIT. These authors conclude that organizations can deploy EGIT by using a holistic mixture of various structures, processes, and relational mechanisms.[4] EGIT structures include organizational units and roles responsible for making IT decisions and for enabling contacts between business and IT management decision-making functions (e.g., IT steering committee). This can be seen as a blueprint of how the EGIT system will be structurally organized. EGIT processes refer to the formalization and institutionalization of strategic IT decision-making and IT-monitoring procedures to ensure that daily behaviors are consistent with policies and provide input back to decision-making (e.g., IT balanced scorecard). The EGIT relational mechanisms are ultimately about the active participation of, and collaborative relationship among, corporate executives, IT management, and business management, and include mechanisms such as announcements, advocates, and education efforts.

The COBIT 2019 framework draws on these insights by proposing that an effective EGIT system should be built from a number of components that work together in a holistic way (i.e., they interact with each other). An EGIT system is effective if it satisfies the relevant governance and management objectives (thereby ultimately meeting stakeholder needs—as explained in the COBIT goals cascade). Components are defined as factors that, individually and collectively, contribute to the effective operation of the EGIT system.

---

[4]Refer to Chap. 2 on Enterprise Governance of IT for additional substantiation.

Fig. 5.4 Components of an EGIT system (ISACA, 2018b)

The COBIT 2019 framework describes seven categories of components (see Fig. 5.4). The most familiar ones are the processes. However, an EGIT system also consists of other related components.

- *Processes* describe an organized set of practices and activities to achieve certain (governance or management) objectives and produce a set of outputs that support the achievement of enterprise goals (through the achievement of alignment goals) (e.g., portfolio management).
- *Organizational structures* represent an enterprise's key decision-making roles or structures (e.g., executive committee).
- *Information flows and items* include all information produced and used by the enterprise. COBIT specifically focuses on the information that is required for the effective functioning of the EGIT system of the enterprise (e.g., business case document, IT strategy document).
- *People, skills, and competencies* are required for quality decision-making, execution of corrective action and successful completion of all process activities (e.g., application support skillset, network support skillset).
- *Policies and procedures* translate desirable behavior into practical guidance for day-to-day management (e.g., privacy policy).
- *Culture, ethics, and behavior* of individuals and of the enterprise that contributes to the success of governance and management activities (e.g., data quality culture).
- *Services, infrastructure, and applications* include the infrastructure, technology, and applications that provide the enterprise with the capacity to govern and manage their information and technology (e.g., data repositories, project management tools).

5.3.3   Dynamic Governance System: Evolutionary Dynamics

ISACA explains that an EGIT system should be dynamic. More specifically, a change in one of the relevant design factors (e.g., a change in the role of IT for the enterprise) might require changes to the EGIT system of the enterprise.

This principle is in line with applying the theoretical lens of the Viable System Model (which is grounded in the theory of management cybernetics) (Beer, 1985) to the EGIT concept.[5] Indeed, EGIT (in its role as controller of the current and future IT use) should have and maintain sufficient capacity to be able to control the (current and future) IT use effectively and this (current and future) IT use should be appropriate so that it remains sustainable in the (changing) external environment. This will ensure the ability to fulfill the general purpose of creating and protecting IT business value. As such, any change in the (current and future) use of IT (e.g., resulting from a relevant IT-related change in the external environment) might require changes to the enterprise's EGIT as well (Huygh & De Haes, 2019). The design factors identified in COBIT 2019 can as such be seen as (internal or external) factors that might trigger adaptation of the enterprise's EGIT.

5.3.4   Governance Distinct from Management: ISO/IEC 38500

ISACA asserts that there is a clear distinction between the governance and management activities and the involved roles/structures within an EGIT system. This principle has been incorporated into the COBIT framework since COBIT 5 and heavily builds on the position put forward by the ISO/IEC 38500 standard on IT governance. As a means to better align the COBIT framework to this global standard, the governance objectives (and therefore also the processes) are explicitly separated from the management objectives (and processes) by means of the *Evaluate, Direct, and Monitor (EDM)* domain. This domain is therefore in strong agreement with the *Evaluate–Direct–Monitor* cycle which is central to ISO/IEC 38500. This governance cycle is composed of three main tasks: (1) evaluating the current and future use of IT, (2) direct preparation and implementation of plans and policies, and (3) monitor, through appropriate measurement systems, the performance of IT (ISO/IEC, 2015).

In most enterprises, governance is the responsibility of the board of directors under the leadership of the chairperson. Management is then responsible for planning, building, running, and monitoring activities (inspired by Deming's PDCA circle "Plan-Do-Check-Act"), in alignment with the direction set by the governing body, to achieve the enterprise's objectives. In most enterprises, management is the responsibility of the executive committee under the leadership of the chief executive officer.

---

[5]Refer to Chap. 2 on Enterprise Governance of IT for additional substantiation.

5.3.5   Tailored to Enterprise Needs: Contingency Analysis

According to ISACA, an EGIT system needs to be tailored to the specific context of the enterprise. This specific context is shaped by several external and internal factors—the so-called design factors (e.g., role of IT, compliance requirements, threat landscape, etc.). ISACA provides detailed guidance on how to use the concept of design factors in the process of designing an EGIT system in its COBIT 2019 design guide.

The COBIT 2019 framework proposes multiple factors that can influence the design of an EGIT system that is tailored to the specific context of the enterprise. These design factors can influence the prioritization of governance and management objectives that are to be met by the enterprise. As such, these factors influence the instantiation of the EGIT components within the EGIT system of the enterprise, resulting in an EGIT system that is tailored to the enterprise's specific needs.

Also recognizing that additional factors might be added to the COBIT framework in the future, the design factors contained in COBIT 2019 are presented in Fig. 5.5.

This principle of tailoring an EGIT system, and the related concept of design factors, is fully in line with the research on IT governance contingency analysis. IT governance contingency analysis deals with understanding the factors that influence the choice for a specific form of IT governance. The rationale underlying this research stream lies in the unanimous recognition that a universal-best IT governance arrangement does not exist (Brown & Grant, 2005), but is instead contingent upon a variety of (internal and external) factors. This research stream therefore heavily draws on contingency theory (e.g., Lawrence & Lorsch, 1967) (Brown, 1997).

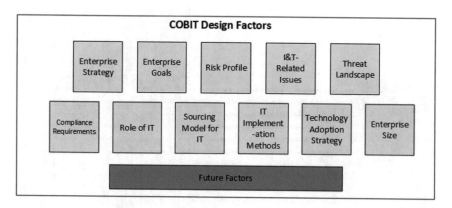

Fig. 5.5   COBIT design factors (ISACA, 2018b)

5.3.6   End-to-End Governance System: IT Savviness

ISACA states that an EGIT system should cover the enterprise end-to-end. This means that the scope of an EGIT system goes well beyond the IT department of the enterprise. Instead, its scope comprises all information processing and technology that the enterprise leverages to achieve its goals and to meet stakeholder needs. The information processing and technology should be treated like any other asset by everyone in the enterprise.

As such, this principle relates to the work of Weill and Ross (2009) on IT Savviness, who assert that business people should take up responsibility in managing IT-related assets. These insights clarify the need for the business to take ownership of, and be accountable for, governing the (current and future) use of IT in creating IT business value. This implies a crucial shift in the mindset of business and IT stake-holders, moving away from managing IT as a "cost" toward managing IT as an "asset" that has the capacity to create IT business value. To put it in the words of Weill and Ross (2009): *"If senior managers do not accept accountability for IT, the company will inevitable throw its IT money to multiple tactical initiatives with no clear impact on the organizational capabilities. IT becomes a liability instead of a strategic asset"*.

The COBIT 2019 framework provides a table of responsibilities and account-abilities for each governance or management objective in which both business roles

Table 5.6   End-to-end responsibilities and accountabilities in "Managed solutions identification and build" (BAI03) (ISACA, 2018a)

B. Component: Organizational Structures

Key Management Practice	Chief Information Officer	Chief Technology Officer	Chief Digital Officer	Business Process Owners	Portfolio Manager	Steering (Programs/Projects) Committee	Program Manager	Project Manager	Project Management Office	Relationship Manager	Head Architect	Head Development	Head IT Operations	Head IT Administration	Service Manager	Information Security Manager	Business Continuity Manager	Privacy Officer
BAI03.01 Design high-level solutions	R		R			A	R	R	R	R		R				R		
BAI03.02 Design detailed solution components	R		R			A	R	R	R			R				R		
BAI03.03 Develop solution components	R		R			A	R	R	R			R						
BAI03.04 Procure solution components	R		R			A						R	R	R				
BAI03.05 Build solutions	R		R			A	R	R	R			R				R		
BAI03.06 Perform quality assurance (QA)	R		R			A	R	R	R			R						
BAI03.07 Prepare for solution testing	R		R			A						R	R		R	R	R	R
BAI03.08 Execute solution testing	R		R			A						R	R		R			R
BAI03.09 Manage changes to requirements	R		R			A	R	R	R		R	R				R		R
BAI03.10 Maintain solutions	A	R		R			R	R	R			R				R		R
BAI03.11 Define IT products and services and maintain the service portfolio	A															R	R		R
BAI03.12 Design solutions based on the defined development methodology	A		R		R		R	R										
Related Guidance (Standards, Frameworks, Compliance Requirements)	**Detailed Reference**																	
No related guidance for this component																		

and IT roles are included. To illustrate this, an example of the management objective "Managed solutions identification and build" (BAI03) is shown in Table 5.6. This table clearly illustrates that both business and IT stakeholders have accountabilities and responsibilities in the context of the management practices belonging to this management objective. Such guidance relates to the component "organizational structures" of an EGIT system (i.e., which, besides processes, is another crucial EGIT component).

To further illustrate, Table 5.7 provides an overview of the roles and organizational structures that are included in the COBIT guidance to effectuate the "organizational structures" component of an EGIT system.

Table 5.7 COBIT roles and organizational structures (ISACA, 2018a)

Role/Structure	Description
Board	Group of the most senior executives and/or non-executive directors accountable for governance and overall control of enterprise resources
Executive Committee	Group of senior executives appointed by the board to ensure that the board is involved in, and kept informed of, major decisions
Chief Executive Officer	Highest ranking officer charged with the total management of the enterprise
Chief Financial Officer	Most senior official accountable for all aspects of financial management, including financial risk and controls and reliable and accurate accounts
Chief Operating Officer	Most senior official accountable for operation of the enterprise
Chief Risk Officer	Most senior official accountable for all aspects of risk management across the enterprise
Chief Information Officer	Most senior official responsible for aligning IT and business strategies and accountable for planning, resourcing, and managing delivery of I&T services and solutions
Chief Technology Officer	Most senior official tasked with technical aspects of I&T, including managing and monitoring decisions related to I&T services, solutions, and infrastructures
Chief Digital Officer	Most senior official tasked with putting into practice the digital ambition of the enterprise or business unit
I&T Governance Board	Group of stakeholders and experts accountable for guiding I&T-related matters and decisions, including managing I&T-enabled investments, delivering value, and monitoring risk
Architecture Board	Group of stakeholders and experts accountable for guiding enterprise architecture-related matters and decisions and for setting architectural policies and standards
Enterprise Risk Committee	Group of executives accountable for enterprise-level collaboration and consensus required to support enterprise risk management (ERM) activities and decisions
Chief Information Security Officer	Most senior official accountable for all aspects of security management across the enterprise

(continued)

Table 5.7 (continued)

Role/Structure	Description
Business Process Owner	Individual accountable for performing processes and/or realizing process objectives, driving process improvement and approving process changes
Portfolio Manager	Individual responsible for guiding portfolio management, ensuring selection of correct programs and projects, managing and monitoring programs and projects for optimal value, and realizing long-term strategic objectives effectively and efficiently
Steering (Programs/ Projects) Committee	Group of stakeholders and experts accountable for guiding programs and projects, including managing and monitoring plans, allocating resources, delivering benefits and value, and managing program and project risk
Program Manager	Individual responsible for guiding a specific program, including articulating and following up on goals and objectives of the program and managing risk and impact on the business
Project Manager	Individual responsible for guiding a specific project, including coordinating and delegating time, budget, resources, and tasks across the project team
Project Management Office	Function responsible for supporting program and project managers and for gathering, assessing, and reporting information about the conduct of programs and constituent projects
Data Management Function	Function responsible for supporting enterprise data assets across the data life cycle and managing data strategy, infrastructure, and repositories
Head Human Resources	Most senior official accountable for planning and policies regarding human resources in the enterprise
Relationship Manager	Senior individual responsible for overseeing and managing the internal interface and communications between business and I&T functions
Head Architect	Senior individual accountable for the enterprise architecture process.
Head Development	Senior individual accountable for I&T-related solution development processes
Head IT Operations	Senior individual accountable for IT operational environments and infrastructure
Head IT Administration	Senior individual accountable for I&T-related records and responsible for supporting I&T-related administrative matters
Service Manager	Individual who manages the development, implementation, evaluation, and ongoing maintenance of new and existing products and services for a specific customer (user) or group of customers (users)
Information Security Manager	Individual who manages, designs, oversees, and/or assesses an enterprise's information security
Business Continuity Manager	Individual who manages, designs, oversees, and/or assesses an enterprise's business continuity capability, to ensure that the enterprise's critical functions continue to operate following disruptive events

(continued)

Table 5.7 (continued)

Role/Structure	Description
Privacy Officer	Individual responsible for monitoring risk and business impact of privacy laws and for guiding and coordinating the implementation of policies and activities that ensure compliance with privacy directives
Legal Counsel	Function responsible for guidance on legal and regulatory matters
Compliance	Function responsible for all guidance on external compliance
Audit	Function responsible for provision of internal audits

5.4 Cobit 2019 Core Model: Governance and Management Objectives

The COBIT 2019 framework identifies 40 governance and management objectives as part of its COBIT 2019 core model (see Fig. 5.6). A governance or management objective always relates to exactly one (governance or management) process. A governance objective relates to a governance process, while a management objective relates to a management process. Additionally, a number of EGIT components of other types (e.g., organizational structures) are included that help achieve the (governance or management) objective.

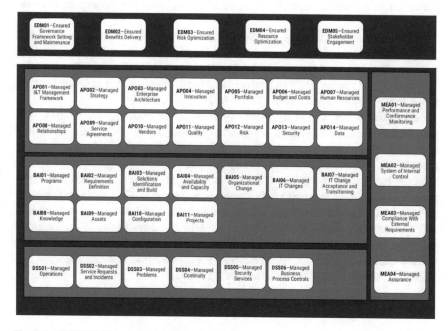

Fig. 5.6 COBIT 2019 core model (ISACA, 2018a)

The governance and management objectives are grouped into five domains. The governance objectives are grouped together in the *Evaluate, Direct, and Monitor (EDM)* domain. The purpose of this domain is for the governing body (i.e., the board) to evaluate strategic options, to direct executive management on the chosen strategic options, and to monitor the achievement of the resulting strategy. The management objectives are grouped into four domains. The *Align, Plan, and Organize (APO)* domain concerns the identification of how information and technology can best contribute to the achievement of the business objectives. An information and technology management framework is required, and specific processes related to the IT strategy and tactics, enterprise architecture, innovation and portfolio management, and data management. Other important objectives in this domain address the management of budgets and costs, human resources, relationships, service agreements, suppliers, quality, risk, and security. The *Build, Acquire, and Implement (BAI)* domain contributes to realizing the IT strategy through identifying in detail the requirements for IT and managing program and projects. This domain further talks about managing capacity, organizational change, IT changes, acceptance and transitioning, knowledge, assets, and configurations. The *Deliver, Service, and Support (DSS)* domain refers to the actual delivery of required services. It contains objectives regarding managing operations, service requests and incidents, problems, continuity, security services, and business process controls. Finally, the *Monitor, Evaluate, and Assess (MEA)* domain includes those management objectives that are responsible for the quality assessment in compliance with the control requirements for all previous-mentioned processes. It addresses performance management, monitoring of internal control, regulatory compliance, and assurance.

As a side note, it should be mentioned that compared to its predecessor COBIT 5, COBIT 2019 includes three new management objectives (and therefore also three new management processes): i.e., APO14, BAI11, and MEA04. Additionally, some governance and management objectives have been slightly changed in name and/or scope (e.g., EDM05, APO10, BAI01, BAI05, and BAI06).

Each governance or management objective is presented in the COBIT 2019 governance and management objectives guide using a similar structure. A description and purpose of the objective is provided as well as its specific goals cascade (i.e., its contribution to enterprise goals through alignment goals) and example metrics for these goals. Then, the EGIT components (i.e., process; organizational structures; information flows and items; people, skills, and competencies; policies and procedures; culture, ethics, and behavior; and services, infrastructure, and applications) which are required to achieve the governance or management objective are discussed in turn. The following subsections illustrate this structure and the material provided in COBIT 2019 for a specific management objective, i.e., "Managed service requests and incidents" (DSS02).

Table 5.8 Description of management objective DSS02 (ISACA, 2018a)

Provide timely and effective response to user requests and resolution of all types of incidents. Restore normal service; record and fulfil user requests; and record, investigate, diagnose, escalate and resolve incidents

Table 5.9 Purpose of management objective DSS02 (ISACA, 2018a)

Achieve increased productivity and minimize disruptions through quick resolution of user queries and incidents. Assess the impact of changes and deal with service incidents. Resolve user requests and restore service in response to incidents

5.4.1   Description and Purpose

For each COBIT 2019 governance or management objective, a short general description is provided which summarizes the core content of the objective. The management objective "Managed service requests and incidents" (DSS02) is described as follows (Table 5.8).

The objective description is then followed by some statements about the general purpose of the objective. Such purpose statement explains the main reasons why an enterprise should consider achieving the objective. For "Managed service requests and incidents" (DSS02), the purpose statement is as follows (Table 5.9).

5.4.2   Enterprise Goals, Alignment Goals, and Example Metrics

The specific goals cascade of each governance or management objective is then provided. This guidance translates the description and purpose of the (governance or management) objective in a more detailed set of goals and metrics at different levels of granularity. As previously mentioned while discussing the COBIT goals cascade, the achievement of the governance or management objective (through implementing an EGIT system consisting of an appropriate instantiation of EGIT components) contributes to the achievement of linked alignment goals, which in turn contributes to the achievement of linked enterprise goals.

Table 5.10 Enterprise goals, alignment goals, and example metrics of management objective DSS02 (ISACA, 2018a)

The management objective supports the achievement of a set of primary enterprise and alignment goals:	
Enterprise Goals	**Alignment Goals**
• EG01 Portfolio of competitive products and services • EG08 Optimization of internal business process functionality	AG05 Delivery of I&T services in line with business requirements
Example Metrics for Enterprise Goals	**Example Metrics for Alignment Goals**

EG01   a. Percent of products and services that meet or exceed
            targets in revenues and/or market share
        b. Percent of products and services that meet or exceed
            customer satisfaction targets
        c. Percent of products and services that provide competitive
            advantage
        d. Time to market for new products and services
	AG05 a. Percent of business stakeholders satisfied that I&T service
	            delivery meets agreed service levels
	        b. Number of business disruptions due to I&T service incidents
	        c. Percent of users satisfied with the quality of I&T service
	            delivery

EG08   a. Satisfaction levels of board and executive management
            with business process capabilities
        b. Satisfaction levels of customers with service delivery
            capabilities
        c. Satisfaction levels of suppliers with supply chain
            capabilities	

Drawing on the concept of the balanced scorecard,[6] the example metrics provided are "outcome measures" for each of the postulated (alignment or enterprise) goals. The alignment goals and metrics can be seen as "performance drivers" for the enterprise goals and their corresponding outcome measures. Using this approach, a cascade can be developed describing how governance and management objectives drive the achievement of alignment goals, which in turn drives the achievement of enterprise goals. As such, this guidance provides a wealth of information to build a balanced scorecard for different IT-related matters in enterprises.

As an example, Table 5.10 illustrates that meeting management objective "Managed service requests and incidents" (DSS02) contributes to the achievement of alignment goal "Delivery of I&T services in line with business requirements" (AG05). This alignment goal could be measured through the outcome measure (i.e., example metric) "Percent of business stakeholders satisfied that I&T service delivery meets agreed service levels". The achievement of alignment goal AG05 then in turn contributes to the achievement of enterprise goals EG01 and EG08, for each of which example metrics (which can be used as outcome measures) are also provided.

5.4.3   EGIT Components

COBIT 2019 states that an EGIT system should be built from a number of interacting components. Components are defined as factors that, individually and collectively, contribute to the effective operation of the EGIT system. An EGIT system is operating effectively if it is achieving the relevant governance and management

---

[6]Refer to Chap. 4 on IT business value for additional substantiation.

objectives (and thereby ultimately meeting stakeholder needs—refer to the goals cascade). The COBIT 2019 framework identifies seven categories of components. The most familiar ones are the processes, as they already have a long development history throughout earlier versions of the COBIT framework. However, an EGIT system also consists of other related components: i.e., organizational structures; information flows and items; people, skills, and competencies; policies and procedures; culture, ethics, and behavior; and services, infrastructure, and applications.

5.4.3.1   Process Component

Each (governance or management) objective directly maps to a single (governance or management) process. The process is further refined in various practices, to provide more detailed guidance. A governance process consists of governance practices, and a management process consists of management practices. To provide even more concrete guidance on how to effectuate the process (and its containing practices), each practice consists of one or more hands-on activities.

Each process practice is accompanied by a number of example metrics that allow to measure the achievement of the practice. These example metrics are thus "outcome measures" of each process practice. Each process practice plays a part in achieving the overall governance or management objective to which the process directly maps.

A capability level is assigned to all process activities within the process practices. In the COBIT core model, this provides insights on the specific activities that are (at least) required to reach a certain process capability level. A process reaches a certain capability level once all activities that are assigned that certain capability level (and the lower capability levels) are performed successfully. This capability measurement is based on a Capability Maturity Model Integration (CMMI)-based process capability scheme, in which capability levels (ranging from 0 to 5) represent a measure of how well a process is performing. The COBIT 2019 performance management approach is discussed in more detail in the next section of this chapter.

To illustrate, the management objective "Managed service requests and incidents" (DSS02) directly maps to a management process that could be referred to as "manage service requests and incidents".[7] This process component, which plays a crucial role in achieving the DSS02 management objective, consists of seven management practices (see Table 5.11).

The first of these management practices, i.e., DSS02.01, is displayed in Table 5.12. Two example metrics are provided that allow to measure the achievement of this specific practice. For instance, the total number of incidents escalated can be used as an outcome measure of this management practice. Providing more concrete guidance on how to effectuate the management practice, five hands-on activities are included. The COBIT 2019 core model assigns

---

[7]As a side note, this exact management process was indeed part of the COBIT 5 process enabler.

Table 5.11 Management practices of management objective DSS02 (ISACA, 2018a)

Management practices contained in the process component of "managed service requests and incidents" (DSS02)
DSS02.01 Define classification schemes for incidents and service requests
DSS02.02 Record, classify, and prioritize requests and incidents
DSS02.03 Verify, approve, and fulfill service requests
DSS02.04 Investigate, diagnose, and allocate incidents
DSS02.05 Resolve and recover from incidents
DSS02.06 Close service requests and incidents
DSS02.07 Track status and produce reports

Table 5.12 Management practice DSS02.01 with example metrics, its containing activities, and related guidance (ISACA, 2018a)

A. Component: Process		
Management Practice	**Example Metrics**	
DSS02.01 Define classification schemes for incidents and service requests. Define classification schemes and models for incidents and service requests	a. Total number of service requests and incidents per priority level b. Total number of incidents escalated	
Activities		**Capability Level**
1. Define incident and service request classification and prioritization schemes, and criteria for problem registration. Use this information to ensure consistent approaches for handling and informing users about problems and conducting trend analysis		3
2. Define incident models for known errors to enable efficient and effective resolution		
3. Define service request models according to service request type to enable self-help and efficient service for standard requests		
4. Define incident escalation rules and procedures, especially for major incidents and security incidents		
5. Define knowledge sources on incidents and requests and describe how to use them		
Related Guidance (Standards, Frameworks, Compliance Requirements)	**Detailed Reference**	
CMMI Cybermaturity Platform, 2018	IA.IP Implement Incident Investigation Processes	
HITRUST CSF version 9, September 2017	11.01 Reporting Information Security Incidents and Weaknesses	
ISF, The Standard of Good Practice for Information Security 2016	TM2 Security Incident Management	
ISO/IEC 20000-1:2011(E)	8.1 Incident and service request management	
ISO/IEC 27002:2013/Cor.2:2015(E)	16. Information security incident management	

capability level 3 to all of these activities. This means that in order for the entire process component of DSS02 to reach capability level 3, (at least) all of these activities need to be performed successfully. Of course, all activities of the other process practices of the process component of DSS02 that have capability level 3 (or lower) assigned to them also need to be performed successfully for the entire process component to reach capability level 3. Finally, references to other guidance (e.g., standards or frameworks) are included for this management practice as well. The detailed reference area cites specific chapters or sections within the related guidance that is recommended.

Table 5.13 Organizational structures component of management objective DSS02 (ISACA, 2018a)

B. Component: Organizational Structures	Chief Technology Officer	Business Process Owners	Head Development	Head IT Operations	Service Manager	Information Security Manager
Key Management Practice						
DSS02.01 Define classification schemes for incidents and service requests	A		R	R	R	
DSS02.02 Record, classify and prioritize requests and incidents	A			R	R	
DSS02.03 Verify, approve and fulfil service requests	A	R	R	R	R	
DSS02.04 Investigate, diagnose and allocate incidents	A	R		R	R	
DSS02.05 Resolve and recover from incidents	A		R	R	R	R
DSS02.06 Close service requests and incidents	A			R	R	R
DSS02.07 Track status and produce reports	A			R	R	

Related Guidance (Standards, Frameworks, Compliance Requirements)	Detailed Reference
ISO/IEC 27002:2013/Cor.2:2015(E)	16.1.1 Responsibilities and procedures

5.4.3.2   Organizational Structures Component

Another key component of an EGIT system is the "organizational structures" component, which includes individual roles as well as organizational structures (from both business and IT). This EGIT component suggests levels of involvement for each of the process practices as described in the process component.[8] Two levels of involvement are included and described: i.e., responsible (R) and accountable (A). When a role or structure is responsible for a certain (governance or management) practice, this role or structure has the main operational stake in fulfilling the process practice and in creating the intended outcome. Such a role or structure would typically be thought of as an answer to the following question: Which role or structure is performing or driving the task? On the other hand, when a role or structure is accountable for a certain (governance or management) practice, this role or structure carries overall accountability for that practice. Such a role or structure would typically be thought of as an answer to the following question: Which role or structure accounts for the success and achievement of the task?

To illustrate, refer to the organizational structures' component of the management objective "Managed service requests and incidents" (DSS02) which is presented in Table 5.13. For each management practice of the process component of DSS02, all roles and structures that are responsible or accountable for the practice are included. For instance, for the management practice "Define classification

---

[8]This illustrates the interaction between EGIT components (in this case the process and the organizational structures), i.e., demonstrating that various EGIT components work together in a holistic way.

schemes for incidents and service requests" (DSS02.01), the chief technology officer is accountable, while the head development, the head IT operations, and the service manager are responsible. Unsurprisingly, seeing as the DSS02 management objective is oriented at the operational level of IT, most of the roles and structures that are accountable or responsible for its management practices are from the IT function of the enterprise (i.e., IT stakeholders).

5.4.3.3 Information Flows and Items Component

This EGIT component provides guidance on the information flows and items for each of the process practices as described in the process component of a certain (governance or management) objective. For each (governance or management) practice, inputs and outputs are described, with indications of origin and destination. An input is information required for the (governance or management) practice to operate effectively and efficiently. An output is information resulting from a successful operating (governance or management) practice. In general, each output (i.e., information flow or item) is sent to one or a few destinations (which typically is another process practice), where it then becomes an input. For some outputs, "internal" is displayed as destination, which means that the information is shared between practices within the same process.

To illustrate, refer to the information flows and items of management practice DSS02.01, which belongs to the management objective "Managed service requests and incidents" (DSS02), as presented in Table 5.14. This management practice requires as input "service-level agreements (SLAs)", which it should receive from

Table 5.14 Information flows and items of management practice DSS02.01 (ISACA, 2018a)

C. Component: Information Flows and Items (see also Section 3.6)				
Management Practice	**Inputs**		**Outputs**	
DSS02.01 Define classification schemes for incidents and service requests	**From**	**Description**	**Description**	**To**
	APO09.03	SLAs	Criteria for problem registration	DSS03.01
	BAI10.02	Configuration repository	Rules for incident escalation	Internal
	BAI10.03	Updated repository with configuration items	Incident and service request classification schemes and models	Internal
	BAI10.04	Configuration status reports		
	DSS01.03	Asset monitoring rules and event conditions		
	DSS03.01	Problem classification scheme		
	DSS04.03	Incident response actions and communications		

management practice APO09.03 (conditional on APO09.03 working effectively). If DSS02.01 is working effectively, it will deliver as output "rules for incident escalation". This specific output is required by the other management practices of the process component of DSS02, as indicated by the label "internal" in the destination column.

5.4.3.4   People, Skills, and Competencies Component

This EGIT component identifies human resources and skills that are required to achieve the governance or management objective. The guidance provided in COBIT 2019 as part of this component is based on the Skills Framework for the Information Age (SFIA) version 6,[9] the European e-Competence Framework (e-CF),[10] and the Institute of Internal Auditors' "Core Principles for the Professional Practice of Internal Auditing".[11] The detailed reference column of this component specifically indicates where additional guidance related to the required skill can be found.

To illustrate, refer to the people, skills, and competencies component of the management objective "Managed service requests and incidents" (DSS02) which is presented in Table 5.15. This guidance presents some skills that are required to achieve the DSS02 management objective. For instance, "network support" is a required skill in the context of this management objective. The detailed reference column provides a unique code that directly links to, in this case, the SFIA guidance on this particular skill.

Table 5.15 People, skills, and competencies component of management objective DSS02 (ISACA, 2018a)

D. Component: People, Skills and Competencies		
Skill	Related Guidance (Standards, Frameworks, Compliance Requirements)	Detailed Reference
Application support	Skills Framework for the Information Age V6, 2015	ASUP
Customer service support	Skills Framework for the Information Age V6, 2015	CSMG
Incident management	Skills Framework for the Information Age V6, 2015	USUP
Network support	Skills Framework for the Information Age V6, 2015	NTAS
User support	e-Competence Framework (e-CF)–A common European Framework for ICT Professionals in all industry sectors–Part 1: Framework, 2016	C. Run–C.1. User Support

---

[9]https://www.sfia-online.org/en/framework/sfia-6.

[10]http://www.ecompetences.eu/e-cf-overview/.

[11]https://na.theiia.org/standards-guidance/mandatory-guidance/Pages/Core-Principles-for-the-Professional-Practice-of-Internal-Auditing.aspx.

5.4.3.5 Policies and Procedures Component

The policies and procedures EGIT component provides guidance on the policies and procedures that are relevant in the context of the governance or management objective. This guidance specifically mentions any relevant policies and procedures, with a description of its purpose and content. If relevant, references to related guidance (e.g., standards or frameworks) are included as well.

To illustrate, refer to the policies and procedures component of the management objective "Managed service requests and incidents" (DSS02) which is presented in Table 5.16. This guidance mentions that a "service request policy" is relevant in the context of the DSS02 management objective. For more specific guidance, the reader is referred to ITIL v3[12] (and more specifically to Chap. 3 of the ITIL Service Operation publication).

5.4.3.6 Culture, Ethics, and Behavior Component

The EGIT component on culture, ethics, and behavior provides guidance on desired elements of organizational culture, ethics, and behavior within the enterprise that support the achievement of a governance or management objective. If relevant, references to related guidance are included here as well.

To illustrate, refer to the culture, ethics, and behavior component of the management objective "Managed service requests and incidents" (DSS02) which is presented in Table 5.17. This guidance states, for instance, that in order to better

Table 5.16 Policies and procedures component of management objective DSS02 (ISACA, 2018a)

E. Component: Policies and Procedures			
Relevant Policy	Policy Description	Related Guidance	Detailed Reference
Service request policy	States rationale and provides guidance for service and incident requests and their documentation	ITIL V3, 2011	Service Operation, 3. Service operation principles

Table 5.17 Culture, ethics, and behavior component of management objective DSS02 (ISACA, 2018a)

F. Component: Culture, Ethics and Behavior		
Key Culture Elements	Related Guidance	Detailed Reference
Enable employees to identify incidents on a correct and timely basis and implement appropriate escalation paths. Encourage prevention. Respond to and resolve incidents immediately. Avoid a hero culture		

---

[12]https://www.axelos.com/best-practice-solutions/itil/what-is-itil.

Table 5.18 Services, infrastructure, and applications component of management objective DSS02 (ISACA, 2018a)

G. Component: Services, Infrastructure and Applications
Incident tracking tools and system

support the achievement of the DSS02 management objective, a mindset oriented at prevention should be encouraged, and that a hero culture should be avoided.

5.4.3.7 Services, Infrastructure, and Applications Component

This EGIT component provides generic guidance (i.e., not mentioning specific vendors or products) on third-party services, types of infrastructure, and categories of applications that can prove useful to support the achievement of a governance or management objective.

Table 5.18 presents the guidance on the services, infrastructure, and applications component of the management objective "Managed service requests and incidents" (DSS02). Unsurprisingly, this guidance states that incident tracking tools can be used to support the achievement of the DSS02 management objective.

5.5 Cobit 2019 Performance Management

ISACA uses the term "COBIT performance management" (CPM) to refer to the activities and methods related to evaluating how well the EGIT system and its components work, and how this can be improved to achieve the required level of performance.

Related to the performance management of processes, COBIT 2019 supports a Capability Maturity Model Integration (CMMI)-based process capability scheme, in which capability levels (ranging from 0 to 5) represent a measure of how well a process is performing. This capability scheme, including the various capability levels and the general characteristics of each level, is presented in Fig. 5.7.

A capability level is assigned to all process activities within (the process practices of) a process component of a governance or management objective, which provides insights on the specific activities that are (at least) required to reach a certain process capability level. Indeed, a process reaches a certain capability level once all activities that are assigned that certain capability level (and the ones that are assigned lower capability levels) are performed successfully.

To illustrate, consider governance objective "Ensured stakeholder engagement" (EDM05). Table 5.19 displays the guidance contained in the COBIT 2019 core model related to the governance practices and their respective activities of the process component of this governance objective. Each process activity is assigned a

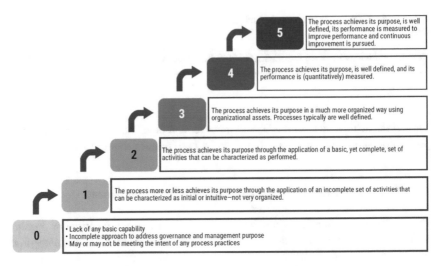

Fig. 5.7 COBIT 2019 capability levels for processes (ISACA, 2018b)

certain capability level. This guidance provides insights on the activities that are required to be performed successfully to reach a certain process capability level. For instance, if management decides that the target capability level of the process component of EDM05 is level 3, all activities that are assigned capability level 2 and 3 need to be performed successfully (i.e., all activities except the ones that are part of the EDM05.03 governance practice). If the target capability level of the process component of EDM05 were level 4, all process activities need to be performed successfully.

Related to the performance management of other EGIT components (i.e., besides processes), COBIT 2019 provides less formal guidance on how their performance can be assessed.[13] For instance, some criteria are provided that can be used for assessing the performance of organizational structures (e.g., the successful execution of the process practices for which a certain role or structure has accountability or responsibility) and the performance of information items (e.g., data quality criteria).

The COBIT performance management approach also introduces the concept of maturity levels. Maturity levels are associated with focus areas (i.e., a specific collection of governance and management objectives and their underlying EGIT components). Hence, a maturity level is a performance measure at the focus area level. A certain *maturity level* (i.e., of a focus area) is achieved once all required *capability levels* (i.e., of the underlying EGIT components) are achieved. This

---

[13]It should be noted that ISACA however states that other governance and management component types—i.e., besides processes—(e.g., organizational structures) may also have capability levels defined for them in further COBIT 2019 guidance (ISACA, 2018b).

Table 5.19 Governance practices of EDM05, with activities and their assigned capability levels (ISACA, 2018a)

Governance Practice	Example Metrics	
EDM05.01 Evaluate stakeholder engagement and reporting requirements. Continually examine and evaluate current and future requirements for stakeholder engagement and reporting (including reporting mandated by regulatory requirements), and communication to other stakeholders. Establish principles for engaging and communicating with stakeholders	a. Date of last revision to reporting requirements b. Percent of stakeholders covered in reporting requirements	
Activities		**Capability Level**
1. Identify all relevant I&T stakeholders within and outside the enterprise. Group stakeholders in stakeholder categories with similar requirements		2
2. Examine and make judgment on the current and future mandatory reporting requirements relating to the use of I&T within the enterprise (regulation, legislation, common law, contractual), including extent and frequency		
3. Examine and make judgment on the current and future communication and reporting requirements for other stakeholders relating to the use of I&T within the enterprise, including required level of involvement/consultation and extent of communication/level of detail and conditions		
4. Maintain principles for communication with external and internal stakeholders, including communication formats and channels, and for stakeholder acceptance and sign-off of reporting		3
Governance Practice	Example Metrics	
EDM05.02 Direct stakeholder engagement, communication and reporting. Ensure the establishment of effective stakeholder involvement, communication and reporting, including mechanisms for ensuring the quality and completeness of information, overseeing mandatory reporting, and creating a communication strategy for stakeholders	a. Number of breaches of mandatory reporting requirements b. Stakeholder satisfaction with communication and reporting	
Activities		**Capability Level**
1. Direct the establishment of the consultation and communication strategy for external and internal stakeholders		2
2. Direct the implementation of mechanisms to ensure that information meets all criteria for mandatory I&T reporting requirements for the enterprise		
3. Establish mechanisms for validation and approval of mandatory reporting		
4. Establish reporting escalation mechanisms		3
Governance Practice	Example Metrics	
EDM05.03 Monitor stakeholder engagement. Monitor stakeholder engagement levels and the effectiveness of stakeholder communication. Assess mechanisms for ensuring accuracy, reliability and effectiveness, and ascertain whether the requirements of different stakeholders in terms of reporting and communication are met	a. Level of stakeholder engagement with enterprise I&T b. Percent of reports containing inaccuracies c. Percent of reports delivered on time	
Activities		**Capability Level**
1. Periodically assess the effectiveness of the mechanisms for ensuring the accuracy and reliability of mandatory reporting		4
2. Periodically assess the effectiveness of the mechanisms for, and outcomes from, involvement of and communication with external and internal stakeholders		
3. Determine whether the requirements of different stakeholders are met and assess stakeholder engagement levels		

distinction between capability levels and maturity levels, as part of the COBIT performance management approach, is visualized in Fig. 5.8.

The various maturity levels and the general characteristics of each level are displayed in Fig. 5.9. In the context of the COBIT 2019 guidance that is currently available, a certain focus area *maturity level* is achieved if each of the process components that fall within the scope of that certain focus area achieve (at least) that certain corresponding *capability level*.

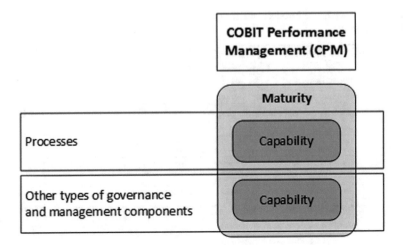

Fig. 5.8 COBIT Performance Management (CPM) (ISACA, 2018b)

5.6   Leveraging Cobit 2019 in Practice

COBIT is a framework that provides generic guidance to assist enterprises in the design and implementation of effective "enterprise governance of information and technology (EGIT)". A thorough understanding of the enterprise is required to benefit from the COBIT framework. Indeed, the generic guidance provided in COBIT 2019 should be filtered and customized into tailored guidance for the enterprise, explicitly taking into account the enterprise's specific context.

5.6.1   Scoping COBIT

The COBIT 2019 framework proposes multiple factors that can influence the design of an EGIT system that is tailored to the specific context of the enterprise. These *design factors* can influence the prioritization of governance and management objectives that are to be met by the enterprise, or the target capability levels of the EGIT components that work together to meet those governance and management objectives. As such, these factors influence the specific instantiation of the EGIT components within the EGIT system of the enterprise, resulting in an EGIT system that is tailored to the enterprise's specific needs. As an example, consider the management objective "Managed continuity" (DSS04). Ensuring continuous IT-related service will likely be more important for a financial services organization (in which there is a critical dependence on IT for the primary business operations) than for a brick factory (in which there might only be dependence on IT for administrative tasks). As a result, the target capability level of the process

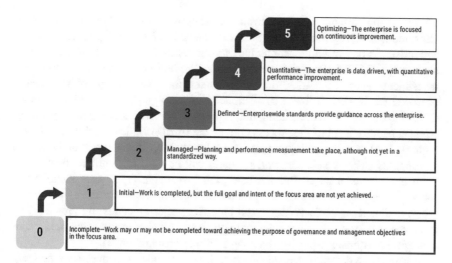

Fig. 5.9 COBIT 2019 maturity levels for focus areas (ISACA, 2018b)

component of the DSS04 objective will likely be higher for the financial services organization than for the brick factory.

It is thus important to scope COBIT down to the specific needs of the enterprise. This should be done by determining priorities in the governance and management objectives. Such a priority ranking can be driven by determining priorities in enterprise goals (i.e., applying the COBIT goals cascade) and taking into account other relevant design factors. For example, when enterprise goal "Quality of management information" (EG07) is considered a high priority for the enterprise, governance objective EDM05 and management objectives APO06, APO11, APO14, BAI09, and MEA01 should receive a high priority ranking in the context of the enterprise's EGIT system. Illustrating another design factor (i.e., threat landscape), an enterprise operating within a high threat landscape will tend to prioritize security-related management objectives (like APO13—"Managed security" and DSS05—"Managed security services").

Once priorities in governance and management objectives are determined, the enterprise can perform a quick assessment of the current "maturity" in meeting those governance and management objectives. Indeed, it makes sense to first focus on those governance and management objectives that were identified as being of high priority for the enterprise but also appear to be low in as-is maturity.

5.6.2 Example EDM02—"Ensured Benefits Delivery"

Once governance and management objectives are prioritized and selected, the generic guidance provided in COBIT 2019 needs to be applied to the specific context of the enterprise. As an illustration, suppose that the governance objective "Ensured Benefits Delivery" (EDM02) was selected as being of high priority for the enterprise. As part of implementing the process component to meet this governance objective, COBIT 2019 states the need to define and communicate portfolio and investment types, categories, and criteria (see the first activity of governance practice EDM02.03 in Table 5.20). This activity is assigned capability level 2 in the COBIT 2019 core model, meaning that it needs to be successfully performed if the target capability level of the process component of EDM02 is capability level 2 (or higher). This specific activity is about understanding which types of IT-related investments can be made and which criteria will be used to prioritize them.

In the case of a major Belgian bank, the investment types were identified as shown in Fig. 5.10. Besides the production budget, there are three investment types: maintenance projects (i.e., small break/fix projects), continuity projects (i.e., enhancements of existing applications) and more complex investments (i.e., major strategic investments typically spanning multiple business units).

For the more complex investments (i.e., funded through the investment budget), the bank agreed upon a set of tangible and intangible investment criteria, an approach based on "information economics".[14] The agreed-upon investment criteria are shown in Table 5.21.

5.6.3   Example APO05—"Managed Portfolio"

Once the investment types and criteria are set, COBIT 2019 proposes in the related[15] management objective "Managed Portfolio" (APO05) to perform a detailed assessment of all program business cases (see the second activity of management practice APO05.02 in Table 5.22).

In the case of the major Belgian bank, for each investment criterion (see Table 5.21—corresponding to Table 5.23), a number of questions are developed. The questions for the criterion "competitive advantage", for example, are: "Does the program deliver competitive advantage?" and "Is the program a necessity to remain competitive?" The criterion is scored by means of a red, yellow, or green color if the average of the underlying questions for a specific IT(-enabled) investment (i.e., the rows in Table 5.23) scores low, medium, or high, respectively. This approach results in a traffic light report for each IT(-enabled) investment, as visualized in Table 5.23.

The scoring is performed by the initiator of the IT(-enabled) investment, which in the case of the bank is the business architect. To obtain an objective measurement

---

[14]Refer to Chap. 4 on IT business value for additional substantiation of "information economics".

[15]Governance objective EDM02 and management objective APO05 are related in the sense that they both are of primary importance for achieving alignment goal "realized benefits from I&T-enabled investments and services portfolio" (AG03).

Table 5.20 Governance practice EDM02.03 and its containing activities (ISACA, 2018a)

Governance Practice	Example Metrics	
EDM02.03 Direct value optimization. Direct value management principles and practices to enable optimal value realization from I&T-enabled investments throughout their full economic life cycle	a. Percent of I&T initiatives in the overall portfolio in which value is managed through the full life cycle b. Percent of I&T initiatives using value management principles and practices	
Activities		**Capability Level**
1. Define and communicate portfolio and investment types, categories, criteria and relative weightings to the criteria to allow for overall relative value scores		2
2. Define requirements for stage-gates and other reviews for significance of the investment to the enterprise and associated risk, program schedules, funding plans, and the delivery of key capabilities and benefits and ongoing contribution to value		3
3. Direct management to consider potential innovative uses of I&T that enable the enterprise to respond to new opportunities or challenges, undertake new business, increase competitiveness, or improve processes		
4. Direct any required changes in assignment of accountabilities and responsibilities for executing the investment portfolio and delivering value from business processes and services		
5. Direct any required changes to the portfolio of investments and services to realign with current and expected enterprise objectives and/or constraints		
6. Recommend consideration of potential innovations, organizational changes or operational improvements that could drive increased value for the enterprise from I&T-enabled initiatives		
7. Define and communicate enterprise-level value delivery goals and outcome measures to enable effective monitoring		4

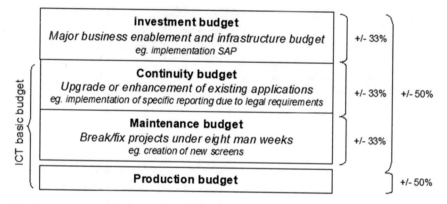

Fig. 5.10 Investment types at a major Belgian bank

and a consistent scoring, all scores of all IT(-enabled) investments are always challenged and overviewed before they are consolidated prior to going for approval to the Executive Committee.

To be able to execute this process, detailed business cases need to be developed for each of the proposed IT(-enabled) investments. A possible approach or template to develop detailed business cases is provided in Table 5.24.[16]

---

[16]Refer to Chap. 4 on IT business value for additional substantiation on business cases and the business case process.

Table 5.21 Investment criteria at a major Belgian bank

Return on investment	Alignment with strategy	Competitive advantage	Necessity (legal, organizational)	Support management
Support future information architecture	Reduction operational risk	Project and organizational risk	Functional uncertainty	Technical uncertainty

Table 5.22 Management practice APO05.02 and its containing activities (ISACA, 2018a)

Management Practice	Example Metrics	
APO05.02 Evaluate and select programs to fund. Based on requirements for the overall investment portfolio mix and the I&T strategic plan and road map, evaluate and prioritize program business cases and decide on investment proposals. Allocate funds and initiate programs	a. Percent of projects in the I&T project portfolio that can be directly traced back to the I&T strategy b. Percent of business units involved in the evaluation and prioritization process	
Activities		**Capability Level**
1. Identify and classify investment opportunities in line with investment portfolio categories. Specify expected enterprise outcome(s), initiatives required to achieve expected outcome(s), high-level costs, dependencies and risk. Specify methodology for measuring outcomes, cost and risk		2
2. Perform detailed assessment of all program business cases. Evaluate strategic alignment, enterprise benefit, risk and availability of resources		3
3. Assess impact of adding potential programs on overall investment portfolio, including changes that might be required to other programs		
4. Decide which candidate programs should be moved to the active investment portfolio. Decide whether rejected programs should be held for future consideration or provided with seed funding to determine if business case can be improved or discarded		
5. Determine required milestones for each selected program's full economic life cycle. Allocate and reserve total program funding per milestone. Move the program into the active investment portfolio		
6. Establish procedures to communicate the cost, benefit and risk-related aspects of portfolios for consideration in budget prioritization, cost management and benefit management processes		

5.7   Summary

In November 2018, the successor of COBIT 5, i.e., COBIT 2019, was officially released. This international framework is aimed at facilitating a flexible, tailored implementation of effective "enterprise governance of information and technology (EGIT)". COBIT primarily is a framework developed by and for practitioners, but it is increasingly incorporating many insights from IT and general management literature, including concepts such as "strategic alignment", "balanced scorecard", "IT savviness", "organizational systems", and "evolutionary dynamics". This chapter aimed to contribute to a better understanding of the COBIT 2019 framework and to provide guidance relevant for practitioners in their endeavors to leverage COBIT 2019 to effectuate effective enterprise governance of information and technology in practice.

Table 5.23 Traffic light report for IT(-enabled) investments at a major Belgian bank

		Investment criteria									
		Return on investment	Alignment with strategy	Competitive advantage	Necessity (legal, organizational)	Support management	Support future information architecture	Reduction operational risk	Project and organizational risk	Functional uncertainty	Technical uncertainty
IT(-enabled) investments	A	Red	Green	Yellow	Green	Green	Green	Green	Green	Red	Red
	B	Red	Green	Green	Green	Green	Yellow	Green	Green	Yellow	Yellow
	C	Green	Green	Green	Green	Green	Red	Green	Green	Red	Red
	D	Green	Green	Yellow	Red	Green	Green	Green	Green	Green	Green
	...										

Table 5.24 Business case template

Cover Sheet	Implementation Approach (How?)
• Program name	• Program plan, milestones, and time frame
• Business sponsor	• Program dependencies
• Program manager	• Enterprise architecture compliance
• Revision notes	• Security policy compliance
• Validation signatures	• Critical success factors
• Approval signature	• Stage gate funding requests
Executive Summary	• Resourcing requirements
• Program context	• Governance arrangements
– Name	**Appendices**
– Business sponsor	• The detailed program plan
– Track record of management team	(including individual project plans)
– Category of investment	• The resourcing plan
– Program description/profile	• The financial plan
• Synopsis of business case assessment	• The benefits realization plan
– Program contribution (value)	(including the benefits register)
– Program plan and timing	• The (organizational) change
– Change implications	management plan
– Key risks	• The risk management plan
– Comparative value summary	(including the risk register)
Introduction/Background (Why?)	
• Opportunity and problem definition (Why?)	
– Problem to be addressed	
– Purpose	
– Strategic contribution	
• Recommended Solution (What?)	
– Scope	
– Business impact	
– Approach	
– Alternatives	
• Value Impact (Attractiveness)	
• Financial and non-financial benefits	
– Description	
– Measures	
– Accountabilities	
• Costs (full economic life cycle, full IT and business costs, best/worst/most likely case)	
• Organizational Change Implications (Feasibility)	
– Breadth and depth of change	
– Organizational capability and readiness	
• Risks and Assumptions and their mitigation (Feasibility)	
– Delivery risks	
– Benefit risks	

Study Questions

1. Explain why COBIT 2019 should be regarded as a framework that enables the implementation of enterprise governance of information and technology (EGIT).
2. Explain the concept of EGIT components as introduced by COBIT 2019.
3. Explain how the (IT) balanced scorecard concept is integrated in COBIT 2019.
4. Explain how COBIT 2019 is in line with the research on IT governance contingency analysis.
5. Explain why COBIT 2019 can be seen as a "holistic" framework for enterprise governance of information and technology (EGIT).
6. Explain how COBIT 2019 accounts for the "evolutionary dynamics" of enterprise governance of information and technology (EGIT).
7. Explain how the performance management of (governance and management) processes can be put in practice by using COBIT 2019.
8. Explain the difference between IT governance and IT management in the context of COBIT 2019 and illustrate with concrete examples.
9. An enterprise considers enterprise goal "Quality of financial information" (EG04) as being of high priority. Which governance and management objectives would deserve particular attention in the context of this enterprise's EGIT system?

References

Beer, S. (1985). *Diagnosing the system for organizations*. West Sussex: John Wiley & Sons.

Brown, C. V. (1997). Examining the emergence of hybrid IS governance solutions: Evidence from a single case site. *Information Systems Research, 8*(1), 69–94.

Brown, A. E., & Grant, G. G. (2005). Framing the frameworks: A review of it governance research. *Communications of the Association for Information Systems, 15*(1), 696–712.

De Haes, S., & Van Grembergen, W. (2009). An exploratory study into IT governance implementations and its impact on business/IT alignment. *Information Systems Management, 26*(2), 123–137.

De Haes, S., Van Grembergen, W., & Debreceny, R. S. (2013). COBIT 5 and enterprise governance of information technology: Building blocks and research opportunities. *Journal of Information Systems, 27*(1), 307–324.

De Wit, B., & Meyer, R. (2014). *Strategy synthesis: Managing strategy paradoxes to create competitive advantage* (4th ed.). Cengage Learning India Pvt. Ltd.

Henderson, J. C., & Venkatraman, N. (1993). Strategic alignment: leveraging information technology for transforming organizations. *IBM Systems Journal, 32*(1), 4–16.

Huygh, T., & De Haes, S. (2019). Investigating IT governance through the viable system model. *Information Systems Management, 36*(2), 168–192.

ISACA. (2018a). *COBIT 2019 framework: Governance and management objectives*.

ISACA. (2018b). *COBIT 2019 framework: Introduction & methodology*.

ISO/IEC. (2015). *ISO/IEC standard 38500: Information technology—Governance of IT for the organization*.

IT Governance Institute (ITGI). (2003). *Board briefing on IT governance* (2nd ed). Retrieved from http://www.isaca.org/knowledge-center/research/researchdeliverables/pages/board-briefing-on-it-governance-2nd-edition.aspx.

Kaplan, R. S., & Norton, D. P. (1996). *The balanced scorecard: Translating strategy into action*.

Lawrence, P. R., & Lorsch, J. W. (1967). *Organization and environment*. Boston, MA: Harvard Business School, Division of Research.

Peterson, R. R. (2004). Crafting information technology governance. *Information Systems Management, 21*(4), 7–22.

Preston, D. S., & Karahanna, E. (2009). Antecedents of IS strategic alignment: A nomological network. *Information Systems Research, 20*(2), 159–179.

Schwarz, A., & Hirschheim, R. (2003). An extended platform logic perspective of IT governance: Managing perceptions and activities of IT. *The Journal of Strategic Information Systems, 12*(2), 129–166.

Steuperaert, D. (2019). COBIT 2019: A significant update. *EDPACS, 59*(1), 14–18.

Van Grembergen, W., Saull, R., & De Haes, S. (2003). Linking the IT balanced scorecard to the business objectives at a major Canadian financial group. *Journal for Information Technology Cases and Applications, 5*(1), 23–45.

Weill, P., & Ross, J. W. (2009). *IT savvy: What top executives must know to go from pain to gain*. Harvard Business Press.

Chapter 6
EGIT Case Study Insights

Abstract This final chapter is structured around case studies that were performed as part of our research activities. All case studies deal with the organization's EGIT arrangement (or system), but each case sheds an in-depth light on certain aspects of EGIT. The first case study contained in this chapter, i.e., the "University of Antwerp" case, deals with board-level EGIT. The second case study, i.e., the "Acerta" case, investigates an EGIT system through the lens of the Viable System Model. Finally, the third case study, i.e., the "De Lijn" case, demonstrates the evolutionary dynamics of an EGIT system (i.e., how and why an EGIT system changes over time).

6.1 Board-Level EGIT at the University of Antwerp[1]

In the "capita selecta" section of the second chapter of this book, the topic of "board-level EGIT" was introduced. Indeed, the board of directors has a crucial role to play in the context of EGIT, as indicated by the definition of Enterprise Governance of IT put forward by this book: "*an integral part of corporate governance for which, as such, the board is accountable. It involves the definition and implementation of processes, structures, and relational mechanisms that enable both business and IT stakeholders to execute their responsibilities in support of business/IT alignment, and the creation and protection of IT business value*". The section on "board-level EGIT" included in Chap. 2 more specifically introduced the antecedents of board-level EGIT, board-level EGIT mechanisms, and the consequences of board-level EGIT. The first case study presented in this sixth chapter deals with board-level EGIT at a real organization. More specifically, this case study demonstrates how board-level IT oversight committees can be established and how such committees relate to the role of the board with regard to the Enterprise Governance of IT.

---

[1]Acknowledgment: This section is based on the doctoral research of Laura Caluwe, and more specifically on an article that was developed in the context of this doctoral research, i.e., Caluwe and De Haes (2019).

6.1.1 Introducing the Case

The University of Antwerp is a relatively young university, founded in 2003, fusing three separate university institutions that date back to 1965. The university is currently responsible for the education of 20,367 students of 116 nationalities. The university staff consists of 5398 people, including professors, assistants, researchers, education staff, and administrative and technical staff. Its three core tasks are research, education, and services.

The central governance structure at the University of Antwerp consists of the rector, 3 central governing bodies, and 9 central advisory bodies. The rector is the university's highest academic official. He is appointed for a four-year term by the board of directors after university-wide elections. The central governing bodies include the board of directors, the executive board, and the board of administration, which is responsible for the daily management of the university. These governing bodies are supported by the central advisory bodies, including the education board, the research board, and the academic council for service to society.

The IT department of the University of Antwerp maintains, manages, and develops the university's IT infrastructure. They provide solutions to support the three core tasks of the university: research, education, and services, but also facilitate secondary processes such as administration and management. In addition, they provide direct support to end users and attend to the maintenance of the infrastructure.

6.1.2 University of Antwerp's Approach for Establishing Board Involvement in EGIT

Like many organizations, the University of Antwerp has become increasingly dependent on IT. This evolution also entails a growing number of IT-enabled investments that need to be carried out by the IT department. The IT department began to struggle with this great number of IT-enabled investments. No central business forum existed to decide which projects would be executed and which would not, swamping the IT department with many requests they could not deliver against. This situation often led to frustration at business side, a tension which was also reported to and known by some board members.

Furthermore, in 2016, a new rector was appointed to spearhead the University of Antwerp. The newly appointed rector strongly believes that the organization should think about long-term developments and how the university can adapt to these developments. More specifically, he stated that he thinks it is the task of the board of directors to create this long-term vision, also regarding IT-related issues.

Accordingly, the University of Antwerp decided to tackle the need to (1) establish a more formal IT portfolio management process that includes all relevant stakeholders, (2) increase the involvement of the board in this process, and (3) ensure a more forward-looking approach.

A widely acknowledged strategy to increase and improve the involvement of the board in IT-related decision-making and control is to enhance its IT expertise (Jewer & McKay, 2012; Parent & Reich, 2009; Valentine & Stewart, 2015). However, due to the nature of the board of directors at the university, there are not many options to thoughtfully alter its composition. When the University of Antwerp initiated more board-level engagement in digital strategy and oversight, only 6 of the 25 members of the board were external directors. The internal directors were appointed after elections among the different university entities and students. From the 6 external members, the university could merely appoint 3. The others were selected by the minister for education, the governor of the province of Antwerp, and the provincial superior of the society of Jesus, which made it difficult to increase the level of IT expertise among board members. Since the first of September 2017, the board is allowed to appoint 3 additional directors. This change will provide the university with the opportunity to slightly alter the composition of the board. As the 3 additional members have not been appointed yet at the time of writing, the future will show whether this new arrangement will result in a higher level of IT expertise at the board of directors.

Due to the limited level of IT expertise on the board, it makes sense to make sure this IT expertise is present and IT-related debates are held in other structures that report to or advise the board. Accordingly, committees were created that include board members and that assist the board in IT-related decision-making and control. Indeed, the creation of an IT oversight or similar committee at board level is a frequently mentioned approach in the academic literature to increase board involvement in IT governance (Coertze & von Solms, 2014; Nolan & McFarlan, 2005; Turel & Bart, 2014). At the university, two such committees were created. One committee, the IT governance committee, considers rather short-term decisions and is in charge of portfolio management of IT-enabled investments. This committee is supported by the investment office. The other committee, the digital strategy think tank, considers the long term from more of an outside-in perspective. The committees are presented in Fig. 6.1.

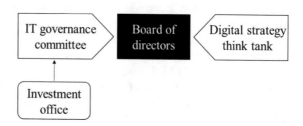

Fig. 6.1 IT oversight committees at the University of Antwerp

6.1.2.1 Guiding Principles

When the University of Antwerp decided to act on the growing need for IT governance mechanisms, a set of guiding principles was agreed upon. These principles include:

- Transparency regarding *investment criteria*: The evaluation of proposed investments should be handled in a transparent way. Clear criteria should be created to decide whether or not to start an investment.
- Transparency regarding the *investment budget*: The size of the investment budget should be known at all times.
- Transparency regarding *individual investments*: For every investment, a business case needs to be developed according to a standard template. Moreover, a business owner is appointed to each investment and no investments can be launched without a business owner.
- Transparency regarding the *investment portfolio*: All investments need to go through the same portfolio decision cycle so that a full and transparent view can be obtained.

These guiding principles were used as a basis to create the board-level IT governance structures that are described in the following sections.

> **Assignment Box 6.1: Understanding EGIT Principles at the University of Antwerp**
> Discuss in group the meaning of these EGIT principles as put forward by the University of Antwerp. Describe which structures, processes and relational mechanisms you would propose to design an EGIT model that allows these principles to be realized in the organization.

6.1.2.2 IT Governance Committee

The IT governance committee was established in 2015 and meets 3 times a year. The main goal of this committee is to manage the IT-enabled investment portfolio more effectively and transparently and make sure it is in line with the overall organization strategy. From a board's perspective, the committee should provide reasonable assurance that the university's IT-enabled investments are in line with the university strategy. Indeed, up until now, the main topic of the committee meetings has been which investments to execute. However, the interviewees indicated that in the future, other topics like project benefits delivery and the IT policy plan could be part of this meeting. Not all IT-enabled investments pass by the IT governance committee. Rather operational investments—like the renewal of certain academic software licenses—are not discussed at this level of the organization, as these would overburden this forum. Instead, the committee focuses on more strategic and innovative projects, which cover about 45% of the entire IT budget.

Due to the democratic nature of the decision-making culture at the university, it is crucial to include a broad delegation of people of the university in this committee. Hence, the goal was to create an entity that would represent all university entities as good as possible. The result is a committee that consists of 15 voting members and 30 advisory members. In addition, the chairman and vice-chairman can invite internal or external experts that act as advisors. The 15 voting members are:

- Rector (chairman);
- Chair of the board of administration (vice-chairman);
- The 4 vice-rectors;
- 3 members of the board of directors;
- 3 members appointed by the Council of Deans; and
- 2 heads of the IT department.

The composition reveals that the board is actively engaged in the IT debate. Four directors were appointed voting members of the IT governance committee (including the rector), and all other directors are also welcome to join. Indeed, at the past committee meetings, attendance ranged from 4 up to 8 directors.

As the heads of the IT department are included in the committee, a certain level of IT expertise is present. However, the goal of the committee is not to go too much into the technical details, but to discuss the investments from a business perspective. Indeed, one of the heads of the IT departments states: "*Within the IT governance committee we present the projects as understandable and as little technical as possible. This is also explicitly mentioned in the IT governance committee charter.*" Of course, the details must be considered at one point. Therefore, it was decided to establish an additional preparatory committee, the investment office.

The *investment office* is responsible for preparing investments to be presented to the IT governance committee. More specifically, a scoring model, which is approved by the IT governance committee, is used to evaluate the fit with the organization strategy, the risks, and the expenditure. This scoring model enables a fairly objective quotation of the investment. Investments are evaluated from a business as well as a technical perspective. For example, the match with the three core tasks of the university (i.e., education, research, and services) is assessed. An overview of all the scoring criteria is shown in Table 6.1. For each of these criteria, underlying questions were developed that allow to come to a "green," "yellow," or "red" score in a consistent way. Green represents a good match, yellow exemplifies a limited match, and red suggests there is no match. In case the investment criterion is not applicable (e.g., an investment in a new online platform for research is not relevant for the education strategy), a "gray" score is used. At the end of this exercise, a scorecard is created, showing the benefits, risks, and expenditure of each investment. The scores are presented using colors, as this enables the reader to evaluate the investment's strengths and weaknesses at a glance.

Table 6.1 Scoring model

Domain	Criterion
Business domain	Strategic match domain education
	Strategic match domain research
	Strategic match domain services
	Administrative streamlining
	Management information
	Marketing/image
	Strategic match ICT policy plan
Technology domain	Strategic IS architecture
	Definitional uncertainty
	Technical uncertainty
	IS infrastructure risk

Table 6.2 IT governance committee agenda, main topics

IT governance committee agenda
Budget overview
Investments: • Investment business case   • Color code resulting from scoring model   • Discussion   • Decision

The investment office does not make any investment decisions but can conclude that a proposed investment is not yet fully defined and matured in the current business case document. As this is merely a supporting committee with a more in-depth focus, it does not reside at the level of the board. The actual decision on whether or not to go through with an investment is made in the IT governance committee. However, the score determined by the investment office is crucial to make this decision. This is reflected in the IT governance committee agenda, which always includes the topics as shown in Table 6.2.

Every meeting, an overview of the IT budget is provided, which is in line with the guiding principles regarding transparency that were established at the beginning of this venture. Furthermore, all investments in need of a go/no-go decision are discussed. First, the investment business case and the color code that is determined by the investment office are presented. Then, the committee discusses the investment. Lastly, it is decided whether or not the investment will be executed.

6.1.2.3   Digital Strategy Think Tank

The other IT governance structure at the top-level of the university is the digital strategy think tank. The current rector started his term in 2016. From the beginning of his mandate, he stated he wants "*an organization that is agile and thinks about future needs,*" and in support of that, he wants to free up the time of the board to execute this task. He argues that *"IT is no longer a supporting frame, it is much more than that. We are at the beginning of an evolution and do not even realize what is in front of us. We need to think about the university in 20 years, IT in 20 years and the society in 20 years."*

In light of these developments, he initiated the creation of the digital strategy think tank which meets several times a year (the meeting frequency is currently undefined; in 2017, four meetings took place).

The goal of this committee is to consider long-term developments that could influence the university. They consider both how emerging technologies can impact the university's business model and strategy, as well as how challenges in society and markets could be addressed levering new technological innovations. One of the topics discussed was the fact that at a certain point in the future, more people will retire than enter the job market, which might trigger companies to hire students before they have finished their master's degree. This development could affect the university, as it might require students to obtain their master's degree in a more flexible way, for example, supported by e-learning. These kinds of digital strategy discussions require a certain level of IT expertise, which is reflected in the composition of the committee. The members of the digital strategy think tank are:

- Rector
- Chair of the board of administration
- 3 professors with IT expertise
- A board member with IT expertise
- 4 members of the IT department

Similar to the IT governance committee, the board of directors is represented in the think tank; the rector and one other board member are included. The difference is that for the digital strategy think tank, they specifically opted to include a board member with IT expertise.

6.1.3 Discussing Board-Level EGIT at the University of Antwerp

Table 6.3 provides a summarizing overview of the two board-level IT oversight committees at the University of Antwerp, their goal, and members.

No consensus seems to exist in extant literature on the role of an IT oversight committee at the level of the board of directors. The roles described in the literature are (1) monitoring of competitors and other organizations with regard to their IT-related activities (Nolan & McFarlan, 2005), (2) monitoring of IT project costs and benefits, risk and compliance and value delivery (Oliver & Walker, 2006), (3) ensuring IT is a topic on the board agenda, and (4) ensuring boards have the necessary information for IT decision-making (Posthumus, Von Solms, & King, 2010). The case of the University of Antwerp indicates that the role of the

Table 6.3 IT oversight committees at the University of Antwerp

Committee	Goal	Members
IT governance committee	Manage IT-enabled investment portfolio more effectively and transparently and align it with overall organization strategy	• Rector (chairman) • Chair of the board of administration (vice-chairman) • The 4 vice-rectors • 3 members of the board of directors • 3 members appointed by the Council of Deans • 2 heads of the IT department
Digital strategy think tank	Keep an eye on the impact of technological developments on the university and consider how societal and market challenges could be addressed leveraging technology	• Rector • Chair of the board of administration • 3 professors with IT expertise • A board member with IT expertise • 4 members of the IT department

committee strongly depends on the needs of the organization. This is in line with the guidance provided in the literature, which incorporates a contingency approach. Yet, current research focuses on the contingency factors that determine whether or not an organization should install an IT oversight or similar committee. The present case study however suggests that a contingency approach can also be taken toward the role of such a committee. At the University of Antwerp, the role of the IT governance committee corresponds to the role described by Oliver & Walker (2006). That is, this committee is mainly responsible for the evaluation of the business cases of IT-related projects. Yet, the role of the digital strategy think tank is different from the roles described in academic literature. This committee's responsibility is to keep an eye on the impact of technological developments on the university and consider how societal and market challenges could be addressed leveraging technology. Hence, it seems that the list of roles described in literature is not exhaustive. Thus, defining the possible roles of IT oversight committees is an interesting topic for future research.

This case study also provides some insights on possible IT oversight committee arrangements. Current research suggests the establishment of one IT oversight (or similar) committee, in some cases supported by the audit or risk committee. Nevertheless, the university decided to create two IT oversight committees at the level of the board. Although this is in conflict with existing guidance, it is an interesting approach as it allows the organization to clearly separate different responsibilities and adapt committee membership accordingly. In this specific case, the responsibilities of portfolio management on the one hand and ensuring a forward-looking, outside-in approach on the other hand are divided over two committees. For the former, i.e., the efficient management of the IT-enabled investment portfolio, the university needed representatives of both business and IT. Furthermore, it was crucial to include a broad delegation of members, covering a wide range of university entities. However, the membership needs of the digital strategy think tank are entirely different. Here, a certain level of IT expertise is crucial as well as the competence to think about long-term strategies. That is why for instance a non-executive director with significant IT expertise is included. Moreover, the type of discussions held at this committee requires a smaller number of members.

In conclusion, an IT oversight committee can take up various roles, depending on the organization's needs. The board can establish multiple committees in order to separate responsibilities. Clearly, membership should be adapted according to the responsibilities the committee assumes.

> **Assignment Box 6.2: Provide Recommendations for the Board-Level EGIT Arrangement at the University of Antwerp**
> Review the board-level EGIT mechanisms at the University of Antwerp and make some recommendations based on the board-level EGIT structures, processes, and relational mechanisms discussed in Chap. 2 (in the "board-level EGIT" capita selecta section).

6.2 Investigating Acerta's EGIT Through the Lens of the Viable System Model[2]

The "capita selecta" section of the second chapter of this book introduced the topic of "viable EGIT." The purpose of leveraging the Viable System Model (VSM) as a theoretical lens to study EGIT is to explain from a theoretical point of view *how* EGIT should be organized for it to be effective and *why*. Indeed, drawing on the VSM provides theoretical insights on *why* IT governance can continue to fulfill its general purpose of creating and protecting IT business value. Furthermore, by drawing on the essential elements of "organization" identified by the VSM, strong theoretical underpinnings are provided for the required functions of an IT governance arrangement, which directly contributes to the practical perspective of *how* to organize effective IT governance. The second case study presented in this sixth chapter aims to describe and diagnose Acerta's EGIT system through the VSM

---

[2]Acknowledgment: This section is based on the doctoral research of Huygh (2019), and more specifically on an article that was developed in the context of this doctoral research, i.e., Huygh and De Haes (2019).

lens. This provides practical insights on how the VSM can be leveraged as a lens for EGIT.

6.2.1 Introducing the Case

Acerta is an HR services provider in Belgium that specializes in advice, computerization and processing of administrative processes for payroll, social security, child benefits, and branch formalities. Therefore, Acerta's customers are enterprises of all sizes and self-employed workers. Nearly 30% of all self-employed workers in Belgium (ca. 270,000) are affiliated to Acerta for the social insurance fund. More than one out of four Belgian private sector organizations (ca. 50,000) use Acerta's payroll processing services. Acerta is also responsible for the payroll calculation of more than one out of three workers within the Belgian public sector, both statutory and contract workers (ca. 220,000). Nearly 13% of people receiving social benefits in Belgium do so via Acerta (ca. 140,000). Acerta has more than 1300 employees spread across 38 offices in Belgium. The firm had a turnover of just over 160 million euros in 2015. Acerta is not a publicly listed company. Instead, it is owned by two shareholders who each own 50% of the shares. In 2015, Acerta's total IT budget was 49 million euros. For 2016, it was set to be 48 million euros, therefore remaining relatively constant. The tendency since 2012 is that Acerta's IT budget lies between 40 and 50 million euros, as this can be supported by their contemporary cost structure. In 2015, ca. 70% of the IT budget was used to "run the business" (i.e., "to keep the lights on," including operational costs and small maintenance projects to maintain existing operations), while ca. 30% was used to "change the business" (i.e., projects for "new IT," both smaller and strategic). Again, the numbers for 2016 are approximately the same. In terms of IT costs, ca. 30% of Acerta's total expenses are IT-related. Therefore, Acerta is very dependent on IT, especially on highly reliable operating systems. Acerta does however not claim to be a front-runner in the application of emerging technologies.

  Acerta developed its own IT governance model, Bita+, an acronym for "business/IT alignment plus". This model is largely developed under supervision of the current CIO, who joined Acerta in 2012. Bita+ is extensively based on his prior experience as CIO of a large Belgian bank. The preparation year for the Bita+ implementation at Acerta was 2013, while the actual implementation started in 2014 and lasted for about 6 months. This fast implementation time can be attributed to the fact that the new CIO already had the blueprint for the Bita+ model developed at the large bank, which was then scaled to Acerta (being approximately 1/10th the scale of the bank). The Bita+ model is not specifically based on a good-practices framework for IT governance (e.g., COBIT). Nevertheless, the CIO states that *"When you would map our processes to the COBIT 5 processes, you would find that approximately 80% of what is contained in COBIT 5 can also be found at Acerta."*

The main trigger for Acerta to implement the Bita+ IT governance model traces back to the preparation stages of a major IT project (>70 million euros) that was deemed to be critical for the company's competitiveness. At that point, the IT governance arrangement available was deemed to be vastly insufficient for dealing with the complexity of the project and the to-be state of Acerta's IT. The prior IT governance system at Acerta was referred to as Bita and essentially consisted of a centralized change advisory board (CAB) as described in ITIL (i.e., a good-practices framework for IT service management). The CAB consisted of four executive committee members who discussed everything IT-related and made all the decisions, resulting in very centralized IT decision-making. This demonstrates the fundamental principles underlying the VSM-based organizing logic for IT governance.[3] Indeed, the current and future IT use should have appropriate variety to remain sustainable in the (changing) external environment, and IT governance accordingly should have sufficient variety to be able to effectively control this current and future IT use.

6.2.2 Controlling the (Current and Future) IT Use at Acerta

This section presents a description of Acerta's EGIT by using the VSM as a theoretical lens. The description is provided for two levels of granularity, i.e., the corporate level and the business domain level.

6.2.2.1 Corporate Level

Table 6.4 maps Acerta's EGIT system at the corporate level to the VSM (sub) systems or functions, and VSM communication channels or variety loops. After providing this general overview, the sections below provide deeper insights on Acerta's IT governance arrangement as seen through the VSM lens.

System 1: Acerta's Current and Future IT Use (Managed at Business Domain Level)

At the corporate level, Acerta controls IT projects (i.e., future IT use—which they refer to as "change IT") and IT operations (i.e., current IT use—which they refer to as "run IT") which are managed locally at the business domain level. Acerta recognizes seven distinct business domains (see Fig. 6.2). The first business domain is "customer approach," which is mainly concerned with distribution. Second, three

---

[3]Refer back to the "Viable EGIT" section as part of the "capita selecta" contained in Chap. 2 of this book.

Table 6.4 Acerta's EGIT system at the corporate level mapped to the VSM functions and variety loops

VSM (sub)systems or functions	IT governance arrangement at Acerta (corporate level)
System 1	• "Run IT" and "change IT" distributed over the seven business domains (resulting in sole ownership) • Activity steering committee (ASC) for each business domain in charge of the management of business domain "run IT" and "change IT" • Business domain intersections (e.g., in the context of IT projects —project interdependencies)

System 2	• Coordinating business domain intersections by means of formal agreements between relevant business domains (for project tasks or subprojects)
	• Enterprise Architecture Forum (EAF):
	  – Coordinating Acerta's "run IT" and "change IT"
	  – Effectuating change management for internal stakeholders
	• IT governance section on Acerta's intranet for coordinating the IT governance approach
	• IT-related standards: ITIL (for IT service management) and PRINCE2 (for IT project management)
	• Release management for coordinating the transition from "change IT" to "run IT"

System 3	• The CIO is a full member of the executive committee • Risk committee as a subcommittee of the executive committee explicitly dealing with IT-related risk matters
System 3*	• Externalized IT audit • IT crisis simulations • Monitoring by exception of IT budget consumption (through financial controllers)

System 4	• Enterprise Architecture Forum (EAF) following up on emerging technologies and their application potential for Acerta
	• Self-awareness:
	  – Central spreadsheet of current and future IT maintained by the EAF
	  – Enterprise architecture (EA) models maintained by the EAF

System 5	• Board-level IT governance:
	  – Yearly presentation of the IT strategy by the CIO to the board of directors
	  – IT-related information part of monthly performance reports received by the board of directors
	• Board of directors contains IT expertise and IT experience (i.e., IT-related board capital)
	• Board members ask critical IT-related questions, especially regarding the business implications of IT-related matters
	• 'New wages engine' board-level monitoring committee (and associated steering committee)

VSM variety loops	IT governance arrangement at Acerta (corporate level)
System 3–system 4 variety loop	• IT strategic planning and budget allocation (LTP) between EAF and executive committee, overviewed by the board of directors

(continued)

Table 6.4 (continued)

VSM variety loops	IT governance arrangement at Acerta (corporate level)
Communication with the environment	• External communication about IT-related matters (i.e., IT-related disclosure) to different stakeholders through annual reports, customer brochures etc.
Command axis	• Bargaining channel: Setting business domain IT budget (mutual process between executive committee and business domain ASC) • Accountability channel (i.e., performance measurement): IT spending monitored by executive committee through financial controllers • Intervention channel (i.e., downward communication of policies): Enforcing legal and corporate IT-related requirements (e.g., IT-security requirements enforced by the risk committee)
Algedonic channel	• Escalation procedures for IT-related crisis situations • Continuously monitoring network security

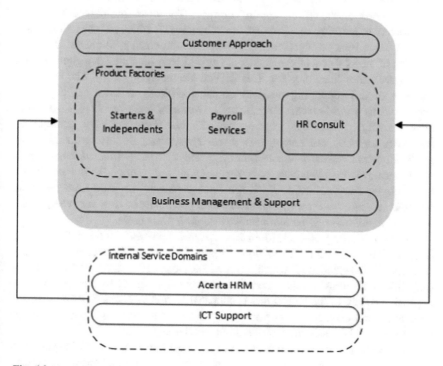

Fig. 6.2 Acerta's business domain architecture

product factories are recognized as separate business domains: "starters and inde-pendents," "payroll services," and "HR consult." Third, the "business management and support domain" focuses on Acerta's financials, intelligence, profitability, and enterprise supporting functions. Finally, "Acerta HRM" and "ICT support" are internal service domains focusing on Acerta's resources and assets. Accordingly, using the VSM as a lens, seven "system 1 operational units" are identified at Acerta's corporate-level system of controlling the (current and future) IT use. Each of these units consists of a set of business domain-level IT projects and IT operations.

In terms of total IT budget, the "ICT support" business domain is the largest. This budget is used for ultimately ensuring the "run IT" of all business domains, e.g., by investing in server infrastructure ('change IT' of the ICT support business domain) and covering the server-related operating expenses ('run IT' of the ICT support business domain). The clear majority of ICT support's IT budget (ca. 75%) is used for covering such operating costs (e.g., electricity bill of the servers). Acerta does not make use of activity-based costing procedures to assign these operating costs to the relevant other business domains, and they are all ultimately covered by the IT budget of the "ICT support" domain. The other business domains are therefore only carrying the costs of the "change IT" initiatives (including small fixes). Charge-back arrangements like activity-based costing, to enable an under-standing of the total cost of ownership, are nevertheless identified as a good practice in IT governance literature (De Haes & Van Grembergen, 2009). The enterprise architect of the supporting business domains critically reflects: *"Charge back arrangements would ensure that the other business units would have a better understanding of the actual cost of 'run IT', like they do for the 'change IT' initiatives, as these are coming out of their own budgets. For instance, when applications are released, it sometimes happens that the old and the new appli-cation are running simultaneously for another few years, thereby needlessly increasing operational costs. If charge back arrangements were used for these operational costs, these transformations would potentially be a lot smoother, as the business domains would be more inclined to limit these costs."*

Of the remaining business domains, "payroll services" traditionally has the highest IT budget (with 17.3 million euros in 2016 about four times larger than "starters and independents," which has the next-largest IT budget). The IT budgets (in millions of euros) of the seven business domains for 2016 are presented in Fig. 6.3. The part of the budget that is allocated to "run IT" consists of operational costs and small maintenance projects (i.e., "to keep the lights on"), while "change IT" consists of IT(-enabled) projects, both smaller and strategic.

An important contemporary example of a project in the "change IT" portfolio is the "new wages engine" project, owned by the "payroll services" business domain. This project is worth over 20 million euros and is directly related to the core business activities of Acerta, making it a very critical strategic IT project. "New wages engine" is deemed necessary to stay competitive in the market. The project started in the first quarter of 2016 and is scheduled to be finished by the end of 2017. The internal financial ERP system is an example of "run IT." This application

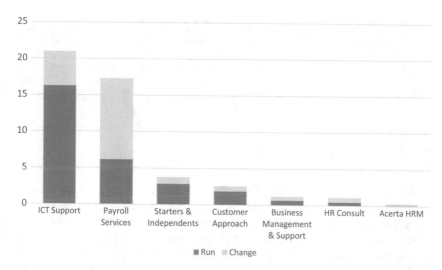

Fig. 6.3 Acerta's IT budget for 2016 (in millions of euros)

is owned by the "business management and support" domain and provides internal financial transparency to all relevant stakeholders.

Each of the seven business domains has a dedicated "activity steering committee" (ASC), which is a structure consisting of the corporate CIO, the business domain managing director, the business domain enterprise architect(s), and the corporate IT governance manager. Each ASC is granted a specific and autonomous IT budget by the executive committee as decided in the long-term financial plan (which is negotiated at the executive committee and ultimately approved by the board of directors). A business domain ASC is responsible for managing the (run and change) IT of that business domain. Accordingly, these seven ASCs correspond to seven "system 1 local management functions." Every IT(-enabled) project (change IT) and IT application (run IT) is owned by a single business domain. The CIO specifically states that the goal of this business domain architecture, and the clustering of (run and change) IT over these business domains, is to enable local autonomy. The managing director of the "payroll services" business domain acknowledges the improvement in local autonomy compared to the previous situation in which IT budgets and IT projects were not assigned to the business domains. Now, the business feels more in control of IT-related budgets and the IT(-enabled) project portfolio.

The yearly planning of an ASC is presented in Fig. 6.4, divided over the four quarterly meetings. In the past, ASC meetings would only occur on a yearly basis. Under Bita+, the decision was made to let an ASC meet on a quarterly basis, to improve its decision-making frequency. The managing director of the "payroll services" business domain states: *"The new frequency of ASC meetings is better. We now understand that discussing the budgeting within a business domain only once each year slowed us down. The frequency of ASC meetings should not be increased*

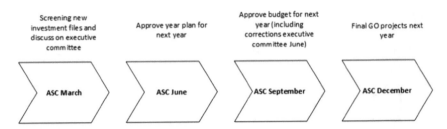

Fig. 6.4 ASC yearly planning (quarterly meetings)

further however, as we have structures directly below it that are covering the more operational aspects." Each ASC meeting starts with a follow-up of the previous quarter, as well as a discussion regarding corrections for the next two quarters.

Based on the above information, seven embedded viable systems are identified at Acerta's corporate-level system of controlling the (current and future) IT use, i.e., one for each business domain. Indeed, the combination of a "system 1 operational unit" (i.e., a business domain's (run and change) IT) and its dedicated "system 1 local management function" (i.e., the business domain's ASC) is an embedded viable system. The total set of these seven embedded viable systems forms system 1 of the system-in-focus (i.e., the corporate-level system of controlling the current and future IT use) and can therefore be referred to as Acerta's (run and change) IT, which is locally managed at business domain level.

The VSM prescribes an "algedonic channel" that is used to raise alarm in case of problems at the level of the embedded viably systems. The IT-related potential incidents at Acerta are classified per impact (from "low" to "very high"). When an incident that is classified as "very high" occurs, the executive committee receives an e-mail from the service management system in real time. The managing director of the "payroll services" business domain, who is a member of the executive committee, says: "*the business implications of the incident are very often clear when reading this automated e-mail. However, it requires a certain competence to understand the link between cause and effect. Nevertheless, I can always immediately gauge the seriousness of the situation based on these e-mails.*" Additionally, Acerta continuously monitors certain aspects at the operational level, especially related to the security of their networks. This is in line with extant research that proposed an automated security monitoring mechanism to be designed and implemented (as an instantiation of the algedonic channel) which has the capacity to trigger an appropriate response so that immediate remedial action can take place (Gokhale & Banks, 2004). Finally, as the CIO is a member of the executive committee, besides being a member of all the business domains' ASCs (and being the managing director of the "ICT support" business domain), it is also ensured that there is attention to IT-related issues at the executive committee level.

System 2: Coordinating (Current and Future) IT Use

Albeit that there formally is no overlap between the business domains' (current and future) IT (i.e., the system 1 operational units), Acerta recognizes that there are links between IT projects (which is internally referred to as "business domain intersections"). This is a direct consequence of assigning the ownership of every IT project (and the resulting "run IT") to a single business domain, while these projects do not necessarily only influence the business domain that holds the ownership. The managing director of "payroll services" explains: *"the projects are always owned by a single business domain, but a given project does not necessarily influence only the business domain which holds ownership. This results in multiple business domain intersections, which is sometimes a little difficult to manage."*

For instance, it is possible that one domain is requested to do something for another domain in the context of an IT project. A formal agreement between both domains is then made by their respective ASC's to coordinate the intersection, and the relevant IT budget is used to compensate the efforts. This formal agreement also contains performance targets (e.g., the time by which the project should be in the testing phase). A recent example of this mechanism at work is related to the strategic project "new wages engine." While this project is ultimately assigned to the "payroll services" business domain, the finance department, as part of the "business management and support" domain, is responsible for certain parts of this project. For this reason, they are in control of a specific subproject of "new wages engine" (for a total of 906,606 euros). Hence, this is an example of an intersection between these two business domains, at the level of a single project.

An important coordination structure is the "Enterprise Architecture Forum" (EAF), which is composed of the enterprise architects of all the business domains and chaired by the CIO. The EAF typically meets every two weeks, but since Acerta is currently in the process of undergoing some major strategic IT-related changes, the frequency of EAF meetings has been increased to every week. The CIO states: *"The enterprise architects essentially have two roles: first, they are responsible for the consistency within their business domain; and second, when they are sitting together under the form of the EAF, they are responsible for the consistency of the whole."* The enterprise architect is a new role that was introduced with the Bita+ system. Not every business domain has a single dedicated enterprise architect. For instance, "payroll services" has two dedicated enterprise architects, as the IT budget for "change IT" of this business domain is considerably larger than that of the other business domains. On the other hand, the internal service domains (i.e., "Acerta HRM" and "ICT support") share an enterprise architect. The purpose of this exercise was to ensure that each enterprise architect would be working full-time.

The EAF is concerned with synergies at the level of Acerta's current and future IT use. Synergies (among system 1 subsystems) can indeed be sought by establishing appropriate system 2 mechanisms (Schwaninger, 2004). For instance, if a new project is requested by a certain business domain, the application opportunities and implications for other business domains is analyzed at the EAF. The managing director of "payroll services" acknowledges the importance of the EAF in ensuring consistency of corporate-level current and future IT use. She states: *"Before the EAF was introduced, it was possible that two different business domains would initiate essentially the same project apart from each other, but for meeting two different business needs. Now, the EAF ensures that the single project meets both business needs, thereby preventing redundancy."* The enterprise architects are viewed by the business as important bridge functions between business and IT. They are technically skilled while also having the ability to talk with the business in a language they understand. Another important coordination function performed by the EAF is (IT-related) change management. In close collaboration with business process owners, the enterprise architects gauge the potential effects of a new system on the internal stakeholders. A mechanism that is frequently used to effectuate (IT-related) change management is "pit-stop sessions," where impacted stake-holders are invited to get them involved with a new system early on and understand the changes it will bring.

System 2 mechanisms provide a service or (non-committal) advice to the system 1 subsystems; i.e., compliance with system 2 mechanisms is essentially voluntary and not mandatory (as would be the case with system 3 mechanisms using the command axis) (Beer, 1985; Hoverstadt, 2010). As such, the EAF would qualify as a system 3 structure if their decisions would be binding. Instead, the EAF has an advisory function (which is nevertheless in practice almost always followed by the business domains), which makes it a clear example of a system 2 mechanism.

Acerta maintains an "IT governance section" on their intranet, containing information about the Bita+ IT governance arrangement. Relevant internal stake-holders can for instance view the IT project portfolios and the investment decisions that are made. This also serves as a coordination mechanism, as employees are hereby informed about the way in which Acerta is governing its IT, with the aim of improving internal transparency and establishing coordinated action. Acerta is also developing an "IT for dummies" section on its intranet, which should ensure that internal stakeholders understand the role of IT for Acerta and the basics of the governance and management of IT at their company. Finally, Acerta employs several IT-related standards, facilitating a standardized way of working: e.g., ITIL for IT service management ('run IT') and PRINCE2 for IT project management ('change IT').

System 3, System 3*, and the Command Axis: Balancing Local Autonomy and Overall Cohesion

The system 3 function guards systemic cohesion by ensuring that the current and future IT use (i.e., system 1) achieves of the general purpose of creating and protecting IT business value. It is effectuated through the executive committee (and its subcommittees like the risk committee) at Acerta. Running the "current state of affairs," the executive committee and its subcommittees make use of the vertical communication channels (i.e., the bargaining channel, the accountability channel, and the intervention channel—together referred to as the "command axis") to each ASC, establishing auto-regulatory coordination mechanisms (i.e., system 2), and the occasional IT-related audits (i.e., system 3*) to accomplish this important task.

The CIO is a full member of Acerta's executive committee, ensuring that IT-related issues are appropriately represented at this level. This arrangement signals that IT is embraced as a strategic partner at Acerta (Valorinta, 2011). Furthermore, allowing the CIO full membership of the executive committee is a viable approach to ensure IT competence at executive committee level (Bradley et al., 2012). At a yearly meeting of the executive committee, a discussion is devoted to the overall IT budget to safeguard consistency with the overall long-term financial plan and to formally approve the investment portfolio. This is a two-way bargaining process, as the managing directors of all the business domains (spearheading their respective ASCs) have a seat at the executive committee and can thereby participate in these discussions. The ASCs of the business domains are then held accountable for the IT budgets they are granted. Financial controllers are assigned to each business domain (and therefore each ASC) to monitor the actual spending of these budgets (i.e., performance measurement). Monthly, the ASC budget consumption is reported back to the executive committee. Monitoring the realization of IT-related benefits tends to happen in an ad hoc fashion at Acerta. Extant literature confirms that this is a notoriously difficult task, largely due to the fact that the identification of expected IT-related benefits is generally perceived as a challenging task (Lin & Pervan, 2003). Indeed, to be able to effectively monitor the realization of IT-related benefits, appropriate success measures should already be developed in the preproject stage (Ward, Taylor, & Bond, 1996). However, the business cases for IT(-enabled) investments at Acerta are rarely used to monitor the realization of expected benefits that are described in them (if any).

Acerta has a dedicated "risk committee" that is chaired by the CIO and of which approximately half of the executive committee is a member. This committee focuses on business risks as well as IT-related risks. The CIO is chairing this committee, as IT-related risks are considered to be a major source of risks for the company. Again, this signals the important role of IT for the organization. The risk committee directly reports to the executive committee. To enable useful discussions of these issues, the business and IT-related risks are presented by means of a "risk map." This risk map is developed as a mutual effort between business and IT stakeholders (i.e., managing directors and the CIO) and classifies all the identified risks on two dimensions: likelihood (of happening) and impact (when it happens). Logically, the goal is to focus first on the risks that have a high chance of happening and a high potential impact when they happen. For instance, "cyber risk: hacking" is an example of an item on the most recent risk map that was classified as belonging to the highest potential impact category and the highest likelihood category.

Additionally, the most important evolutions on the risk map are separately discussed using four risk categories: "increasers," "decreasers," "new," and "gone."

The responsibilities of the risk committee are classifying these risks, as well as creating and maintaining the risk policy and the risk management strategy. The progress in the business domains of the proposed risk mitigating actions is also followed up by this committee. When communicating the IT-related risks to the executive committee, special attention is devoted to making sure that the business implications are very clear. This is of course safeguarded to a large extent by the fact that both business and IT stakeholders are involved in developing the risk map and classifying the risks. The risk committee is responsible for enforcing certain risk- and security-related policies. For instance, there are hard IT security-related policies (e.g., password policies and policies of logical access security), which are communicated to the employees using the intranet. These policies are also audited accordingly (i.e., system 3*). Failure to comply with these policies is considered a labor offense. This again demonstrates the difference between system 2 mechanisms (with which there is a voluntary compliance) and using the command axis to enforce IT-related policies. Nevertheless, both approaches are used by system 3 to control the "operational variety" at the level of system 1.

At Acerta, external IT auditing is formalized by means of a contract with a third-party IT auditing company, which provides full coverage (e.g., security audit, project audit, method audit, etc.). In cooperation with an external IT consultancy company, Acerta also organizes a real-life IT-related crisis simulation two times each year. The last edition of this test involved a hacker who claimed having stolen confidential information from their servers about one of Acerta's largest customers. These crisis simulations provide an excellent way to gauge the as-is state of the responsiveness to such situations. Internally, the executive committee, via the financial controllers, can audit the budget consumption of each of the ASCs when deemed appropriate (i.e., by exception). In practice, this almost never happens, because of the internal financial transparency provided by the financial module of the ERP system. Monitoring by exception differs from the regular performance measurement in the sense that it is not exercised at regular intervals, but only when deemed appropriate by the executive committee. The identified system 3* mechanisms at Acerta obey the good practices that such mechanisms should adhere to; i.e., they are sporadically used, and all the relevant stakeholders are aware of their existence (Espejo & Gill, 1997). As such, these mechanisms fulfill their role in reducing the variety that system 3 must control through the command axis.

System 4: Sensing/Anticipating Environmental Change, Communicating with the Environment, and Self-awareness

At Acerta, scanning of emerging technologies is one of the responsibilities of the "Enterprise Architecture Forum" (EAF) (i.e., composed of the four enterprise architects of the business domains and chaired by the CIO). The importance of the capacity to sense and anticipate relevant changes related to advances in IT and the business opportunities created by emerging technologies has been explicitly identified in extant research (Weill & Ross, 2004). However, it is acknowledged that

Acerta is not continuously scanning its environment for strategic opportunities and threats rooted in emerging technologies, as Acerta's use of IT is more geared toward being highly operationally reliable instead of being a front-runner in the application of new technologies. Nevertheless, potential applications of emerging technologies are placed on the agenda of EAF meetings. Recent discussions regarding emerging technologies at the EAF were for instance about big data, Internet of things, and in-memory technologies. The enterprise architect clarifies: *"Discussing emerging technologies at the EAF is organized more or less ad hoc. If I must put a frequency on it, I would say that these issues are discussed 4 or 5 times a year at the EAF."* To support following up on emerging technologies, the enterprise architects: (1) are encouraged to attend Gartner workshops, (2) have access to Gartner reports (e.g., hype cycles), and (3) are encouraged to proactively identify courses they would like to attend. In summary, the EAF is responsible for gathering (IT-related) information that can be used to prepare Acerta for the future.

Acerta uses multiple channels to communicate with external stakeholders about the way in which it is leveraging and controlling its (current and future) IT. First, the annual report has been used in the past to be transparent about certain IT-related matters. Nevertheless, this document never contained specific information about how Acerta effectuated IT governance. For the last two years, Acerta released a very brief annual report, containing only the most essential company information. The CIO states: *"For us, the annual report is a nice document when printed, but when we hand it out, people put it somewhere and then it just starts gathering dust. Nobody is really doing anything with that document."* IT governance transparency is not seen as a priority at Acerta, despite the fact that it is an emerging research topic in IT governance literature (De Haes, Huygh, & Joshi, 2017; Joshi, Bollen, & Hassink, 2013) and the possible positive effects it can have for a firm (Chatterjee, Richardson, & Zmud, 2001). While the annual report is generally the preferred medium for IT governance-related disclosure (Joshi et al., 2013), this medium is clearly not deemed important at Acerta. This vision of lesser importance of the annual report could potentially be explained by the fact that Acerta is owned by two shareholder groups that each own 50% of the company. This might be different for a company that is publicly listed and has a larger number of minority shareholders. Instead, Acerta focuses its IT (governance)-related disclosure more toward its customers, using several channels. For instance, Acerta communicates its quality labels to its customers using commercial brochures. Customers are sometimes even allowed to be actively involved. For instance, a very important customer of Acerta is allowed to audit IT-related matters at Acerta on regular intervals.

To ensure self-awareness, a central spreadsheet of Acerta's current and future IT is maintained by the EAF. Without this information centralized, there would be a clear risk at redundancy when proposing new investments. The EAF, in collaboration with ICT architects and business process owners, is also responsible for modeling Acerta's enterprise architecture (EA). This is guided by an EA framework based on Capgemini's "Integrated Architecture Framework (IAF)." Multiple types of stakeholders are involved in EA modeling, as the framework is built around four quadrants: business architecture, ICT architecture, business design, and ICT design.

The enterprise architect explains: "*We do use the EA models when gauging the applicability of new ideas, however, these models are not maintained on a continuous basis. With each major IT project, however, there is a boost to get them up-to-date.*" Related to the self-awareness of IT governance, the as-is maturity of the IT governance mechanisms and practices comes to mind. At Acerta, formal maturity assessments of IT governance practices are not conducted. The IT governance manager explains: "*It is very difficult to formally assess the maturity of IT governance structures and processes. Nevertheless, you get a feeling of the maturity when attending meetings of IT governance structures.*" Despite the fact that it is considered difficult, it is a good practice to gauge the maturity of IT governance mechanisms and practices, to enable proactive improvements (ISACA, 2018).

System 3–System 4 Feedback Loop: IT-Related Strategic Decision-Making

In the context of Acerta's corporate system of controlling the current and future IT use, the feedback loop between system 3 and system 4 is essentially about corporate-level IT strategic planning. This is a mutual process between different stakeholders [i.e., enterprise architects and the CIO in the EAF (system 4) and managing directors of the different business domains in the executive committee, also including the CIO (system 3)]. The EAF, in performing its system 4 function, senses the current state of the environment and anticipates potential future states (e.g., emerging technologies that could potentially transform the industry), while the executive committee (system 3) has clear insights on "the present" (e.g., in terms of feasibility given the current resources available). Discussions are then held at the executive committee, where the CIO represents the system 4 function (and as such the process is mutual between system 3 and system 4). This strategic decision-making process ultimately results in Acerta's IT strategy (which is formulated to be in line with Acerta's overall business strategy—i.e., IT strategic alignment), as well as an associated IT budget (which is part of the long-term financial plan) to execute this strategy. These strategic decisions then dictate the playing field for the lower-level recursions (i.e., the individual business domains). The strategic decision-making process is overviewed by system 5 (i.e., board-level IT governance), to ensure that the resulting decisions are in line with the overall direction, values, and purpose of the organization (Beer, 1985; Espejo & Gill, 1997).

   Related to the system 3–system 4 feedback loop (and more specifically related to the information about (potential) changes in the external environment that serves as input to this feedback loop), the enterprise architect of the supporting business domains mentions: "*We have the feeling that a part of such discussions at the EAF remains unheard by the executive committee. The enterprise architect then should proactively discuss this with the managing director of a specific business domain. I think that these discussions could be brought to the executive committee in a more proactive fashion.*" This seems to point in the direction of a small imbalance between system 3 and system 4, resulting in the fact that relevant changes in the environment are sometimes ignored (i.e., system 3 slightly dominates system 4) (Achterbergh & Vriens, 2002).

System 5: Board-Level IT Governance

At Acerta, IT is considered to be a business enabler. The managing director of the "payroll services" business domain acknowledges an improvement from the old "Bita" to the new "Bita+" arrangement in that regard. She states: *"IT is now regarded more as a business enabler. In the past it was regarded more as a cost center. I think the establishment of the EAF was very important in changing the business' perception of IT. The enterprise architects are talking with the business in terms of application opportunities, which is a major improvement compared to the past."* This statement relates to the role of IT for the organization. Determining and understanding the role of IT for the organization has been identified as an important IT-related decision in the context of an organization's IT governance arrangement (Weill & Ross, 2004).

Despite the widespread agreement between researchers and practitioners on the need for board involvement in IT governance, it appears to be more the exception than the rule in practice (Andriole, 2009; Huff, Maher, & Munro, 2006; IT Governance Institute (ITGI), 2003; Turel, Liu, & Bart, 2017). The need for board-level involvement in IT governance is said to be dependent on the role of IT for the organization (Jewer & McKay, 2012; Nolan & McFarlan, 2005). As Acerta considers IT to be a business enabler, its board should evidently be involved in IT governance (Nolan & McFarlan, 2005). Acerta's board of directors contains IT expertise and experience, which is considered to be a good practice to enable board involvement in IT governance (De Haes & Van Grembergen, 2009; Nolan & McFarlan, 2005; Valentine & Stewart, 2013). Specifically, Acerta's board contains a member who owned and managed an IT company, as well as an independent director who has an IT audit and IT consultancy background. This hence ensures the existence of IT-related "board capital" (Hillman & Dalziel, 2003). The CIO confirmed that putting directors with IT expertise and experience on the board of directors was done on purpose, driven by the recognition of Acerta's IT intensity.

Board-level IT oversight at Acerta is effectuated for instance through an annual presentation of the IT strategy (i.e., resulting from the decision-making at the level of the system 3–system 4 variety loop) by the CIO to the board of directors. Extant literature has identified such presentations as a potential approach to effectuate supervision of IT strategy formulation (Bradley et al., 2012; Huff et al., 2006). The directors can then ask critical questions regarding the business implications of the IT strategy. Both issues are linked, as in order to be able to ask critical questions, board members need to have at least some expertise on the business implications of IT (Nolan & McFarlan, 2005). Nevertheless, the CIO states that *"when communicating with the board, it is very important to discuss the matters at hand in business language. If IT-related matters are discussed in technical jargon at board-level, the directors will not understand the issues and automatically think the proposal is bad.*" The CIO furthermore adds IT-related comments to the monthly performance reports that the board of directors receives. In VSM terms, the system 3–system 4 feedback loop indeed needs to be monitored by system 5 (Beer, 1985), which directly relatés to the crucial monitoring function of the board in the context of IT governance (Benaroch & Chernobai, 2017). It is for instance considered crucial to ensure that the (current and future) IT use is consistent with the organization's mission, strategy, values, norms, and culture (Weill, 2004).

Acerta realized that the major strategic IT(-enabled) project "new wages engine" is of crucial importance to the success of the organization (and could even endanger the survival of the organization if things go awry). In response, a specific sub-committee was established at the level of the board of directors to monitor this critical project. Approximately half of the members of the board of directors is a member of this committee, as well as the CEO. The CIO directly reports to this committee on a quarterly basis. As this important project is also partially co-sourced in partnership with an external company, a steering committee was implemented that directly reports to this board-level project monitoring committee with the goal of managing the relationship with this co-sourcing partner. Among the members of this steering committee are also representatives of this external partner.

6.2.3   Business Domain Level

Drawing on the VSM's underlying concept of recursivity, i.e., the unfolding of complexity throughout various levels of granularity, a business domain's ASC (i.e., a "system 1 local management function" within the corporate-level system of controlling the (current and future) IT use) serves as metasystem at the next-lower-level recursion, i.e., the business domain-level system of controlling the (current and future) IT use. Taking a recursive view at the unfolding of complexity enables the controlling of IT at the business domain level to be examined more closely. The unfolding of complexity reflects specific choices regarding how the current and future IT use will be controlled throughout various levels of granularity (i.e., corporate level, business domain level, etc.). It was identified that Acerta's corporate-level system of controlling the (current and future) IT use contains 7 embedded viable systems (i.e., one for each business domain). For instance, there will be a separate viable system of controlling the (current and future) IT use of the "payroll services" business domain. Drawing on the concept of recursivity, the ASC of "payroll services" as such maps to the metasystem at this level of recursion.

Within each business domain-level system of controlling the (current and future) IT use, the "business domain managing director" will act as system 5, setting the overall direction, values, and purpose of the business domain. In practice, this entails translating what is set at the corporate level (for Acerta as a whole) to the business domain.

System 4 at the business domain level is instantiated by means of a "domain council." A unique domain council exists for each of Acerta's seven business domains. The enterprise architect of a given business domain is the chair of the domain council of that business domain. The domain council is responsible for conducting a prestudy about a problem statement that arises, and for discussing potential IT-related solutions. The enterprise architect can personally propose ideas, but also acts as a contact point for other stakeholders. For each idea, an "idea-report" will be drafted, which is a small one-pager that discusses a potential solution for a certain need. A standardized idea report template exists, containing three sections: "as-is," "to-be," and "cost estimates."

There can be multiple triggers for ideas that are discussed at the domain council, e.g., a modification required for legal/compliance reasons, a technological change, a business need, etc. At the domain council, the business is frequently involved in the discussions, to ensure business/IT alignment. For instance, relevant business process owners are always attending domain council meetings. The other attendees of a domain council meeting tend to vary, depending on the ideas that are being discussed. In practice, more technically oriented actors are often invited to domain council meetings (e.g., ICT architects), as they have technical expertise and/or experience that is relevant to the discussion at hand. The frequency of domain council meetings depends on the specific business domain. For instance, the domain council of "payroll services" meets on a more regular basis than the domain council of "HR consult," as the former domain is larger in terms of IT budget and consequently has more ideas in the pipeline. When the domain council finished the prestudy for a given idea, it will be presented by the enterprise architect to the business domain's ASC.

A business case is developed for each project idea. The enterprise architect is accountable for developing the business case and bringing it to the level of the ASC. This process will be initiated first at the domain council, and external stakeholders can be asked to participate when deemed appropriate (e.g., financial controllers to check if the financials are realistic). The contents of a business case tend to differ depending on the investment size. For more expensive IT projects, business cases are developed in greater detail. Extant literature asserts that the comprehensiveness of a business case is related to the success of the investment that it describes (Ward, Daniel, & Peppard, 2008). A business case at Acerta usually contains projected numbers for budget, timing, and scope. Additionally, the expected impact on business goals is discussed. Especially this latter information is discussed more in-depth if the project is considered more important. In a recent project that was about upgrading Acerta's entire server infrastructure for instance, the goal was to increase operational efficiency by lowering operational costs. These projected numbers were included in the business case. Especially if the aim is to actually measure benefits realization in the post-project stage, the expected benefits should be carefully identified as part of the business case (i.e., in the preproject stage) (Ward et al., 1996).

At the level of the system 3–system 4 feedback loop within a business domain, "portfolio management and prioritization" is instantiated, which is overviewed by the managing director of that business domain (to ensure coherence with the overall direction, values, and purpose—of Acerta in general and the relevant business domain in specific). Within the budget that was assigned to each business domain's ASC (i.e., by the executive committee at the corporate level), the prioritization of projects will indeed be done within the ASC, considering the input of the domain council (largely based on the prestudies). As the enterprise architect is also a member of the ASC, this feedback loop is indeed mutual between the system 4 and system 3 functions. A first draft project prioritization is always prepared by the enterprise architect to guide a prioritization meeting of the ASC. The managing director of the "payroll services" business domain stresses the importance of careful IT project prioritization, as *"there are always more project ideas than there is budget in any given year."* When a business case is too expensive to be funded through an ASC's allocated IT budget, but the project in question is considered to be of strategic importance, the business case can be brought upwards (i.e., to the next-higher-level of recursion). Indeed, the business case can be presented to the executive committee, or even to the board of directors, via the business domain managing director (who has a seat at the executive committee). Recent examples of business cases that escalated this way are the "new wages engine" project (payroll services business domain), and a hardware upgrade of the entire server infrastructure (ICT support business domain).

The entire business domain ASC will instantiate the system 3 function, responsible for (1) resources and performance targets negotiation, (2) IT performance measurement, and (3) enforcing IT-related policies (i.e., "command axis") within a given business domain. Within the constraints of the IT budget that is assigned to the business domain by the executive committee, resource bargaining exists for individual IT projects (i.e., future IT use) and maintenance envelopes (i.e., current IT use). The consumption of these budgets is then monitored accordingly. The IT-related policies that are to be enforced can be business domain-specific, or corporate policies flowing down directly from the corporate-level system of controlling the (current and future) IT (e.g., the IT security policies).

A business domain's available IT budget is divided in different chunks by its ASC (see Fig. 6.5). Specifically, each budget is divided over the following categories: "break and fix," "functional maintenance," "projects," and "investments." The break and fix part of the budget is used for system maintenance and solving small defects. The functional maintenance part of the budget is oriented at small enrichments, i.e., small enough that it will not be treated as a separate project (at Acerta the rule of smaller than 20 man-days is maintained, where a man-day is considered to cost 600 euros). Projects are equal or larger than 20 man-days and are formally contained in the long-term financial plan. Finally, investments are those projects that are large enough to require formal approval of the board of directors. This last category is specifically aimed at meeting an important business objective or strategic goal and often leads to an increase in assigned IT budget, as "investments" often are projects of a magnitude that cannot be funded through a business domain's annual IT budget. The business cases for "investments" often represent a

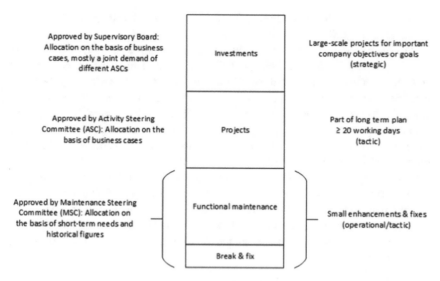

Fig. 6.5 IT budget breakdown (*Note* the relative sizes of the parts do not reflect proportions of the IT budget)

joint demand by multiple ASCs. This was for instance the case with the recent investment concerning the server infrastructure upgrade.

Each ASC has a "maintenance steering committee (MSC)" directly below it. This structure meets once each month and is responsible for the "break and fix" and the "functional maintenance" parts of the IT budget (i.e., related to the "current IT use" of a business domain). The business domain application owner is the chairman of an MSC. The exact composition of an MSC is to be decided by the chairman. It is however required that the IT governance practice of "bringing relevant business and IT stakeholders together in the structures" is followed (as is required for all IT governance structures at Acerta). Additionally, each business domain has a dedicated "service meeting" (which is ITIL-based). Acerta service desk representatives (i.e., internal and external helpdesks), the application manager, and the team leader ICT together form this structure and organize meetings to monitor and safeguard the service quality of Acerta's current IT use.

When an idea is approved and prioritized within an ASC, the project can be launched. At this point, a PSC is put in place for project execution; i.e., a project workforce consisting of both business and IT stakeholders, chaired by a project leader and overviewed by the enterprise architect of the business domain that has ownership of the project. This structure generally meets every two weeks, but this can vary depending on the project, or the phase the project is in. One of the PSC members is an ICT delivery manager, who is responsible for appointing the resources to the different project tasks. A business change leader is also involved to include the business perspective (e.g., to enable business process re-engineering). The PSC also consists of ICT architects who are executing the project tasks. The enterprise architect has a monitoring function within a PSC and returns feedback to the level of the ASC.

The current and future IT use at the business domain-level is divided into "run IT" (i.e., current IT use) and "change IT" (i.e., future IT use), which are managed accordingly by different structures. Therefore, two embedded viable systems are identified within each business domain: (1) the "run IT" system 1 operational unit, which is managed by the business domain's MSC and the business domain's service meeting (together instantiating this system 1 local management function), and (2) the "change IT" system 1 operational unit, which is managed by business domain PSCs. Auto-regulatory coordination (system 2) within a business domain is established by means of the business domain enterprise architect (who is responsible for the coordination within his or her business domain). Additionally, release management ensures the smooth transitioning from "change IT" to "run IT."

This concludes the discussion of Acerta's IT governance arrangement at the business domain level, as seen through the VSM lens. This is summarized by means of Table 6.5.

Assignment Box 6.3: Leveraging the VSM as a Theoretical Lens to Describe an EGIT System

If you have access to an organization, use the VSM as a theoretical lens to describe that organization's EGIT system. Specifically consider how the complexity of controlling the (current and future) IT use is unfolded over different levels of granularity (e.g., inter-organizational level, organizational level, business domain level etc.)

6.2.4 Increasing the (Managerial) Variety of Acerta's EGIT

Resulting from the VSM-based analysis of Acerta's organizational system of controlling its (current and future) IT use, some potential future attention points related to variety engineering were identified. Specifically, the following actions related to these potential attention points can be considered by Acerta to further improve the managerial variety of their organizational system of controlling the (current and future) IT use (i.e., the variety of their EGIT). As such, this section presents a diagnosis of Acerta's EGIT by leveraging the VSM as a theoretical lens.

- While, in the context of IT performance measurement, the monitoring of IT-related costs seems to be completely under control at Acerta, the monitoring of IT-related benefits realization can be improved. Measuring the realization of IT-related benefits is notoriously difficult, which is largely due to the fact that the identification of expected IT-related benefits is generally perceived as a challenging task (Lin & Pervan, 2003). Therefore, the business case process

Table 6.5 Acerta's EGIT system at the business domain level mapped to the VSM functions and variety loops

VSM (sub)systems or functions	IT governance arrangement at Acerta (business domain level)
System 1	• Project steering committees (PSC) for managing IT projects (i.e., future IT use) • Maintenance steering committee (MSC) and service meeting for managing current IT use
System 2	• Release management for smooth transitioning from future IT use to current IT use • Enterprise architect responsible for coordinating the current and future IT use within the business domain
System 3	• Activity steering committee (ASC)
System 3*	• Monitoring by exception of IT projects in the pipeline • IT-related audits, project audits, etc.
System 4	• Domain council, which is responsible for conducting a prestudy about a certain need within a business domain
System 5	• Business domain managing director • Translation of Acerta's overall direction, values, and purpose to the specific business domain
VSM variety loops	IT governance arrangement at Acerta (business domain level)
S3–S4 variety loop	• IT project portfolio management and prioritization, which is overviewed by the managing director of each business domain
Communication with the environment	• External communication with business domain-specific customers
Command axis	• Bargaining channel: Dividing the business domain's IT budget into categories: "investments," "projects," "functional maintenance," and "break and fix" • Accountability channel (i.e., performance measurement): IT spending of MSC and PSCs monitored by financial controllers • Intervention channel (i.e., downward communication of policies): Enforcing IT-related policies within a business domain
Algedonic channel	• For instance, when certain things in an IT project go awry, the PSC can directly report to the ASC in general and the managing director in specific

should ensure that the foundation for assessing the performance of the project in the post-implementation stage can be established. Indeed, a business case should be regarded as more than merely a formal document that becomes obsolete after formal project approval (Maes, De Haes, & Van Grembergen, 2015). Indeed, for proper benefits management, post-project evaluation is required to determine if the expected benefits are realized. To enable such a post-project review, appropriate success measures should already be developed in the preproject stage (Ward et al., 1996).

• The sensing/anticipating of environmental change related to emerging technologies and the discussions regarding their application potential is currently an ad hoc process at Acerta. As it is acknowledged that Acerta's contemporary use of IT is geared toward being highly operationally reliable instead of being a front-runner in the application of emerging technologies, this current arrangement is not necessarily problematic. However, as the role of IT for Acerta would evolve more toward applying IT innovatively to explore new business opportunities, this process might benefit from becoming more systematic. Indeed, a more proactive stance toward emerging technologies might then be required. A limited (system 4) ability to sense the current state of the environment (using the alpha communication channel), or to anticipate potential future changes (using the beta communication channel), will ultimately result in suboptimal strategic decision-making at the level of the system 3–system 4 variety loop. Indeed, when system 4 is weak (i.e., not of requisite variety) or missing, the system will have difficulties to readily respond to changing circumstances (i.e., adaptation). This situation has been explicitly identified as a functional pathology related to system 4, referred to as "headless chicken" (Pérez Ríos, 2010).

- Directly related to the previous point, the EAF feels that the information they provide related to emerging technologies and their application potential sometimes remains unheard by the executive committee. This points at a small imbalance between system 3 and system 4, resulting in the fact that relevant IT-related changes in the environment are sometimes ignored (i.e., system 3 slightly dominates system 4) (Achterbergh & Vriens, 2002). In the context of an organizational system of controlling the current and future IT use, the system 3–system 4 variety loop needs to work particularly well if the organization considers itself to be a front-runner in applying IT innovatively to explore new business opportunities. In that case, the organization requires a proactive stance toward sensing/anticipating emerging technologies and the related application potential. Such a proactive stance requires the monitoring of the environment for strategic opportunities and threats on a (quasi) continuous basis (Overby, Bharadwaj, & Sambamurthy, 2006). The connection between system 4 and system 3 then also needs to be optimized to be able to readily respond to these strategic opportunities and threats. As Acerta claims to be primarily oriented toward high operational reliability however, the variety running through this loop will be significantly lower than if it were a front-runner in applying IT innovatively to explore new business opportunities. However, in the case of evolving toward the latter situation, the contemporary arrangement of the system 3–system 4 feedback loop might prove to be insufficient (i.e., not of sufficient variety).

- IT governance transparency is currently not seen as a priority at Acerta. However, academic literature emphasized its importance and positive effects for firms, especially in industries where IT plays a strategic role (Chatterjee et al., 2001; De Haes et al., 2017; Joshi et al., 2013). As such, Acerta might need to put additional effort into IT governance transparency, or the transparency on IT-related matters, if the pervasiveness of IT for Acerta further increases. In that regard, Acerta should identify its relevant external stakeholders and ensure appropriate IT (governance)-related transparency or disclosure which would instantiate the alpha communication channel.

- Related to the self-awareness of Acerta's organizational system of controlling the (current and future) IT use, two attention points can be identified. First, enterprise architecture models are currently not being maintained on a continuous basis. As such, Acerta is not equally self-aware at different points in time (i.e., enterprise architecture models tend to be updated while preparing for large IT-enabled change). Second, maturity assessments of IT governance mechanisms and practices are not conducted at Acerta. However, such assessments enable proactive improvements to the IT governance arrangement (ISACA, 2018). As such, this could be important in ensuring and maintaining an appropriate variety of Acerta's EGIT.
- One of the approaches through which board-level IT oversight is effectuated at Acerta is the annual presentation of the IT strategy by the CIO at a meeting of the board of directors. As the role of IT for Acerta would become more geared toward applying IT innovatively to explore new business opportunities (i.e., an increasing operational variety of Acerta's current and future IT use), this arrangement might prove to be insufficient to ensure an appropriate board-level oversight of IT-related matters. In other words, the involvement of the board of directors might need to be significantly increased in that case. A possible action could be to establish a board-level committee chartered with setting direction toward, and being in control of, the (current and future) use of IT. Such a committee (e.g., labeled "IT strategy committee," "IT oversight committee," or "IT governance committee") would comprise directors with specific expertise and make specific recommendations to the board (IT Governance Institute (ITGI), 2003; Nolan & McFarlan, 2005).

Assignment Box 6.4: Improving the (Managerial) Variety of EGIT
Use the EGIT structures, processes, and relational mechanisms provided in Chap. 2 of this book to provide alternatives for the way in which Acerta is controlling its current and future IT use. Specifically consider alternative ways to further increase the variety of Acerta's EGIT.

This exercise can also be approached using the COBIT 2019 framework as introduced in Chap. 5 of this book.

6.3 Evolutionary Dynamics of De Lijn's EGIT[4]

This section further draws on the topic of "Viable EGIT" that was introduced in the "capita selecta" section of the second chapter of this book. Therein, it was described that leveraging the VSM as a theoretical lens for organizational systems of

---

[4]Acknowledgment: This section is based on the doctoral research of Huygh (2019).

controlling the current and future IT use allows incorporating the evolutionary dynamics of EGIT. More specifically, the theory of management cybernetics underlying the VSM implies that the variety of the (current and future) IT use should be appropriate so that it remains sustainable in the (changing) external environment and that the EGIT arrangement should have sufficient variety to be able to control the (current and future) IT use effectively. The third and final case study presented in this sixth chapter aims to demonstrate the evolutionary dynamics of De Lijn's EGIT system through the theoretical lens of management cybernetics (which is underlying the VSM). This provides practical insights on how and why an EGIT system changes over time.

6.3.1   Introducing the Case

De Lijn was founded in 1991 as a direct consequence of the regionalization of public transportation in Belgium. The organization is responsible for public transportation in Flanders by means of trams, busses, and the subway. The Flemish region is its major shareholder, holding 81.55% of shares. De Lijn had 8050 employees at the end of 2017, of which 1664 were working part-time. De Lijn's IT department, "ICT central services," employs 140 FTEs and is structured in the following divisions: project management office, applications, infrastructure, and architecture. Each division is then further structured in cells. The infrastructure division, for instance, is further structured into a network cell, a server cell, and a desktop cell (see Fig. 6.6). De Lijn's total IT budget for 2019 is 28.5 million euros. The majority of this, 24 million euros (or approximately 84%), is used to cover ICT central services' operational expenditure. The remaining 4.5 million euros (or approximately 16%) is assigned to ICT central services' capital expenditure. Additionally, approximately 17 million euros is released for the so-called strategic IT-enabled business projects. These funds are coming directly out of the budgets of

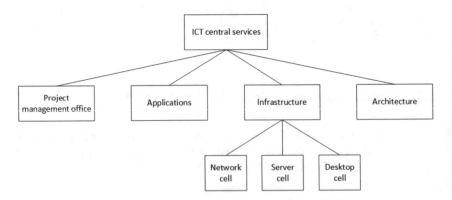

Fig. 6.6 Structure of De Lijn's IT organization

individual business units (e.g., marketing). Therefore, De Lijn's total IT spending for 2019 will be around 45.5 million euros.

ICT central services is a full-fledged business domain in the contemporary organization. The CIO is its managing director and has a seat at the executive committee. Over the years, the growing importance of ICT central services was increasingly recognized, as digital technologies started to play a more pervasive role in the public transportation industry (e.g., real-time information, mobile tickets, etc.). The head architecture, who started out as IT infrastructure manager at De Lijn in 1994, reflects: *"In the early days, ICT central services was merely providing operational support. The increasing pervasiveness of IT in our business context enabled a growing importance of ICT central services. In the contemporary organization, IT is represented at the executive committee and is at least of tactical importance. Each monthly executive committee meeting has IT-related matters on the agenda. I expect that this trend will continue, and ICT central services will evolve even more towards being of strategic importance for De Lijn."* The changing role of IT for the organization did not only influence the importance of ICT central services. It also triggered changes in the way De Lijn governs its IT. The CIO explains: *"In 2010, De Lijn did not even have a central list of IT projects that were in the pipeline. It goes without saying that there was also no transparency regarding the budgets and the costs of these projects. We work with formal budgets since 2012. You could say that, before that, the person who yelled the hardest at a project prioritization meeting ultimately got his or her project proposal approved."* This clearly demonstrates the fundamental principles from management cybernetics underlying the VSM-based organizing logic for IT governance. Indeed, the role of IT for organizations is increasingly transforming from merely providing operational support toward being a (strategic) business enabler (Buchwald, Urbach, & Ahlemann, 2014). From a management cybernetics point of view, this reflects an increasing variety of the (current and future) IT use, which translates to the need for an increasing variety at the level of the EGIT arrangement to be able to effectively control this (current and future) IT use.

Chatterjee, Richardson, and Zmud (2001, p. 58) argued that *"[...] the portion of industries in which IT serves a transformational role is likely to increase."* Based on this forecast, they encouraged firms to continuously evaluate the suitability of their IT governance arrangement, as a heightened transformational role of IT within an industry would put heightened requirements on the IT governance arrangements of firms active in that industry. This argument is entirely in line with the theory of management cybernetics underlying the VSM. Indeed, a heightened transformational role of IT within an industry represents a change of environmental variety that is relevant to the organizational system of controlling the (current and future) IT use of firms active in that industry. To ensure that their current and future IT use remains sustainable in that industry, the role of IT in these firms will likely change. Accordingly, the IT governance arrangement should have an appropriate capacity to remain in control of these changes at the level of the firm's current and future IT use. This as such provides theoretical insights on why an EGIT system changes over time.

6.3.2   A Longitudinal View of De Lijn's EGIT

De Lijn started an organizational effort to redesign its EGIT arrangement in 2017. At that point, it was recognized that the contemporary way of controlling its (current and future) IT use would be too simplistic to be successful in how they envision their future business environment. Indeed, the CIO expects an increasing pervasiveness of IT in the public transportation industry. The chief marketing officer shares this belief, stating: *"Without an increasing focus on digital, De Lijn will most likely become an obsolete player in the mobility market of the future."* This shared belief at the executive management level (i.e., regarding the (future) role of IT for the public transportation industry in general and De Lijn in specific) gradually results in more IT-enabled business projects in the pipeline at De Lijn (i.e., increasing variety of the current and future IT use or "operational variety") and a higher-variety approach to IT governance (i.e., increasing "managerial variety"). At the moment of writing, the blueprint of the to-be state of the IT governance arrangement is completed, and the first steps toward implementation are being taken. Below, a more in-depth discussion is presented related to how De Lijn prepares for an envisioned future of digital transformation.

6.3.2.1   Triggers and Lessons Learned from the Past

Multiple external triggers lead to an understanding of the need for redesigning the way in which De Lijn controls its (current and future) IT use (i.e., De Lijn's EGIT). In other words, multiple changes in environmental variety were recognized. De Lijn perceives a changing business context. The number of parties that are offering mobility services is increasing, often supported by digital technologies. Following the European liberalization rules, De Lijn will have to ensure by 2020 that it can work as efficient, flexible, and competitive as the private sector. De Lijn should be capable of being competitive with any given private company, as the government could decide to privatize (parts of) public transportation. However, travelers' satisfaction levels recently dropped from 72% (2016) to 64% (2017). Additionally, disruptive technologies like autonomous vehicles and disruptive services like Transportation as a Service (TaaS) are affecting the public transportation industry. Such (digital) disruptions might directly impact De Lijn's core business, requiring a (digital) transformation to remain competitive in a (digitally) transforming industry. The chief marketing officer explains: *"The reality of a digitally transforming business environment might significantly alter our role in the mobility market. We increasingly understand that there is a need for our role to evolve towards assisting people in a sustainable and inclusive manner to move from point A to point B in the most appropriate way. To achieve this, digitization becomes very important (for instance building platforms, good internal data, capturing external data). Digital platforms will become increasingly important to collaborate with other important mobility players (e.g. NMBS [railway company], bicycle-sharing system providers etc.)"*

In addition, several "lessons learned" from the past were identified that are incorporated in this redesign of De Lijn's EGIT. A first consideration is that the agility of strategic planning at De Lijn needs to be improved, to allow for a faster response to a changing business context. At all times, a relevant up-to-date version of the business strategic plan should be available to ensure that direction is provided to the business domains and the alignment of strategies can be achieved. Strategic planning at De Lijn should also consist of more long-term thinking based on scenario planning. A second consideration relates to improving IT-related exploration. IT-related innovations need to be researched and proposed more proactively, preferably coordinated from within "ICT central services." A third consideration is related to the agility of the projects in the (IT) project portfolio. De Lijn has experienced multiple instances of IT-related business projects in the past that ran for multiple years without meeting the initial expectations. When the organization started to run some agile projects that delivered results in short timeframes, many stakeholders in the organization started to realize that a mind shift was required. The fact that this agile way of working quickly delivered tangible results, combined with the fact that many stakeholders were dissatisfied with working for multiple years on a project that might not even deliver upon its original objectives, led to a rapid adoption of an agile mindset to project management within De Lijn.

6.3.2.2   Update of Strategic Plans

De Lijn has recently updated its overall business strategy (mainly in response to the above-mentioned external triggers). The strategy was validated by the executive committee at the spring seminar of 2018 and has two major focus areas: operational excellence and customer centricity. When drafting De Lijn's most recent IT strategic plan (i.e., version 2016–2020) in 2015, this updated business strategy was not yet available, resulting in an "expression barrier" problem for IT strategic alignment (Weill & Broadbent, 1998). With an updated business strategy available, the IT strategic plan is currently being reconsidered, although the feeling exists that the choices taken in the former IT Strategic plan will not require many changes to ensure supporting the achievement of the new business strategy. Ensuring IT strategic alignment, the reconsidered IT strategic plan will contribute to both focus areas of the business strategy.

The dual focus of the business strategy (i.e., operational excellence and customer centricity) relates well to the concept of "IT ambidexterity," or "bimodal IT". In fact, the reconsidered IT strategic plan emphasizes the bimodal use of IT. To enable effective bimodal IT use, EGIT should provide sufficient control for both modes (Haffke, Kalgovas, & Benlian, 2017).[5] Accordingly, the belief that De Lijn's IT use needs to evolve more toward bimodal lies at the core of its redesigned EGIT

---

[5]Refer to the "ambidextrous EGIT" section as part of the capita selecta presented in Chap. 2 of this book.

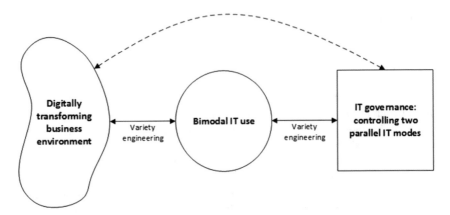

Fig. 6.7 Maintaining viability through variety engineering at De Lijn

arrangement. Relating this to the theory of management cybernetics (Fig. 6.7), De Lijn perceives a digitally transforming business environment (i.e., environmental variety is increasing). To continue to create and protect IT business value (i.e., general purpose of the organizational system of controlling the (current and future) IT use) in such a digitally transforming business environment, De Lijn chooses to evolve toward bimodal IT use (i.e., increase the operational variety). Indeed, the variety of the use of IT should be appropriate so that it remains sustainable in a (changing) external environment. Accordingly, the EGIT arrangement is being redesigned (i.e., increase managerial variety) so that the variety of this arrangement is appropriate to effectively control the bimodal IT use.

With bimodal IT, the challenge for "ICT central services" will be to continue delivering on its original objectives of reliable and secure IT services, while simultaneously achieving its digital transformation objectives (Haffke et al., 2017). To better achieve these digital transformation objectives, it was decided to change the organizational structure responsible for managing the IT project portfolio. More specifically, this responsibility moves from within "ICT central services" to the corporate level. Indeed, one of the primary goals of redesigning the EGIT arrangement at De Lijn is to increase the agility of the projects in the IT project portfolio. The head architecture explains: *"In the past, when major IT-related business projects were approved, the project would simply consume the assigned budget for the next 3, 5 or 7 years, without any adjustments or responsiveness. The project then continued as initially planned, no questions asked. In a digitally transforming world, such inertia is detrimental."*

6.3.2.3 Changes at the Organizational Level

To increase standardization and efficiency in managing De Lijn's project pipeline, project portfolio management has moved to the corporate level for all projects.

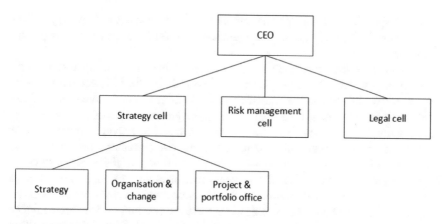

Fig. 6.8 Corporate-level strategy cell, risk management cell, and legal cell

A "strategy cell" has been implemented at the corporate level, which deals with strategy formulation, organizational change, and project and portfolio management (Fig. 6.8). The project prioritization method employed by the executive committee will also be changed. The goal is to have the method based on a more comprehensive evaluation, encompassing both a cost and a value perspective (as opposed to the previous situation of predominantly using a cost perspective). This is a response to the feeling that the project prioritization method dominantly focused on the cost aspect of the project proposals, without explicitly considering in specific terms how much value a project would generate. This also requires tailoring the business case process at De Lijn. In the past, benefits management was experienced to be notoriously difficult at De Lijn as the expected benefits were vaguely formulated in the business case, or not even included at all. The strategy cell will formally follow up the business cases and will trigger updates of a business case when deemed necessary. This way, business cases will have a longer lifecycle, which is considered a good practice in IT value management (Maes et al., 2015).[6]

Another important responsibility of the strategy cell will be strategy formulation. The cell will provide templates for strategic plans and will trigger and coordinate the strategy formulation process of the business domains. The so-called spring seminar at the executive committee will be formally used to adjust the overall business strategy, which should result in an updated business strategy on a yearly basis. The strategy cell then coordinates the strategy formulation process of the business domains, ensuring that all strategic plans are updated and aligned appropriately. This should therefore avoid the expression barrier problem that existed during the formulation of the latest IT strategic plan (see supra). Overall, these changes related to strategic planning at De Lijn should result in a better responsiveness to changes in the external environment. The fact that the corporate strategy

---

[6]For additional insights, refer to the section on the business case process in Chap. 4 of this book.

cell is responsible for both project and portfolio management and strategy formulation should ultimately ensure the alignment between the strategy and the project pipeline.

A comprehensive road map for the marketing business domain was recently constructed, which was augmented by ICT central services to identify the IT services needed to achieve the identified business targets. For instance, one of the targets of the marketing road map is the improvement of the real-time passenger information by taking into account surrounding traffic to provide a more accurate estimated time of arrival. This is expected to improve customer satisfaction levels, thereby contributing to the customer centricity focus area of the business strategy. Until recently, this modeling of a business road map and the supporting IT road map was only done for marketing, as this business domain is most involved in the digital transformation of the organization. Nevertheless, these efforts are currently being extended toward other business domains (e.g., operations). This shows that the organization is increasingly thinking ahead, or preparing for the future, and acknowledging the important role of IT in that context.

A corporate-level risk management cell has also been established, responsible for identifying and following up all risks (including project-related risks of the IT(-enabled business) projects). The maturity of the risk management process will also be improved, ensuring that there will be appropriate insights on the likelihood and impact of the identified risks (which previously was not formalized).

6.3.2.4 Changes at the (Functional) Level of ICT Central Services

In the new structure of "ICT central services" (Fig. 6.9), a "solution strategy" cell is included. This EGIT structure formally brings together the enterprise architects and the business analysts and has been assigned the following responsibilities: coordinating the entire IT landscape (e.g., consistent use of standards and documenting IT-related matters in a formalized and standardized way), following up on emerging technologies and evaluating their application potential, and enterprise architecture modeling. The head architecture became the head solution strategy and remains responsible for IT strategic planning (which is now coordinated at the corporate

Fig. 6.9 Re-organized structure of ICT central services

level by the strategy cell—see supra). Each business analyst will still be appointed to a specific business domain, but they are now formally brought together under the umbrella of this new EGIT structure. In the past, business analyst meetings were ad hoc and informal. The new arrangement should therefore improve the coordination of business requirements stemming from different business domains. Furthermore, formally bringing the enterprise architects and the business analysts together, the solution strategy cell should improve the efficiency of the process from a business analysis (i.e., responsibility of the business analysts) to a project proposal (i.e., responsibility of the enterprise architects).

ICT central services' new structure also includes a "solution delivery" cell. This is the former applications division of ICT central services (refer back to Fig. 6.9), but now augmented with "business relationship managers". The business relationship managers are appointed to a specific business domain and will actively check if the business is satisfied with the as-is state of the current IT use (i.e., IT operations and services). They are the internal service-level managers and provide a low-threshold point of contact for the business. The business relationship managers will connect to the business analysts, as a dissatisfaction with the as-is of IT operations might need to be translated into new requirements.

As the project and portfolio office operates at the corporate level, the "planning and governance" cell of ICT central services will have the responsibility of being its administrative center (e.g., administrative responsibilities in dealing with cloud computing service providers). The "IT security cell" is simply a new name for the EGIT structure formerly known as "IT security board," remaining responsible for defining, communicating, and enforcing IT security-related requirements. The IT infrastructure cell remains unchanged, responsible for managing IT operations (i.e., current IT use).

This concludes the discussion of the evolutionary dynamics of De Lijn's EGIT system through the theoretical lens of management cybernetics (underlying the VSM). As such, this case study provided practical insights on how and why an EGIT system changes over time.

> **Assignment Box 6.5: EGIT Evolutionary Dynamics**
> Use the EGIT structures, processes, and relational mechanisms provided in Chap. 2 of this book to provide recommendations for further increasing the variety of De Lijn's EGIT. Take a deep-dive in the specific issue of board-level EGIT.
>
> This exercise can also be approached using the COBIT 2019 framework as introduced in Chap. 5 of this book. Take a deep-dive in the specific situation in which there is an increasing amount of IT-enabled project proposals to be prioritized.

Assignment Box 6.6: De Lijn's Evolving EGIT Arrangement and COBIT 2019 Design Factors
Refer back to Chap. 5 in which the COBIT 2019 framework was introduced. Identify which of the COBIT 2019 design factors apply to this case study on the evolutionary dynamics of De Lijn's EGIT arrangement. Explain how they manifest specifically at De Lijn.

6.4   Summary

This final chapter presented several case studies that were performed as part of our research activities. While all case studies had the organization's EGIT arrangement (or system) as overall focus, each case study provided specific insights on certain aspects of EGIT. The first case study contained in this chapter, i.e., the "University of Antwerp" case, dealt with board-level EGIT. The second case study, i.e., the "Acerta" case, investigated an EGIT system through the lens of the Viable System Model. Finally, the third case study, i.e., the "De Lijn" case, demonstrated the evolutionary dynamics of an EGIT system (i.e., how and why an EGIT system changes over time).

Study Questions

1. Discuss some key considerations in establishing a board-level EGIT arrangement.
2. Discuss how the unfolding of complexity (in controlling the current and future IT use) is arranged at Acerta.
3. Discuss some approaches leveraged by De Lijn to increase the variety of its EGIT arrangement.
4. Discuss how the "De Lijn" case links to "ambidextrous EGIT" (refer back to Chap. 2—section on capita selecta).
5. Discuss how the evolutionary dynamics of EGIT can be linked to the concept of design factors introduced in the COBIT 2019 framework (refer back to Chap. 5).

References

Achterbergh, J., & Vriens, D. (2002). Managing viable knowledge. *Systems Research and Behavioral Science, 19*(3), 223–241.

Andriole, S. (2009). Boards of directors and technology governance: The surprising state of the practice. *Communications of the Association for Information Systems, 24*(1), 373–394.

Beer, S. (1985). *Diagnosing the system for organizations.* West Sussex: Wiley.

Benaroch, M., & Chernobai, A. (2017). Operational IT failures, IT value destruction, and board-level IT governance changes. *MIS Quarterly, 41*(3), 729–762.

Bradley, R. V., Byrd, T. A., Pridmore, J. L., Thrasher, E., Pratt, R. M., & Mbarika, V. W. (2012). An empirical examination of antecedents and consequences of IT governance in US hospitals. *Journal of Information Technology, 27*(2), 156–177.

Buchwald, A., Urbach, N., & Ahlemann, F. (2014). Business value through controlled IT: Toward an integrated model of IT governance success and its impact. *Journal of Information Technology, 29*(2), 128–147.

Caluwe, L., & De Haes, S. (2019). Board engagement in IT governance: Opening up the black box of IT oversight committees at board level. In *Proceedings of the 52nd Hawaii International Conference on System Sciences.*

Chatterjee, D., Richardson, V. J., & Zmud, R. W. (2001). Examining the shareholder wealth effects of announcements of newly created CIO positions. *MIS Quarterly, 25*(1), 43–70.

Coertze, J., & von Solms, R. (2014). The board and CIO: The IT alignment challenge. In *HICSS 2014 Proceedings.*

De Haes, S., & Van Grembergen, W. (2009). An exploratory study into IT governance implementations and its impact on business/IT alignment. *Information Systems Management, 26*(2), 123–137.

De Haes, S., Huygh, T., & Joshi, A. (2017). Exploring the contemporary state of information technology governance transparency in Belgian Firms. *Information Systems Management, 34*(1), 20–37.

Espejo, R., & Gill, A. (1997). *The viable system model as a framework for understanding organizations.* Retrieved from http://www.moderntimesworkplace.com/good_reading/GRRespSelf/TheViableSystemModel.pdf.

Gokhale, G. B., & Banks, D. A. (2004). Organisational information security: A viable system perspective. In *Australian Information Security Management Conference 2004 Proceedings* (pp. 178–184).

Haffke, I., Kalgovas, B., & Benlian, A. (2017). Options for transforming the IT function using bimodal IT. *MIS Quarterly Executive, 16*(2), 101–120.

Hillman, A. J., & Dalziel, T. (2003). Boards of directors and firm performance: Integrating agency and resource dependence perspectives. *Academy of Management Review, 28*(3), 383–396.

Hoverstadt, P. (2010). The viable system model. In M. Reynolds & S. Holwell (Eds.), *Systems approaches to managing change: A practical guide* (pp. 87–133). London: Springer.

Huff, S. L., Maher, M., & Munro, M. (2006). Information technology and the board of directors: Is there an IT attention deficit? *MIS Quarterly Executive, 5*(2), 55–68.

Huygh, T. (2019). *Investigating IT Governance through the Viable System Model* (doctoral dissertation). University of Antwerp, Antwerp, Belgium.

Huygh, T., & De Haes, S. (2019). Investigating IT Governance through the Viable System Model. *Information Systems Management, 36*(2), 168–192.

ISACA. (2018). *COBIT 2019 framework: Introduction & methodology.*

IT Governance Institute (ITGI). (2003). *Board briefing on IT governance* (2nd ed.). Retrieved from http://www.isaca.org/knowledge-center/research/researchdeliverables/pages/board-briefing-on-it-governance-2nd-edition.aspx.

Jewer, J., & McKay, K. (2012). Antecedents and consequences of board IT governance: Institutional and strategic choice perspectives. *Journal of the Association for Information Systems, 13*(7), 581–617.

Joshi, A., Bollen, L., & Hassink, H. (2013). An empirical assessment of IT governance transparency: Evidence from commercial banking. *Information Systems Management, 30*(2), 116–136.

Lin, C., & Pervan, G. (2003). The practice of IS/IT benefits management in large Australian organizations. *Information & Management, 41*(1), 13–24.

Maes, K., De Haes, S., & Van Grembergen, W. (2015). Exploring the business case process for IT enabled investments. *International Journal of IT/Business Alignment and Governance, 6*(2), 14–30.

Nolan, R., & McFarlan, F. (2005). Information technology and the board of directors. *Harvard Business Review, 83*(10), 96–106.

Oliver, G. R., & Walker, R. G. (2006). Reporting on software development projects to senior managers and the board. *Abacus, 42*(1), 43–65. https://doi.org/10.1111/j.1467-6281.2006.00188.x.

Overby, E., Bharadwaj, A., & Sambamurthy, V. (2006). Enterprise agility and the enabling role of information technology. *European Journal of Information Systems, 15*(2), 120–131.

Parent, M., & Reich, B. H. (2009). Governing information technology risk. *California Management Review, 51*(3), 134–152.

Pérez Ríos, J. (2010). Models of organizational cybernetics for diagnosis and design. *Kybernetes, 39*(9/10), 1529–1550.

Posthumus, S., Von Solms, R., & King, M. (2010). The board and IT governance: The what, who and how. *South African Journal of Business Management, 41*(3), 23–32.

Schwaninger, M. (2004). Methodologies in conflict: Achieving synergies between system dynamics and organizational cybernetics. *Systems Research and Behavioral Science, 21*(4), 411–431.

Turel, O., & Bart, C. (2014). Board-level IT governance and organizational performance. *European Journal of Information Systems, 23*(2), 223–239.

Turel, O., Liu, P., & Bart, C. (2017). Board-Level information technology governance effects on organizational performance: The roles of strategic alignment and authoritarian governance style. *Information Systems Management, 34*(2), 117–136.

Valentine, E., & Stewart, G. (2013). The emerging role of the Board of Directors in enterprise business technology governance. *International Journal of Disclosure and Governance, 10*(4), 346–362.

Valentine, E., & Stewart, G. (2015). Enterprise business technology governance: Three Competencies to build board digital leadership capability. In *HICSS 2015 Proceedings*.

Valorinta, M. (2011). IT alignment and the boundaries of the IT function. *Journal of Information Technology, 26*(1), 46–59.

Ward, J., Daniel, E., & Peppard, J. (2008). Building better business cases for IT investments. *MIS Quarterly Executive, 7*(1), 1–15.

Ward, J., Taylor, P., & Bond, P. (1996). Evaluation and realization of IS/IT benefits: An empirical study of current practice. *European Journal of Information Systems, 4*, 214–225.

Weill, P., & Broadbent, M. (1998). *Leveraging the new infrastructure—How market leaders capitalize on Information Technology*. Boston: Harvard Business School Press.

Weill, P., & Ross, J. (2004). *IT governance: How top performers manage IT decision rights for superior results*. Harvard Business Press.

Weill, Peter. (2004). Don't just lead, govern: How top-performing firms govern IT. *MIS Quarterly Executive, 3*(1), 1–17.

Printed in the United States
By Bookmasters